The Best Little Boy in the World Grows Up

The Best Little Boy
in the World Grows Up

Andrew Tobias

Random House

New York

All rights reserved under International and Pan-American
Copyright Conventions. Published in the United States
by Random House, Inc., New York, and
simultaneously in Canada by Random House
of Canada Limited, Toronto.

Grateful acknowledgment is made to the following for permission
to reprint previously published material:
Los Angeles Times Syndicate: Excerpt from "Trophy Boys," from the
August 18, 1997, issue of *New York* magazine. Copyright © 1997 by
New York Magazine. Distributed by Los Angeles Times Syndicate.
Reprinted by permission.
Warner Bros. Publications U.S. Inc.: Excerpts from "Whatshername,"
by Paul Stookey, Dave Dixon, and Richard Kniss. Copyright ©
(renewed) by Pepamar Music Corp. (ASCAP). All rights reserved.
Used by permission of Warner Bros. Publications U.S. Inc.,
Miami, FL 33014.

Library of Congress Cataloging-in-Publication Data
Tobias, Andrew P.
The best little boy in the world grows up / Andrew Tobias.
p.   cm.
Sequel to: The best little boy in the world / John Reid.
ISBN 0-375-50111-8
1. Tobias, Andrew P.   2. Gay men—United States—Biography.
I. Reid, John. Best little boy in the world.   II. Title.
HQ75.8.T6   1998
305.38´9664´092—dc21
[B]   98-22912

Random House website address: www.randomhouse.com

Printed in the United States of America
on acid-free paper
2 4 6 8 9 7 5 3
First Edition

Book design by Tanya Pérez-Rock

Not long ago, I was invited to speak at my high school's second annual gay and lesbian awareness assembly—six hundred ninth through twelfth graders. When I was sitting where they were sitting, I told them, not an hour went by that I did not think of my one central mission in life: never having anyone find out the horrific truth.

And there I was, telling virtually the entire school.

A couple of months later, I was asked to be a trustee. Boy, has the world ever changed.

This book is the story of that change, at least from my small window on it; and a thank-you note to those—very possibly including you—who through their goodwill and open minds have helped change it.

This book also explains how I kidnapped Scot, why I am not secretary of the treasury, and some ways we might be able to change the world still further. But hang on.

The Best Little Boy in the World Grows Up

1

"What do you mean, 'Proposed Epilogue'?" my editor at G. P. Putnam & Sons asked a quarter century ago when he had finished reading the final draft of *The Best Little Boy in the World*.

We had just gotten through a long discussion—I wouldn't call it a fight—where I was trying to persuade him to let me use "The Red Crayon" as my pen name, which he said was stupid. (How would it be alphabetized in *Books in Print*—under Crayon?) And now we were on to the fight—I wouldn't call it a discussion—over what to call the last section of the book. To me, this was even more important.

The pen name thing I just thought was clever, and might cause reviewers to focus on an anecdote in the book about how once, when I was about eleven and *incredibly* sheltered . . . I mean *incredibly* sheltered, and even more incredibly afraid someone would discover My Secret . . . I had been at a party where we were all given crayons and paper and instructed to write some really terrible word. The slips of paper—all anonymous—would then be collected, and the hostess, also about eleven, would read some dumb fill-in-the-blanks story about a princess. (This was back in the days before most eleven-year-olds had beepers and subscriptions to *Wired*.) So, being the best little boy in the world, and crouching back there behind the couch with my crayon and scrap of paper, I did exactly what I was told. I wrote the absolute worst word I could think of. And then our hostess began reading.

"So the . . . toilet . . . princess and the . . . booger . . . prince went down to the . . . slimeball . . . fountain and"—all was going well until our hostess, looking at the next word to be inserted, burst into tears and went running from the room.

Something told me she had come to my scrap of paper. I began to sweat. *"Okay!"* her mother yelled, storming back into the room. *"Which one of you has the red crayon?!"*

Agh! The red crayon! It was *supposed to be anonymous.*

Anyhow, it seemed to me that the manuscript I had just submitted to G. P. Putnam's had in a sense all been written with that red crayon . . . a book about things that—as strange as this may seem only twenty-five years later—were all but unmentionable.

So I just thought The Red Crayon was a more than apt pen name. And if it was different . . . if it didn't fit the established mold . . . well, wasn't that sort of the whole point? Wasn't that my life? And if it was a little on the cute side, what else was new? My college roommate Hank, as I called him in the last book—who went on to become mayor of Cincinnati, incidentally—always used to kid me about that. "Is it any good?" I'd ask him of whatever I'd most recently written. (In college, we'd coauthored a book called *The Ivy League Guidebook.*) "Well, it's . . . cute," he'd say.

So, cute I could live with. But my editor, who had already agreed to acquire this literary masterwork for $5,000, was not amused. I could publish the book under my own name or under a pen name, but not under the name of a crayon. Not only was it too cute, it just wasn't remotely practical or possible. "So forget it."

So I did. I went instead with the name John Reid, which was the Lone Ranger's real name (if you believe, as on some level I surely did, that the Lone Ranger was real). What was he trying to *hide* behind that mask . . . *his* deep dark secret? Did you ever see *him* with a babe? He was just riding around with Tonto being *good* all the time. Only later would I discover that John Reid (spelled differently—Reed—but pronounced the same) was also the name of the famous Soviet-sympathizing American journalist Warren Beatty portrayed in *Reds* (making me not just a homo but a commie)—as well as the name of at least three men who wrote outraged letters to G. P. Putnam & Sons, fearful that someone might actually think this disgusting book had been written by *them*.

One even threatened to sue.

I don't know anyone named Crayon who would have sued.

But the pen name, though I cared deeply about it, was an argument I was willing to lose. The fight over this "Proposed Epilogue" thing was much more important.

"Just call it Epilogue," my editor said, growing testy.

"I can't," I said.

"Why not?"

"That makes it sound like fact; but it's not fact. It's *proposed* fact."

I *planned* to tell my parents I was gay, and I *expected* they'd say that as far as they were concerned, I was still the best little boy in the world—but I had not yet in fact actually stepped up to the plate and made the announcement. My manuscript had gotten a little ahead of my real life.

"Well, then, fine," said my editor. "By the time the book comes out, it *will* be fact. So call it Epilogue. There's no such thing as a Proposed Epilogue."

"There is now!" I insisted.

After all, why not? How could this possibly matter to my editor? Surely it had nothing to do with selling the book or how it would be listed in *Books in Print*. But it was crucially important to me, because I had spent my entire life trying to be the best little boy in the world, trying never to lie . . . and I had written the rest of the book, though disguised (it was Harvard, not Yale—that sort of thing), just as honestly as I possibly could, preposterous as that may sound to those of you who read it. (Yes, really: I was eighteen and a sophomore in college when I learned, by accident, to masturbate. One has to be honest-and-then-some to admit such things, even under a pen name.)

"Look," he said. "If you don't want to call it Epilogue, call it Chapter Sixteen."

This man was entirely missing the point. But after much back-and-forth I gave in. I figured, Well, this just gives me no out. I *must* tell them now, before the book appears, or else the book is dishonest. And they *must* say it's okay, or else I'm in deep trouble. Not only would I have the impossibility of losing their love and respect, I'd have the guilt of knowing that the entire two-sentence last chapter of my autobiography—"*I told them. They said that so far as they were concerned, I was still the best little boy in the world*"—was a lie.

I was virtually certain, having known them well for nearly twenty-five years, that their reaction would be as described. And I couldn't go any longer without telling them, anyway. It's one thing to keep the secret under ordinary circumstances. But to keep it when you were publishing a *book* about it, for crying out loud?

So I swallowed hard and agreed to Chapter 16.

A practical, courageous person at that point would have scheduled a dinner with his parents to tell them forthwith. That way, the matter would be resolved; and in the dread event their reaction were *not* as written, there'd be time to correct Chapter 16 in galleys (just before moving to Australia).

I *am* a practical person—very much so—but not particularly courageous.

I put it off.

After all, there would be nearly a year before the book actually hit the bookstores. In case this news would hurt the folks as much as I feared (though I was confident they'd still love me), why spring it on them any sooner than need be? I wasn't being a coward; I was being a good son!

The galleys arrived, and it was time to tell them. I just couldn't find the right moment.

A prepublication excerpt appeared in *New York* magazine (and they lived in New York). And I didn't tell them.

Of course, the excerpt was by "John Reid," and he went to Yale, not Harvard. But I got calls from friends I hadn't talked to in years—high school friends!—congratulating me on the excerpt. "Uh, what do you mean?" I would ask. "Well, the style is unmistakable," they'd reply.

All right, it wasn't dozens of calls, maybe just two. But if two high school friends I hadn't seen in years could figure it out, surely the Supreme Court (as I affectionately thought of them), who *subscribed* to this magazine—who bragged to all their friends that I was *on the masthead* of this magazine—would surely pick up on it, too.

For several weeks I was jumpy when the phone rang. But the dread call never came.

And then advance copies of the book arrived and I hadn't told them, and then it hit the stores (with a resounding "plip") and I hadn't told them, and then it was reviewed in *The New York* freaking *TIMES,* for crying out loud, and I hadn't told them.

I felt guilty; I felt odd (although perhaps I also felt a slight sense of living-dangerously exhilaration); and I just sort of pushed it to the back of the list of important things I definitely was going to do. Like writing a will.

In short, I lied.

I had *not* told them.

Uh-oh.

2

The *Best Little Boy in the World* came out in 1973, when I was twenty-six. *I* had come out all of three years earlier, the summer of my twenty-third birthday. It had only taken me a dozen years from the time I first realized—instinctively, at age ten or so—that that *word* my father and his friend were using with such distaste as they walked through the TV room applied to *me*.

Don't ask me how I knew. I was a gifted child.

And yet it *didn't* apply to me. I *wasn't* a homosexual, for crying out loud. I just felt a tremendous attraction to boys my own age and none at all—I mean *none*—to girls of any age.

I wasn't stupid, so I never told anyone about this. But it was the very essence of who I was. There wasn't a moment growing up that I wasn't consciously compensating for it. It was as if I had been a secret agent in a foreign country. Everything I said, every glance—I *never* looked longingly at what I longed for—it all had to pass through the censor.

I coped. In high school, I was on the soccer team, I was on the swimming team, and when my time for the 400-yard freestyle began to slacken rather than improve (chlorine poisoning, perhaps), Coach Kramp (honest! Harry Kramp—good guy) suggested I go out for wrestling instead. So junior year, I wrestled.

(I happened to be in the league's toughest weight class—137. Early on, our captain, also in that weight class, had his neck broken. Against all reason, and after only a few weeks' practice, I was now wrestling varsity in the 137-pound weight class for Horace Mann School. Coach Quinn would tell everybody else to get in there and kill. But when it was my turn, he'd rub my shoulders and just keep reminding me they get only three points if they win but *five* points for a pin. *Stay off your back.* Sometimes I did, sometimes I didn't.)

Junior year was also when I began thinking about going out into the real world.*

For this, I was utterly unprepared. For one thing, I couldn't do the Twist. Dancing with girls was something that made me so nervous and self-conscious, I lost what little sense of rhythm and agility I otherwise possessed—which made me all the more nervous that people would see there was obviously something wrong with me, which made me all the more inept. When it came to guy talk and nudging my buddies to check out the hot stuff coming up the street, I lived in constant terror. I didn't know which the hot stuff was. At any moment I was in danger of saying something so unbelievably inappropriate as to blow my cover.

I had no idea what I would do with my life—or how I could even have a life. Everyone normal dated and fell in love and got married and had kids, and that was what I would have to do—but it was, I knew, completely impossible. My sex drive had been multiplied by minus one, as I came to think of it—the equation was the same, but all the signs had been reversed. *And,*

---

* In high school, college seems like the real world.

as best I could tell, I was the only one. Again, I was not stupid (well, not completely stupid). I knew what a homosexual was: I had seen pictures in comic books—the pale, skinny person with long blond hair lying on the beach furtively, behind a boulder, beside the dark-bronzed bodybuilder. But this was not me. Kiss another guy? Cowboys don't kiss.

I took periodic melodramatic walks, talking with myself about suicide, though never, I think, seriously considering it. There was no need for that yet—any *given* day I could negotiate quite well. Horace Mann was then still an all-boys day school, and on weekends our family went up to a fairly remote country place where, for all my friends knew or cared, I was a heterosexual love machine. My parents could see I didn't want to talk about my social life, and also that I had a date every blue moon—a necessary torture. They must have just figured I was a late bloomer and, like a lot of teenagers, possessive of my privacy. Who had time for girls, anyway? I was competing to get into college.

My folks made it simple. They said I would go to Harvard. What if I don't get in? I asked. They—modest people about everything except their children—said I *would* get in. Well, what about a safety school? (Like Yale, I am tempted to add.) Shouldn't I apply to one of those? No, they said; I was going to Harvard.

And Harvard, bless its heart, said okay. (The fact that my brother, Goliath—not his real name—had paved the way and would graduate summa cum laude the June before I arrived as a freshman probably didn't hurt, either.)

At Harvard, though I loved almost every minute of it, I was consumed with my cosmic problem. Running the student business conglomerate or sitting in a Slavic Literature class—I majored in Slavic Languages and Literatures, which for me meant reading *War and Peace* in English, in the Cliff Notes edition—my secret was as uppermost in my mind as sex is in any young man's mind. Perhaps you saw *Europa Europa*. It is based on the true story of a young Jewish boy who was sent from home to escape the Nazis but wound up at a school for promising Hitler Youth, his very survival dependent on never letting *anyone* know his true identity. Imagine—circumcised—how terrified he must have been even of taking a shower. Everything he heard and said had to pass in and out of his brain through a filter, multiplied by minus one.

This is effectively how the don't-ask, don't-tell folks want us to live. It's dishonest, and it takes a toll.

I didn't know any gay men at Harvard—or didn't think I did. I later learned that my Winthrop House classmate next door, Nat Butler—whose heart was beating no more than thirty feet from mine for three years—was going through much the same thing I was, thinking *he* was the only one in the world who had this terrible secret. And that two of Winthrop's best-liked tutors, Barney Frank and John Newmeyer, were gay (though Barney was as closeted as I was). And that my freshman proctor had been gay—indeed, that there had been gay parties going on *in the basement of my freshman dorm,* even as I was agonizing three floors up.

To all this, I was oblivious.

More than that, I was a fairly severe homophobe. The one or two people I did wonder about, I treated with contempt, as almost any red-blooded American boy did back then—and there was nothing I wanted more than to be a red-blooded American boy.

Yet how could I square that with the fact that I was in love with two of my roommates?

On one level, I "knew" there probably were other people like me—regular guys who liked guys—much as we "know," mathematically, that there is probably other intelligent life in the universe. But how do you make contact? Guess wrong, and you're finished. (It was actually Nat Butler's *roommate* I was suspicious of—wrongly, as it turns out.) I spent hours thinking of ridiculous schemes—anonymous random social science surveys I would send out, with replies to a P.O. box. Except that my survey wouldn't be sent out randomly at all, but to a select few. And they wouldn't be anonymous, either. Any fool could code them with imperceptible markings. And if one of them . . . if only . . . if . . .

Of course, I never did any of this. In four years at Harvard I remained 100 percent bottled up inside.

Only once that I can recall did I think of actually talking to anyone. I went to the office of Rusty Kothavala, the highly popular instructor of Nat Sci 10—Rocks for Jocks—and also the proctor who had lived in the basement of my dorm, Pennypacker Hall, with his wife and daughter. There was something simpatico about him I felt I could trust, and I was *so* depressed, *so* lonely and despairing, I went to his office, sat down, and began to talk. I was nineteen; he was thirty-two.

I can't remember what I talked about, except that it was probably not geology and it was definitely not "my secret." I came *that close,* but had trained myself too well. This was one secret agent they'd never catch.

"Oh, I remember it well," Rusty told me in his pleasing singsong cadence when I called thirty years later. "You hemmed and hawed for about half an hour—it dawned on me that maybe this was what was bugging you, but I felt it would be wrong to pry unless you brought it up first."

"But—but—" I sputtered, with questions about his wife and, well, everything else.

"The Sixties were terrific fun," he said, cheerily. "I was at Harvard getting my Ph.D. and remember I just stumbled onto a place in Boston opposite the bus station, a bar called the Punch

Bowl, a big place with flashing lights. I was sort of wide-eyed and hesitant, and when I got to the door, the bouncer looked at me and said, 'Yeah, this is the place.' "

He had discovered the Punch Bowl through good old-fashioned legwork. "I spent a week going to downtown bars every evening until I found a gay one." Once there, he ran into all sorts of undergraduates, grad students, proctors, faculty—it was a widespread network. Scores and scores of people. How big were the parties he had at Pennypacker? "Maybe thirty people, something like that."

And upstairs I slept.

Rusty got married in 1963, the year before I arrived. In fact, it was his wife-to-be who helped him come to terms with himself. He had been all contorted and conflicted and finally told her. "Good Lord," he recalls her asking. "Is that all? Here I thought you were one of these international criminals or something."

And gay parties in the Pennypacker basement? *Wasn't he afraid of being caught?*

"I believed it was perfectly all right to be gay. And I figured if people weren't tuned in, they wouldn't see it, so there was nothing to be concerned about. But I was also clear that I was not going to become sexually involved with any of the students, so that was easy. Following those simple rules, it was really all quite a breeze."

Not for me, it wasn't. And not for my friend Bill—or so I surmise, anyway. I never talked with him about any of this. No one did. But a few years later, after he had finished Harvard College and Harvard Medical School and was beginning his residency, he put a shotgun in his mouth. I was completely at a loss. How could anyone have done that, let alone someone so extraordinarily successful, handsome, and popular? (Everyone loved Bill.) My *straight* friends—his roommates, who knew him better than

I had—came to the conclusion that he did it because he was gay and couldn't deal with it.

It wasn't that Bill *seemed* gay. He was a varsity sprinter, a skier, a strong, manly guy, albeit shy with women and something of a loner. And not from Greenwich Village or some other Gomorrah—he was from rural Pennsylvania. But this is what his roommates, who knew him best, considered the most likely cause. As I've thought back on it over the years—wondering, too, whether he would be alive and how my own life might be different if we had dared go further than playful arm-punching—I've come to the conclusion they were probably right.

Even today, nearly a third of teenage suicides are thought to be gay kids unable to live in a world that despises them—though I like to think that in light of the last few years' remarkable progress that figure may have begun to drop.

A couple of years after graduating, I did manage to "come out"—with extreme trepidation—to one of my closest straight friends. And then to another and another. (It got easier; I got more confident.) At twenty-two, I still had not had sex with anyone, male or female, as I went around spilling the beans.

In the book, I said John Reid worked for IBM. Actually, he had gone on to work for a company called National Student Marketing Corporation, where he—I—worked crazy hours (no time for a social life, I could tell my folks truthfully) and where I was now obsessed with *two* things: my secret, of course, which was ever-present, but now, also, my stock options, which with just six months left before I could exercise them were worth $400,000 (about $1.5 million in today's money).

The full extent of my gay life at this company was a guy named Glenn, whom I fantasized wrestling to the floor of my office and . . . and . . . well, I was a pretty good wrestler but had no clue what might come after that. Of course, this was only fantasy. In a million years I would never have done it, or even told him I was attracted to him. It was a different time. (Nor could Glenn risk encouraging me. Years later I was astonished to learn he had been a "practicing homosexual" all the time I was fantasizing.)

I was the company's lowliest vice president, with forty employees and an office on the thirty-fifth floor of the Time & Life Building. I had a beautiful secretary, Maggie, whose awesome young body made me extremely nervous—but who was so genuinely nice, and who seemed to like me so much, I managed to overlook it. On December 31, 1969—New Year's Eve, the most reliably awkward, depressing night of the year for someone living the kind of life I was—I took her out as my date. I can't remember where we went but do remember taking her home before she would have liked, and not coming upstairs. Today, this is the stuff of *Seinfeld* episodes, where Elaine tries to get that guy to "switch teams," but he's perfectly *happy* on that team, and it's all pretty much out in the open and funny. ("They *like* their team," Jerry advises Elaine, or words to that effect.) But back then it was horrible. I didn't want to hurt Maggie's feelings, yet I could hardly tell her the truth. And I *certainly* couldn't come upstairs and switch teams for the night. It was as unthinkable to me as it must be to Jesse Helms to mess around with Sam Nunn.

Anyway, I got her home, out in Queens somewhere, and kept the cab for the long ride back into Manhattan. Maybe I got home at three. I'm not clear what happened for the next few hours, but I think what must have happened is that I dropped a tab of mescaline and went to sleep. I would like to stress this was a *long* time ago (and it was, for all practical purposes, the Sixties, even though technically it had become the Seventies a couple of hours earlier). For those of you who don't know, mescaline is like acid—and not ordinarily taken at bedtime.

This is what I had been doing for fun . . . a better term

might be "release" . . . during my intense stint at National Student Marketing. Most Sundays, I'd do a tab of mescaline. Alone. For me, it was akin to a religious experience, and a time to explore the depths of my cosmic, melodramatic soul. Who was I going to be? How was I going to survive? I remember going to see *Easy Rider* one Sunday afternoon, alone—and sitting through two complete showings without ever budging from my seat.

Easy Rider is deep.

Every second weekend or so, I would take the Eastern Airlines Shuttle up to Boston, to visit my college friends, who'd rented an old town house in Back Bay: 331 Beacon Street. Strings still reached all the way from the fifth-floor bedrooms down to bells in the kitchen in case you wanted to ring for tea— not that they had any servants to ring for or drank a lot of tea. Indeed, they didn't even have furniture, beyond beds and a couple of thrift-shop sofas and rugs in this giant house, all of which they rented for $600 a month.

It was so cool. How I longed truly to fit in.

Anyway, I must not have slept much or at all that New Year's morning, and soon I was hailing a cab to La Guardia. I wasn't sure what time the first shuttle departed, but no matter: I was just completely drawn to Boston and my friends.

Finally, at either six or seven, I guess, it was time to brave the cold sunrise and climb the stairs to the plane. I will never forget a freshly shaved, bright-eyed senior Eastern Airlines pilot crisply welcoming me aboard—unshaven and deep into my own head.

"Congratulations, young man," he said, reaching to shake my hand. "You are the first Eastern Airlines Shuttle passenger of the decade."

Startled, I mumbled something, hoping he couldn't tell I was tripping or homosexual—both seemed so obvious to me— and took a seat.

Then I began thinking about it, and although there were

presumably others boarding planes in Boston and Washington at approximately the same time, I chose to believe that I was indeed the first Eastern Airlines Shuttle passenger of the decade. And—not being much of a pioneer in anything else—I thought that was pretty neat. It would give me something amusing to tell the guys when I got to Boston (not that anyone but me would be awake for many hours), and presumably Eastern would be sending me some kind of trophy. When nothing came, I wrote Frank Borman, astronaut–turned–Eastern Airlines CEO, and months later received a beautiful hand-lettered, felt-framed commemorative certificate. I still have it.

A sort of testimonial, if you will, to my having been one remarkably screwed-up young adult.

And yet, with the help of these psychedelic Sundays, I did finally loosen up—first, enough to tell a handful of my closest straight friends, almost all of whom took it well, and then, finally, enough to actually *do* something about it.

But for that I needed a cover.

Harvard Business School, I decided, would be perfect.

My fortune in stock options had disappeared when it turned out that NSMC's accounting was fraudulent. The president and a guy from Peat Marwick went to jail. I went off to Harvard Business School.

When asked why, I told people I wanted something "respectable" to do while I regrouped.

In fact, I wanted something respectable to do while I came out.

It was the summer of 1970. I had just turned twenty-three. Suddenly, I was like someone from the Soviet Union inside a Western supermarket for the first time. You should have *seen* me careening up and down the aisles.

So, no, it wasn't IBM. I picked IBM as part of John Reid's disguise thinking it combined the white-shirted seriousness of

Harvard Business School with the excitement of a Wall Street star. (NSMC's stock had risen in eighteen months from its $6 initial public offering price to $140 before it collapsed.)

But why a disguise at all? Why a pen name?

On the one hand, once I finally did break out of my shell I was soon bursting with indignation—and with a book that just had to be written. It was astonishing! There was a whole world out there "everybody" knew about but *nobody* knew about. It was so hypocritical! It was so unfair! It was such an amazing story! Soldiers were gay, priests were gay, teachers were gay—*headmasters* were gay—executives and tax attorneys were gay, movie stars were gay, cops were gay, Roy Cohn was gay. Alexander the Great was gay, Da Vinci was gay, Tchaikovsky was gay, Herman Melville was gay. John Maynard Keynes was gay. *J. Edgar Hoover was gay!* There were millions of decent Americans leading elaborate double lives that almost no one knew about. Parents went to their graves never knowing their children. (And children sometimes went to their graves never knowing their parents.) So much deception! So much shame! And *why*? What had *I* done wrong, for crying out loud? What had *any of us* done wrong to have been born the way we were? (Or if not born, then "determined" in the first few years of life.) And how did it hurt anyone if we simply were ourselves?

It was, as I say, an amazing story, and I had gone to schools whose mottoes were, respectively, *Magna est veritas et praevalebit* ("Great is the truth and it shall prevail") and *Veritas* ("Truth"), and here was a truth of monumental proportions sitting there like a big fat emperor with no clothes. I had read *1984*. I knew about truths that dare not be spoken, and the urgent need to speak them anyway and overthrow tyranny.

The point is, by the time I was finishing up my MBA, I *had* to tell this story.

On the other hand, this was 1972. To have used my real name would have required far more courage than I had. It would also have exposed my parents to embarrassment I would never willingly have caused them.

So The Red Crayon wrote it, and in complete secrecy.

Just as I had taken the summer off before starting Harvard Business School to write a book about my National Student Marketing experience—*The Funny Money Game*—so I now took the summer off before going to work for *New York* magazine to write a book about *this* experience.

It had been my vague notion to become some sort of entrepreneur. At Harvard Student Agencies, I had helped build the fledgling publishing business, which was centered around *Let's Go: The Student Guide to Europe.* At NSMC, I had started a business that rented refrigerators, cheap, to student governments. It was a win-win for everyone. I still get excited thinking about it.* Once I had my MBA, I thought someone would give me a new venture to launch, much like the refrigerator business or *Let's Go.* Instead, I got offers from Boston Consulting Group, *Fortune,* and *New York.*

In 1972, an offer from Boston Consulting Group was pretty much first prize. Yet how would I fit in? I couldn't see myself golfing with clients and swapping stories about our wives. Now that I actually had a private life, I couldn't imagine trying to pretend I was someone other than who I was. No, if I had a shot at happiness, writing was probably the better avenue. *Fortune* was alluring—good money, great magazine, the chance to do important stories. But *New York,* for which I had already written, and on whose cover I had already appeared inside a soap bubble about to burst ("Confessions of a Youth Marketeer"), was the sentimental favorite. Clay Felker had energy and vision no one could match; his partner Milton Glaser was a genius. And Shel-

---

* My two passions: refrigerator rentals and auto insurance reform. I am unquestionably an exciting guy.

ley Zalaznick, Clay's managing editor, was wise, gracious, funny, and welcoming. So that's where I went. But not before writing my book.

I moved down to New York, to a little apartment on Sullivan Street—with walls so thin I learned what little I know about straight sex from my neighbors—and spent the summer writing. There and in Massachusetts. In total secrecy. Banging away on a portable manual typewriter.

When the Supreme Court asked what I was doing, I told them I was "writing the great American novel." Everyone of that era knew such novels never actually got written, let alone published. But that was okay. It was an answer. They knew I'd be writing for *New York* come the fall, and were proud of that—their son the writer (Goliath, meanwhile, had become their son the anthropologist)—so what harm could it do?

Sure enough, I admitted around Labor Day, I hadn't really gotten anywhere with the novel. I'd just stuck it in a drawer. Someday maybe I'd come back to it.

But in fact I had written something explosive. Or so it seemed to me.

When I called my agent (thanks to *New York* and *The Funny Money Game,* I had an agent), I said only that I needed to see him. I had written a book, I said, but the identity of the author must be kept secret. Would he look at it on that basis?

I handed him the manuscript—he, as dignified and WASPy a heterosexual as you will find anywhere—and held my breath. No one in the world had read it but me.

Today, of course, one might casually hand it to any agent—or choose a gay agent, for that matter. But apart from my not knowing any gay agents back then, it wouldn't even have occurred to me. It had not dawned on me that there would be a gay audience for *The Best Little Boy in the World.* Or at least that was not the point. Gay people already *knew* this story. In my mind's eye, it was always straight people I was writing the book for—all the good people who, I was sure, if they just knew the truth, would (a) be astounded and (b) rally round to right the wrongs and change the world.

In fact, as it happened, only about six straight people read the thing, especially in the early years (one of them, thankfully, was my agent), whereas gay readers have kept it reliably in print all this time. But I was only half wrong. Especially in the last few years, the good people I had in mind have, for the most part, gotten the message (though only those six got it from me), and many have rallied round just as I thought they would. We're not there yet, but we've come a long way. *Magna est veritas et praevalebit.*

3

My agent placed the book with G. P. Putnam's. Everyone else turned it down. And while my editor was happy to have it, scuffles over the pen name and Epilogue notwithstanding, Putnam's sales force, as I learned later, was not. Well, really! What would you expect? This was a book about *that*. And most of the sales guys were nice straight men of a certain age who, like my dad and his friend going through the TV room while I watched cowboys whip out their guns and vie for dominance, *just didn't talk about that*.

Today, of course, we talk about anything—and in the middle of the day, on TV ("Mothers who date bulimic daughters' boyfriends—next *Leeza*"). Back then, discussion of homosexuality was just beginning, and in the most tentative way.

Today, every bookstore has a whole section of "Gay and Lesbian Studies." Back then, there was Gore Vidal's *The City and the Pillar*. Okay, and a few others—but scattered around the store, and with no sign pointing to them, so how would you even know?

What's more, *The Best Little Boy in the World* was not a book that would be backed by a publicity tour. The author couldn't very well go around with a bag over his head. And Putnam's was not about to advertise it.

To my surprise, it did get reviewed in *The New York Times,* and quite generously. The reviewer, David Brudnoy, I would later learn, was himself gay. (Was that cheating?)* No doubt helped by David's review, the book's small first printing sold out in fairly short order. Putnam's, perhaps chastened by the response of its sales force, declined to do a second.

To force its hand, I took some ads in the closest thing there was back then to a national gay magazine—*After Dark,* a magazine that never specifically said anything about being gay, but it was a *dance* magazine, for crying out loud (or so I remember it)—and I got about 1,500 mail orders, which Putnam's grudgingly went back to press to fulfill. But they weren't interested in taking it any further. The subsidiary-rights person, I learned through a friend, actually discouraged a paperback sale. A few years later, I sold the paperback rights myself.

Via the publisher—who forwarded them to my agent, who forwarded them to me—I got a lot of letters. "Dear 'John,' " many of them began. "I can't believe it—you wrote my story." It seems there were a lot of best little boys in the world out there.

Twenty-five years later, I still get letters every now and then. One fellow even told me not long ago that the book saved his life. He says he used to sleep with a loaded gun by his pillow every night—not because he feared intruders, but because he was an aide to a highly conservative, homophobic Missouri congressman, and the tension in his head between who he was

---

* David, in case you don't know, has since become a rightly beloved New England institution: a conservative/libertarian radio talk show host whose near-death AIDS experiences, and the extensive national publicity that resulted, he recounted in 1997 in *Life Is Not a Rehearsal.*

and who he was supposed to be was all but unbearable. Somehow, *The Best Little Boy in the World* helped him break out of his shell, quit his job, and start doing something positive. I have no illusions I actually saved his life. But however small its grain of truth, such a story obviously trumps any royalty. (And is both tax- and commission-free.)

Now I have to stop and tell you something very spooky. By way of background, you need to know that the classic lesbian "coming out" novel is *Rubyfruit Jungle,* by Rita Mae Brown. I came upon it in paperback only several years after it had been published. My overwhelming impression when I read it was that it might just as easily have been titled *The Worst Little Girl in the World.* The author was everything I was not—mischievous, tough, profane, worldly, poor, female, orphaned, brave, and secretly attracted to *girls.* Really, the two books, hers and mine, are almost a yin-and-yang set: both first published in 1973 (by separate publishers), both first reprinted in paperback in 1977 (likewise), both continuously in print ever since.

Okay, no need to fall off your chair. I grant you that's just moderately spooky at best. But wait.

In the first book, I wrote about going to "Camp Winnepesaukee." It was actually Camp Wigwam, in Maine, and Richard Rodgers actually wrote one of the camp songs, and Einstein actually vacationed there for a week—all this long before my time, though perhaps not long before my dad was Best Camper 1933—*so I'll have no snickering about Camp Wigwam.* I loved Camp Wigwam. I went on to become a counselor for a year, and today one of my campers from that era runs the camp. My partner, Charles, and I went up this past summer to visit.

Well, one of my own counselors at Wigwam was a very cool guy named Jerry Pfeiffer, captain of the tennis team at the University of Florida at Gainesville, if memory serves, who seemed to take more than a casual interest in my fourteen-year-old bod.

But that couldn't have meant anything, because he had this equally cool girlfriend, a proud Southerner, also on the Florida tennis team, whom he'd gotten a job as a counselor at our sister camp, Hiawatha. (I'll have no snickering about Hiawatha, either.) The two of them were obviously going at it hot and heavy. I know, because on a couple of occasions I even had to double-date with them—Jerry took me and my little Camp Hiawatha girlfriend out to the movies along with him and his gal.

Her name? Yes! Rita Mae Brown.

I had no clue she was gay; nor she, I. We had absolutely no contact after that summer until long after publication of our books.

Now: In a country of 200 million people, what were the chances that a deeply repressed little upper-middle-class New York best little boy in the world would find himself double-dating in Harrison, Maine, with a poor orphaned Southern worst little girl in the world—and that they would be more or less the only two people out of 200 million to write "coming out" autobiographies back before it became a genre, and that these two books, in hardcover and then again in paperback, would come out—totally independent of each other, from separate publishers—at almost exactly the same time?

Of course, unlike the best little boy in the world (hereafter: TBLBITW), Rita Mae Brown had the courage to use her real name.

No, I had still not told my parents.

Before every phone call, I'd do a little rehearsal, thinking of the accomplishments I could offer them—what I was writing for *New York* magazine, mainly—and perhaps some white lie about my social life if one was needed.

I certainly couldn't tell them about the goings-on at Sullivan Street or, later, at London Terrace—let alone out on Fire Island. (I think I told them I went to the Hamptons.) What? And break their hearts? They were *so proud* of me. And so protective. If you think it's tough news for a parent to hear today, imagine what it was like in the Seventies, when the only gay "role models" were the characters in movies who minced for a laugh or hanged or shot themselves. Or were *so* unnaturally fond of their mothers that they kept them in rocking chairs, long after they were dead.*

But neither could I fail to tell them. What? And lie to them all my life? Or have them hear it from someone else? Surely they eventually would. I did have a book out about this, after all. We did live in the same city.

And so the battle would rage in my head, with me never quite finding the courage or the right moment, always aware that once spoken, the words could never be unspoken.

Everything else in my life was going well. Not my love life, entirely—I'll get to that—but everything else.

Finally, one Sunday, writing an Afterword for the paperback, which would be out shortly, and almost thirty years old, I could take it no longer. It was just too preposterous. The book was coming out in paperback and *still* I hadn't told them?

I picked up the phone, dialed the number in Westchester (it was Bedford Village, not Brewster), and when my mother answered I said, almost this abruptly ("You told them over the *phone*?" my friends marvel at my lack of grace): "Mom, listen. I really apologize if I should have told you years ago, and I really apologize if I shouldn't be telling you until years *from* now, and of course I realize you may already know anyway, but I just feel as if I have to tell you—I'm gay."

I don't remember the words exactly, but that was the gist of it. I do remember her words exactly. They were: "Don't tell your father."

---

* Norman Bates may or may not have been gay, but Tony Perkins was.

She whispered this urgently as Dad went to pick up the extension in the other room.

"But—"

"Promise me!"

Good son that I was, or wasn't, or wanted to be, I was left with my mouth open but nothing coming out.

The subject, which Mom and I soon met over lunch to discuss, made her very uncomfortable. And a little frosty. We were not a family that *had* problems, and certainly not one that aired them.

(I was thirty-five before I learned that my mother has a brother. I was driving her and *her* mother up the West Side Highway, listening out of the corner of my ear as they talked about what, if anything, to send "your brother" for his birthday, thinking perhaps they must have meant *my* brother—Goliath— but finally making sense of it and almost driving off the road. "*Wait* a minute," I interrupted. "Are you saying you have a brother?" I knew of course about my mother's brother Previn, who had been killed in the war, and after whom I had been middle-named*—but a *living* brother? "Yes," my mother said in a way that suggested she didn't care to discuss it. "Why do I only know about this *now*?" I asked. "You never asked," she said. Basically, they had just drifted apart. His converting from Judaism had something to do with it, I think, though we were anything but religious—and so he was *just not discussed*.)

I'm not saying Mom was Mary Tyler Moore in *Ordinary People,* but her reaction to my news had that flavor. Of *course* she loved me, but this was a part of my life she just didn't want to know about. She certainly didn't want to risk making my father miserable by my telling him.

·   ·   ·

---

* I am Andrew Previn Tobias and, yes, André Previn is my second cousin, which must make Woody Allen my third-cousin-in-law-once-removed-by-adoption.

Well, now.

Ahem.

This was not exactly the way the Epilogue was supposed to read.

With time, of course, it did play out just as expected. Today, in fact, my mother jokes that while she certainly loves Goliath's wife, she does wish he could have found someone like Charles. And not just because Charles gets her the clothes he designs wholesale. (Though we are all human.)

So this is not to knock my mother. But appearances are important to her. She winces every time my age surfaces, let alone my older brother's, because she realizes that armed with this information, people are less likely to assume that she's younger than we are. I actually overheard her once talking to someone about Goliath. "How *old* is he?" she asked, as if this were the kind of trivia no mother could possibly be expected to recall. "I don't know—thirty-something." This was not, strictly speaking, true.

As for the appearance of a gay son—well, *she* accepted it, but what sense did it make to let others know? Like Dad.

So for more than a year, if you can believe it, I did not tell my father. It was now a secret among me, my mom, all my gay friends, most of my straight friends, my brother (who was lovely about it), my agent and editors, and Lord knows who else. And Mom seemed to think this was the best of a bad situation.

And in that respect, though she adored and admired my father totally, as he did her, I think she underestimated him.

I say this because after nearly two years of continued avoidance/deception, I finally got her permission to tell him. She asked that I do it on one of those rare occasions when she would be out of town—a board meeting in Hawaii. She thought he might be able to handle it better if he had a little space.

I called my dad in Bedford and, having learned it was best not to do this over the phone, asked whether he wouldn't mind stopping up a little early on his way back into the city on Sunday. And so late Sunday afternoon, he came. I still remember him sitting on the couch in my "office," the only such solo visit to my place I can ever recall him making.

I was not scared. I was nervous, but by now had become sufficiently confident in who I was, professionally and personally—and I had enough faith in him—that if anything, I think I felt excited. Wasn't *this* gonna be dramatic!

Leaning forward in a swivel chair that had cost me twenty bucks at a used furniture store, I spilled the beans as sensitively and sensibly as I could.

"Well?"

The thing is, there wasn't much of a reaction. It was, essentially: "Okay. Thanks for telling me." He didn't seem terribly uncomfortable, but neither did he show much interest in discussing it.

"That's it? I mean, I've been dreading telling you this for twenty years—I was sort of expecting more of a reaction. Aren't you, say, a little surprised?"

He said that by this time he wasn't all that surprised—after all, I had never really had any women in my life. He said he wasn't thrilled by the news, but basically all he cared about was that I be happy.

"Well," I said, certain that there was *some* way here to provide the drama I seemed to require after all these years of anguish, "would it surprise you to know I've written a book about it? And that it was reviewed in *The New York Times*?"

This surprised him.

I gave him a copy; he went home, possibly took two aspirin, and called me in the morning.

When he called, he was crying—which was much more drama than I had wanted. This was a man who did not cry. He had stayed up all night reading the book—twice. It was, he said, the best thing I had ever written.

"So, gee, Dad," I asked, choking up a little myself. "Why are you crying?" Well, he was crying because he loved me so much and felt so bad I had been through all that misery and he hadn't picked up on it or been there to help me with it.

Stop. This is getting schmaltzy, and neither my dad nor I was of a particularly schmaltzy stripe. So suffice it to say I assured him as forcefully as I could that he had absolutely nothing to feel bad or guilty about—that the whole *point* had been to hide it from him, and that the more important point was that it had all worked out okay! I was happy! Life was great!

And it *was* great, in no small measure, because of my wonderful parents and upbringing.

Mom came back a day or two later. Dad told her the news.

My mother's recollection all these years later is that when he did, she said that, well, like him, she really wasn't too surprised. She apparently never let on just how unsurprised she was.

They hoped it wouldn't make my life too difficult.

From then on, while the subject still wasn't one my folks were eager to discuss in much detail, the huge cloud of anxiety had been lifted.

One of my fondest memories, a few years before Dad died—it would have been around 1980—was of bringing my then boyfriend, Scot Haller, up to Bedford for Thanksgiving and introducing him for the first time. After a couple of hours, my dad pulled me aside and said, "He seems like a very fine young man."

4

S cot *was* a very fine young man, but before I tell you about Scot I need to tell you about Ed. And, before that, about how lonely I was before I *met* Ed.

The thing is, acknowledging that you're gay, if you are, and coming to accept it is only part of the challenge. Learning to have reasonably uninhibited, mutually satisfying sex is another part.* Making and keeping great friends is even more important—like many gay men, I have a terrific extended family. But the real trick, needless to say, gay or straight, is finding someone to share your life with and making that work.

That first summer—my Summer of '42, as I called it in the last book, although it was actually the summer of 1970—I embarked on all these various missions with a vengeance. By the end of the summer, I had met "Chris." Chris was at Harvard

_____

* In the first book, I suggested that if the road to good sex leads from Lisbon to Leningrad, I was, at that writing, lost someplace in the Pyrenees. Today, Leningrad's name has been changed back to St. Petersburg and I have visited three times—but only physically, sad to say, not metaphorically. Metaphorically, I'm someplace in Bavaria by now. But with my hormones not raging quite as they were at twenty-five, Bavaria's just fine. Good beer.

Law School—not Harvard Business School, as I had said in that book—*I* was at Harvard Business School—and he was my first boyfriend. It didn't last very long, because of Golden Boy—who was a senior at Tufts and Chris's best friend, but let's not rehash all *that* painful mess. Yet to this day, when I call Chris and say . . . "Hiiiiiiii" . . . in that fake deep-voice drawl we use only with each other, and only for this one word . . . or when he calls me and says . . . "Hiiiiii" . . . we instantly know who it is and break into a laugh. We're three thousand miles apart and six months may have passed since the last call, but that "Hiiiiii" is all it takes. Chris—once a teenage Senate page for Strom Thurmond, no less—graduated from Harvard, became an associate at Pillsbury, Madison & Sutro in San Francisco, then a partner at the leading Silicon Valley law firm, where he got options in some of those early Silicon Valley start-ups, then left all that to go to divinity school, and today is a lawyer and "medical ethicist" for one of the large hospital chains. He's been with his current partner, a bright young man who loves music and works in a music store, for nine years.

Golden Boy went from Tufts, where he'd been president of his senior class, to Arthur D. Little, the consulting firm, and from there to Harvard Business School for *his* MBA. Then on to Doyle Dane Bernbach, the ad agency, where he was assistant to the president for a while and then worked in administration. During this time he was on the board of the Martha Graham Dance Company (a subscriber to *After Dark,* no doubt), and he was a frequent denizen of the baths. When you're as good-looking as GB was, it's easy to have sex with lots of attractive people. And when it's easy to have sex with lots of attractive people, having sex with lots of attractive people can become addictive—which makes it all the more difficult to find that one special person you want to be faithful to. In a way, I'm fortunate not to have been that good-looking. And where my less-than-10 looks didn't save me from wild or anonymous sex, my prud-

ishness generally did. Anyway, as you can surely tell from this
buildup, GB's health problems began early, with a thing called
Bell's palsy that paralyzed one side of his face. It was his cue to
leave New York and find a different life. At one point, with his
health failing and the money running out, he actually went to
live with Chris for six months. Friendships run deep in the gay
world. Eventually, he returned to Cape Cod to live with his parents. He died in 1988.

Mr. Paranoia—while I'm running through the last book's
cast of characters—got his architecture degree from Harvard and
is alive and well in Middle America, winning awards and being
published in all manner of journals. He's on the board of the
local art museum, a sought-after lecturer, a principal in his own
small firm—nurtured by a small circle of straight and gay
friends, kept company by a trusty canine, and considerably less
paranoid about "being found out" than he once was. "Oh,
Andy," he says in his distinctive, emotion-laden way when I rib
him about it. "Everybody knows. I just don't want to make a
big thing about it." And sex? He's just largely thrown up his
hands about that by now. His playing-around days have long
been over, and he seems content to be alone. As his pal, I'd pre-
fer to think of him coupled in a loving relationship. But in com-
paring his life with that of many of my other straight and gay
friends, I'd say, on balance, he's as happy and centered as most,
more productive than all but a few. And who knows? The right
adoring grad student may yet come along one day.

I wasn't looking for an adoring grad student when I arrived in
New York, I was looking for Mr. Right. I was like a lot of other
young men and women, in other words. My type? Well, Tom
Cruise—or his then equivalent—is an easy, shorthand way to
give you an idea. Dazzling, funny, strong, confident, nice.

And there actually were some people like that in New York

twenty-five years ago. But how many of them were gay? And how to meet them? And—the real zapper—what were the chances they could ever possibly feel the same way about me?

Chris had been largely such a guy, and still is. The problem with Chris—and this is a problem one frequently encounters with relationships—is that he was human. Humans burp. Humans can be boring. Humans don't always want to mess around when you want to, and sometimes want to when you don't. This is never a problem with unattainable partners; they are flawless.

Humans, moreover—especially gay humans, I suspect—are not always sexually compatible. Yes, with men and women there must be endless variations, too. At a three-day Young Presidents Organization "university" extravaganza I once attended as a speaker, the most popular session was not the one on the future of Soviet oil production or mine on insurance but—over-whelmingly—the one entitled "Passive Men, Wild Women." So even I realize that the dominant partner in a straight rela-tionship is not always the guy. I know, for example, of a New York media personage (you'd recognize his name) who likes to be diapered by his dominatrix. But I think complete compati-bility between two guys may be even tougher than between a guy and a gal.

In any event, the point is this: As terrific as he was, Chris wasn't perfect. And though neither of us cared a hoot about di-apers, we weren't perfectly sexually compatible.

When one is twenty-three, one is looking for perfection. At least I was. And one is a horny little bastard, and tempted by for-bidden fruit, which is how Golden Boy and I wound up spend-ing one of the hotter nights of my life there in my Harvard B-School dorm room—though I remained completely loyal to Chris that night in everything other than fact.

Well, all this is recounted in tedious detail in *The Best Little*

Boy in the World. My point here is, simply, that if Chris, handsome and charming as he was, wasn't quite right for me, you can imagine the challenge of finding someone who was.

It was into that search that I threw myself when I reached New York in 1972 to begin my magazine-writing career.

Writing for *New York* was easy, once I got used to working on my own, at home most of the time, without much structure. My pieces ranged from a story about the phone company (which was actually doing a pretty good job, I thought—"Sorry, Right Number," the editors titled it) and a profile of *Barron's* columnist Alan Abelson ("The Smartest Man on Wall Street") to one about bank capital adequacy* (would the banks collapse? nah) and another about solar energy (Clay put a gorgeous girl on the cover, floating in a pool, soaking up the sun). I wrote profiles of music mogul Ahmet Ertegun, real estate mogul Sam Lefrak, and Paramount Pictures mogul Frank Yablans. I profiled a famous "gold bug," James Dines, whom Clay put on the cover with antennae coming out of his temples. "Does Bear Stearns Have a Deal for You?" asked one piece. "How Tall Is Robert Redford Really?" asked another. (A terrific guy, but not very tall.)

Before accepting the job, I had staked out another beat as well.

"You know, Shelley," I somehow summoned the nerve to say to *New York*'s Sheldon Zalaznick over lunch as I was being hired—cheeks burning in the supercooled (pre-OPEC) restaurant air—"if I come to work for you, I'd like to be able to write about one other area besides money and business."

---

* It was in regard to this article that I got a phone call from a woman at Citibank identifying herself as John Reed's secretary. At the time, Reed was one of Citicorp's young stars; since 1984, he's been its chairman. "Mr. Reed is giving a speech and plans to refer to your article and basically wanted me to find out: Who are you?" I came *so close* to saying, "Who am I? I'm John Reid!"

"Oh yes?"

"Well, I'm not sure that I would, and maybe just under a pen name, but . . ."

Somehow, very awkwardly, I got the thought out.

Fine, Shelley said calmly, offering me a roll.

As it happens, John Reid did only two such pieces for *New York* before the magazine was sold and we all moved on to *Esquire.* One was the aforementioned excerpt from *The Best Little Boy in the World.* The other, a year or two later, was called "How Gay Is New York?" although the real question it attempted to answer was more specific: How many New Yorkers are gay?

Of course, it was no secret by then to anyone I worked with, or virtually anyone I knew—except my parents—who John Reid was. What *was* very much unknown, yet intriguing to try to deduce, was just how many of our fellow citizens were gay or lesbian. I thought that by exploring this I might help people see the naked emperor . . . show our importance to the city . . . impress on our politicians the size of our constituency. The city had at least one gay congressman at the time, and I was certainly not the only gay writer for *New York,* but these things could not be publicly acknowledged.

Figuring out how tall Robert Redford is was easy: You measure him. (After much blocking and tackling by his loyal press agent, a very good-natured Redford allowed me to visit him on the set, joked about how meaningless my life was if *this* is what concerned me—why wasn't I writing about the environment?—and let me stand eye to eye with him to more or less figure out that he's five-nine, maybe five-ten. *The New York Times* had reported he was six-two.) Figuring out how many New Yorkers are gay was quite different. Even if I had had the resources to ask a large scientific sample, how many would have answered honestly?

Today the fear and shame are lifting fast. (A member of Harvard's class of 1971 notes that where only 2 percent of his classmates identified themselves as gay in the twentieth reunion survey, that number had jumped to 7 percent by his twenty-fifth.) But back in 1974, this was not the case. Nor did I have the resources to conduct surveys, in any event.

Also—what's gay? What's lesbian? In my mind, someone who fantasizes primarily about people of the same sex is gay or lesbian, whether he or she acts on those desires or not. And in my mind, there is a continuum, from 1, say, which would be entirely gay, like me, to 10, which would be entirely straight. How do you count someone who is a 3, happily married with wonderful children—but generally fantasizing about men when sleeping with his wife? I know some terrific people like this (a bit tortured, but terrific). Are they straight? Gay?

So it was obviously not possible to get any sort of clear-cut answer. Yet after rambling on for pages about the number of gay bars in New York and doing all sorts of oblique extrapolations (if each bar is visited by two hundred patrons a night, on average, and the average patron goes out twice a week . . .), statistically ludicrous but colorful, I did try to make some sense of it.

Basically, I had two substantive things to go by.

The first, having nothing specifically to do with New York, was Kinsey. Alfred Kinsey and his colleagues did have the resources to ask thousands of people about their innermost sexual secrets in the 1940s—in-depth interviews conducted with such skill and persistence, and with such assurances of confidentiality, that Kinsey was convinced he got the truth. He found that an astounding 37 percent of all males had, at one time or another, achieved orgasm in a same-sex situation (mostly playful adolescents involved in essentially meaningless masturbation, no doubt) . . . that 10 percent were predominantly gay in their orientation . . . and that a hard-core 4 percent back in the Forties were actually living gay lives, having sex exclusively with other men.

(Women, for whatever reason, he found, were only about half as likely to have a predominantly homosexual orientation.)

Decades later, in the midst of the gays-in-the-military debate, someone came out with a widely publicized study pegging the number of gay males at 1 percent. The thought was that we were *such* a small minority, it really was okay to ignore or discriminate against us. But this figure had been arrived at simply by sending folks out with a clipboard and *asking* them. Hello— are you homosexual? Based on the same methodology, one might presume that the number of shoplifters is zero and that straight men never cheat on their wives. ("Hello, sir? I'm calling to ask a few questions for a survey. Do you cheat on your wife?")

The 1 percent proponents also spread the word that Kinsey had done his research on prison populations—of all things—and so *of course* his numbers were skewed by deviants and perversion. Hasn't anyone seen *Fortune and Men's Eyes*?

But this was not the case.

To begin with, while 17.97 percent of the 5,300-man sample that underlay Kinsey's startling findings had spent some time in jail, Kinsey did not interview any penitentiary prisoners until *after* publishing the male volume. So his findings weren't based on interviewing prisoners. More to the point, startled by the high numbers, Kinsey himself tested and retested the results. "It has been our experience," he wrote, "that each new group into which we have gone has provided substantially the same data. Whether the histories were taken in one large city or another, whether they were taken in large cities, in small towns or in rural areas, whether they came from one college or another, a church school or a state university or some private institution, whether they came from one part of the country or from another, the incidence data on the homosexual have been more or less the same."

Long after Kinsey died, the Kinsey Institute reexamined his data, excluding all prison and jail histories. Sure enough, according to the report it published in 1979, the numbers still worked out about the same.*

So whether it's nature or nurture or whatever else, the general ballpark of 10 percent guys, 5 percent gals—which would suggest a blend of 7.5 percent overall—may be about right.

With benefit of hindsight, I can tell you that of the 110 boys in my class at Horace Mann, at least four live exclusively gay lives (well, three—the fourth jumped out a window). That's the 4 percent Kinsey would have predicted. Of my remaining 106 classmates, with most of whom I've lost touch, who knows?†

Anyway, the first thing I had to go on for my *New York* article was the Kinsey research. But how should his data be adjusted for New York? Surely more gay men had been drawn to the city from Minnesota, say, than from the city *to* Minnesota. (The young men drawn to Minnesota are from Montana.) It's always been easier to meet people—and to live anonymously—in a big city. No American city is bigger than New York.

Maybe for those who are relatively young the proportions don't vary much from town to town—that makes sense. There's no reason more New Yorkers would necessarily be *born* gay. And maybe Americans were less mobile in the Forties than today. But by the mid-Seventies—or the late Nineties, for that matter—it was reasonable to think that quite a few gays and lesbians had moved to places like San Francisco and New York.

---

* I am indebted for these insights to Dr. C. A. Tripp, a remarkable octogenarian who worked closely with Kinsey for nearly a decade and who is almost surely the leading living authority on his work. Kinsey himself was the married father of four, one of the nation's first Eagle Scouts (a best little boy?), and consumed with homoerotic desires, which, after a suitable period of self-flagellation, he acted upon with enthusiasm.

† Suicide is by no means reserved for the homosexual. Tragically, one of my straight high school classmates also jumped out a window several years ago—as did the wife of a straight friend of mine, who had hanged himself.

So might the numbers be twice as high in New York as else-where? That would notch it up from 7.5 to 15 percent—a million New Yorkers, give or take.

The second set of concrete data I had to work with was the 1970 Census data. Naturally, there was no column for "sexual orientation." But there was a column for "never married." And it was interesting to compare the proportion of never-marrieds at different ages in different neighborhoods. How come, especially when you get above age thirty, the difference in the number of never-marrieds is so stark between Staten Island, say, and Brooklyn Heights? I have no degree in social science or demography, but I can tell you why: *There are no gay people in Staten Island.* Well, almost none.

And I knew another thing: Beyond a certain age, there are almost no straight males in Manhattan who couldn't be married if they wanted to be. Never married? Never even tried it once? There will be exceptions, of course; but the main thing driving the variation in statistics for never-married males in various parts of New York is, quite simply, sexual orientation.

Anyway, using Staten Island as a "control" for the number of never-marrieds one might expect in a straight population, and making a bunch of other (to me) reasonable assumptions, I deduced that something like 750,000 of New York's 7 million-plus citizens were gay. Give or take.

Looking at the nation as a whole, if Kinsey was right, then something approaching 20 million Americans are gay or lesbian—at least in their heart of hearts, if not their daily lives—or will be when they grow up. That, in turn suggests that a *majority* of Americans either are gay or lesbian or have close relatives, friends, or colleagues who are.

In my own case, I would count as close relatives two parents, a brother, a sister-in-law, a niece, an aunt, and three cousins—as well as two grandmothers who loved me a lot but had died before I let anyone know I was gay. That's eleven. Close straight friends? I'm unusually fortunate in this regard, but let's say a dozen. Colleagues? Let's say another dozen. So in my case, there might be thirty-five people—straight—who didn't know until I told them that someone they cared about was gay.

Multiplying 20 million gay Americans by 35 gives you a number—700 million—that is silly because of all the overlap. (Many of "my" 35 will, knowingly or not, have other gay relatives, friends, and colleagues.) But the point is: Most Americans actually do like and care about gay people. Relatives, friends, teachers, pupils, coworkers, bosses, employees, movie stars, priests. They often just don't know it.

And of course the ones least likely to accept it *are* the least likely to know it, because they're the ones it is most intimidating to come out to.

Most of my free time in what I think of as my *New York* magazine years I spent trying to meet some significant portion of those 750,000 New Yorkers, knowing that surely, somehow, somehow . . .

But in the most tentative and least courageous way, part of me was also caught up in the nascent struggle for our civil rights.

Nothing meant more to me in high school and college—and beyond—than what I guess might be called the traditional civil rights movement. Martin Luther King, Jr., is a hero to *any* American. So I don't mean to freeload off the suffering of millions of slaves and their descendants, many of whom remain, through decades of continued discrimination, disadvantaged. But it was beginning to dawn on me, perhaps more slowly than on most, that there really were some similarities here and that we really did have rights and that, in America, there was a process—in no small part illuminated for us by Dr. King and others—by which to attain them.

So when I was asked by an activist to join NYPAC, I said yes. NYPAC was a short-lived, elite little group whose initials must have stood for "New York Political Action Committee"— ain't *that* a bold, in-your-face, unmistakably gay moniker, though perhaps it was right for its time. There were about thirty of us, some more out than others, and the idea was to interview candidates for public office and issue endorsements.

To me, the group's usefulness wasn't in discerning where the candidates stood on "our issues." I certainly had no illusion our endorsement could sway elections. To me, NYPAC's value lay, quite simply, in exposing these leaders to a group of gay men and women they may never have knowingly encountered. Because the paradox, of course, was that the gays and lesbians they *could* readily identify, or from whom they were routinely receiving demands, were in almost every instance the gays and lesbians with whom they could least easily relate.

This is not to imply that the rights—or even the ideas—of us yuppies were or are any more important than those of drag queens rollerskating down Christopher Street blessing the crowd with fairy dust from their magic wands. (This sort of thing made me *very* nervous when I was younger. I was astonished to meet Rollerina at Fire Island one time, out of uniform, and to find out that he was, in fact, quite a nice guy; worked for Merrill Lynch or something like that.) But opening minds and changing attitudes is a gradual process. It was time, we felt, that our political leaders met *us,* who represented what may have been the largely silent majority of gays and lesbians in New York.

Among us were lawyers, journalists, and businesspeople. We had a judge, Dick Failla, since lost to AIDS; and a tenured lecturer at the City University of New York, Virginia Apuzzo, since named assistant to the president for Administrative and Management Affairs (she runs the office-building/hotel/travel aspects of the White House). As one of the younger—and shyer—members of the group, I rarely said anything, but always wore a suit. Dick and Ginny, by contrast, though respectful and soft-spoken, were completely eloquent. They had a tremendous impact.

Mario Cuomo came. In 1977, he was vying with Congressman Ed Koch for the Democratic mayoral nomination. He might remember it differently, if he remembers it at all, but my sense was that he had never in his entire adult life encountered anything like this. He entered Bob Livingston's Upper East Side penthouse apartment "here," in terms of knowledge and empathy, and left *here,* six paces closer to comfort and concern. Was he ready to storm the barricades? No. But you could almost see the surprise in his eyes as he realized he was dealing with people very much like . . . well, very much like himself. One assumes it was not Mario who authorized, let alone dreamed up, the VOTE FOR CUOMO NOT THE HOMO slogan that would appear, years later, when he was challenged for the governorship by Koch.

The night Koch came to meet with us, the lights went out in mid-discussion. Power had, in fact, gone out at that moment up and down much of the East Coast. Koch handled it with his trademark humor and aplomb, as—elevators frozen—everyone trooped down twenty flights of stairs in the dark and out onto the street.

Later, Koch would become mayor, and with great courage, it seemed to me, given all the rumors, he signed an executive order banning discrimination in city hiring based on sexual orientation. He had me up to his little apartment for dinner one night and began by telling me a story that seemed unrelated to anything in the news. It was about someone who had screwed him once long ago, and about how he, Ed, had retaliated with devastating impact. The story ended with a sweet smile and the words "I never forgive and I never forget." Or that was the essence of it, anyway. Being quite slow when it comes to things like this, I remember thinking, *huh?* Only hours later did I realize this must have been a ground-rules-setting story with which he had initiated acquaintanceships hundreds of times.

The emperor had no clothes, it seemed to me, but in this case he was a helluva good emperor, great for the city and its people, and I voted for him with enthusiasm. Subsequently, he came up to my apartment a couple of times for dinner with me and Dick Failla and a handful of other young gay professionals. When I now tell Charles that I cooked dinner for the mayor of New York—Charles, who never met a place setting he couldn't improve or a flower arrangement he couldn't perfect, not to mention what he can do with the actual food—his mind boggles. Left to my own devices, my normal place setting consists of whatever container I'm eating out of. My normal meal involves, at most, six minutes in the microwave. But it's true. With no caterers or "help" of any kind, I'd stick a big roast beef in the oven (the only two times I ever actually lit the oven, I think), open six cans of gourmet black bean soup, adding extra sherry (my special touch, albeit suggested on the label), bake a dozen potatoes, uncork the red wine—my sense was that the mayor, like me an enthusiastic eater, enjoyed it just fine and that everyone else was too distracted by his presence to pay much attention either way. His stories were illuminating and delightful. Ask a question, offer a compliment, and off he went. Though he may have had a fault or two, New York has rarely if ever had a more competent, engaging, successful mayor—or, following twelve years of service, ex-mayor.

If only I had had a "co-host" for these dinners.

5

We have all known loneliness. I think my own loneliest moment may have been on a winter evening senior year in college with my two roommates up at Killington, in Vermont. We had gone skiing—I, for the first time in my life. The day itself, while cold and wet, and nervous-making for someone trying not to look too dorky in front of his much cooler roommates, had gone well enough. What got me was trying to negotiate the "après-ski" that night, scoping out chicks at the dance bar, and having to pretend I was loving it, man—loving it! In fact, I was hating it. I was inadequate, I didn't fit in, my life was a complete deception, and in a few months I'd no longer have Harvard's wonderful prudishness to fall back on (no female visitors allowed in the dorms much of the time). What was I going to do? I feigned sleepiness and headed back for the lodge—"See you guys later." As I crunched back through the cold crisp air, under the stars, feeling so left out, I realized that my life was absolutely, completely hopeless. I sat down in the snow, alone, and cried.

Now, five years later, life had improved immeasurably. I had gay friends—in particular, Chris, never more than a phone call away—and I had straight friends I could talk to honestly. Life didn't seem the least bit hopeless. In fact, it seemed pretty terrific most of the time.

But how terrific, really, if you don't have someone to share it with?

Thus many evenings, like single young city dwellers of whatever sexual orientation, I would go out to the bars or out on dates or, occasionally, to parties.

Once in a while I would "score," but not nearly as often as I would have liked. The guys I was attracted to were the superstars. They either weren't attracted back or, when perhaps they were, I was generally too nearsighted to see it. (I didn't know much, but I knew not to wear my glasses. And I was far too skittish to put contact lenses on my eyeballs.) It was also hard because I'm not a big drinker; because I don't have a lot of patience for small talk; because I was not as fascinating on the topic of automobile insurance as I am now—and, mainly, because I needed my sleep. Sure, at three or four in the morning I might have been able to stagger home with one of those guys or gone off someplace for anonymous sex. But even in those days I liked to be in bed by one. And unless forgetting a partner's name years after the fact renders it anonymous retroactively, I have never been into anonymous sex.

The people I did connect with were people I liked. Many remained friends long after we stopped messing around. But none of them totally clicked, as in: Mr. Right. Well, to put it in TV terms, look how many women Jerry went through in his quest for the right one! Look how many men Elaine went through! And George? Don't get me started on George!

On top of all the other problems, there was this: I was only turned on by guys at least a little younger than me. I'll never forget, that first summer up in Boston at age twenty-three, accidentally going to bed with a guy who turned out to be twenty-six. When I heard that, I got out of there *real* fast. A dirty old man! To my enormous relief—I really didn't know at the time how this would work out—I found that as my own age crept up, so did the age range of people I found attractive. Today, I'm proud to tell you, I *do* find some twenty-six-year-olds attractive. Even better, I find one forty-year-old very attractive. He's sort of a better-looking Kevin Bacon (and I've always liked Kevin Bacon).

But the age thing is not a small problem, because a *preponderance* of guys like younger guys (or younger gals, for that matter), and, well, not everyone can be younger than everyone else. Only in Lake Wobegon can everyone be above—or in this case below—average. So that's a problem. And because I was even more hung up on this than most—and for whatever reason was really, really turned off by older guys coming on to me—I have always dreaded *being* that older guy and coming on to a younger guy who might feel the same way. Even knowing in my head that there are lots of twenty-four-year-olds who'd love to be hit on by twenty-eight-year-olds—and even some twenty-eight-year-olds who don't mind at all when the right forty-five-year-old appears—it's something I've never been easily able to grasp in my gut.

So let's see: Guys my own age or older were out because they were too old. And guys younger than me were out because—in my view if not theirs—*I* was too old. That left: Nobody.

Ain't life grand?

Not to say I didn't manage. I really did make some great friends, including some intimate ones; really did have some hot times, which Charles says are not appropriate to describe in this book, and he's right, so I won't. I can *allude,* maybe.

There was the guy I met in Tucson when I was covering the national zookeepers' convention and staying, to keep expenses low, at the YMCA. Whoa! There was the New York Stock Exchange executive into a boxing fantasy that kept us both interested for more than a few dates. There was the shirtless young Paramount executive I met while wearing the garb of an Egyptian foot soldier at a theme party on Fire Island. He was twenty-four, I was twenty-six. We had a very good time (and I discovered he looked great in a suit as well), but I found myself wanting to get away pretty fast afterward . . . until a week or two later, when we'd be drawn together like magnets . . . and then wanted to get away . . . and then a week later . . . The rhythms of our attraction clearly had a lot more to do with "appetite" (want/sate, want/sate) than with love (which is at once more enduring and more complex). Oh gosh, and there was Chubb—who was anything but. And that adorable junior at Princeton (who is now a judge, I was delighted to learn recently). Remember all that dating you did in high school and college? That's what this was for me—making up for lost time.

So I'm not saying I don't have good memories from my single years, but the fact remains that much of the time I was lonely. This is really embarrassing, and the sophisticates in the crowd are going to barf, but I remember lying on the couch in the high-ceilinged, unfinished-cedar living room of Dirty Pool, the Fire Island house I took a half-share in one of those early summers, feeling almost as blue as I had up at Killington.

That's not the embarrassing part. The embarrassing part is that—with everyone else in the house off at the disco or wherever—I would be listening, over and over, to Neil Diamond singing the score from *Jonathan Livingston Seagull*—which would actually have been a pretty great movie if they hadn't let the seagulls talk. Big mistake. But Neil Diamond's singing was just fine. "You may find him; yes, you may find him . . ." There was something to the soaring sweep of the music that—well, don't give me that superior chortle. Your songs may be different, but you know you have them, too.

We all have them, I imagine, and I can almost date my periods of cosmic yearnings by the songs.

"What kind of fool am I? Who never fell in love?" I would sing to myself as an eleventh grader, consumed with the impossibility of it all, walking up Madison Avenue, hoping to bump into one of my cooler classmates. (It's not that I had never fallen in love—I had been in love with one boy or another ever since elementary school—I just could never tell anyone about it.)

"It's heavenly . . . heavenly . . ." Johnny Mathis would sing as I looked out over the Charles River, a college senior, letting all the love songs bathe over me, and yearning, yearning. *Heavenly* is one of the top ten albums ever recorded in the history of time. I still love it. (I may have been its only fan not even to have suspected that Johnny Mathis might be gay. I did know he was black.)

My other album senior year, which without question occupies one of the other nine spots on the since-the-world-began top ten, was Peter, Paul, and Mary's *Album 1700*. Listening to it, even today, remains a religious experience. "Take your place on the Great Mandella" confirmed that we must resist the Vietnam War—and racism and injustice and all the other evils of the world. Not that I didn't have tremendous respect for the guys who did go fight, but I knew I couldn't, knew that that war was crazy.* And there was that beautiful, sad, mystical song that began: "This house goes on sale every Wednesday morning . . . and taken off the market in the afternoon." Imagine: a real estate song—ostensibly, at least—that rips your heart out.

There was even one song—well, one line in one song—that seemed to be speaking to me. It all spoke to me, but I mean, to *me*. It's in the preamble, where Peter or Paul is singing—more like conversing casually—and asking an old pal, "How's the

---

* Fortunately, I had this humongous varicocele that kept me out of the draft. If you're a doctor, you know what that is. If not, you don't want to. (It's largely gone now, anyway. Forget the surgery—just wear a jock.)

preacher? How's Don? Did he go back to school? No kidding! I thought he was gay." This is just incidental—he's trying to make small talk to disguise his real interest ("oh and, yeah, while I think of it, do you remember—not for myself, for a friend—that girl that I went with, before I got married, a couple of times at the end? What's her name?")—but *hold on!* Did I hear that right? "No kidding! I thought he was *gay.*"

To begin with, I don't think I had ever heard that word in a song before—or much of anywhere else. Back then, the word you heard was *homo.* But the main thing was how little it seemed to mean either way. He obviously liked Don, never mind that he thought he was gay (it was probably the preacher who turned out to be gay), and in any event it was no big deal. How's Don? Married? "No kidding! I thought he was gay." (Of course, a seven-word lyric is not room enough to go into the possibility that he married even *though* he was gay.)

I don't know why that one little lyric didn't free me more. Perhaps because it was just one little lyric. There was no 800 number on the album to call to talk to the character in the song who seemed so comfortable with friends he thought were gay. But I suspect even that little shred of acceptance helped me realize there were straight friends I could eventually talk to about this, as I eventually did.

Today, of course, gay people and gay role models are much in evidence. Mayors march in Gay Pride parades. And there is the President of the United States, not just some character in a song, saying directly, not just obliquely, that we're okay. There was none of that back then. When I was in college, the "Stonewall riot," which kicked off the modern gay rights movement, June 28, 1969, hadn't even occurred. It was still all just a huge 20-million-person secret. Nor, even after that riot, were things at first very quick to change.

How's the preacher? How's Don? Did he go back to school? No kidding! I thought he was gay . . .

． ． ．

Anyway, at Fire Island, that summer of my twenty-sixth year, it was *Jonathan Livingston Seagull*.

Fire Island is to New York what Provincetown is to Boston. Sort of. I had been out to Fire Island once, Memorial Day weekend 1971, while I was still in B-School, and hadn't liked it. It was cold and rainy. It was ridiculously expensive. Almost everyone was much older than me, including the forty-year-old lawyer who was my host. (I trusted him not to come on to me because—one—he couldn't possibly imagine someone would be attracted to a person so old and—two—he knew me through serving on a charity board with my mother. This was before any briefs had been presented to the Supreme Court. The irony of her inadvertently having been my ticket to Fire Island was not lost on me.) The few guys my own age or younger tended to be . . . well . . . not cowboys, not preppies, not my type.

I ultimately did meet a young Texan that weekend named Randy Green, who was not a cowboy—and certainly not preppy—but who in his jeans and boots and mustache (though I don't usually like mustaches), and given the fact that I had, in my misery, dropped half a tab of mescaline (remember, this was 1971, and thus technically still the Sixties), filled the bill. We were very different—part of the appeal, no doubt—not least because he apparently did find ancient forty-year-olds attractive and, at a later date, got it on with my host. (Though I found this distasteful, I remember thinking it might bode well for me should I ever become forty myself.) Randy went on to almost make it as a photographer, with a show at OK Harris Gallery in 1978 and a feature on the cover of *American Photographer* magazine. We stayed friends from that weekend until, nearly twenty years later, like so many of my friends from this era, he died.

． ． ．

That early exposure having turned me off to Fire Island, I spent the next summer in New York and was skeptical when, over the following winter, I got a call from an associate editor at *Fortune,* Peter Vanderwicken, who'd previously been *Time*'s Detroit bureau chief and, before that, *Time*'s national economic correspondent. We should have lunch, he said.

"Why?" I asked.

He allowed as to how he liked my work in *New York,* and *of course* we should have lunch—meet him at Toots Shor's.

So I showed up, never having been to Toots Shor's—the old Sinatra-and-everybody-else-straight hangout—and Peter, a nice old bald guy in his early thirties, was charming and funny and enthusiastic and then, about halfway through lunch, said I should take a share in the house he and some others had rented on Fire Island.

It seems he'd read the excerpt of *TBLBITW* in *New York* and realized—not even having gone to high school with me— that the style was so much like my financial writing (it wasn't! I don't use nearly so many . . . ellipses . . . in my financial writing!) that it had to be me, and he wanted me in the house.

One thing led to another, and before you know it, I was a half-share Fire Islander. And because I was not about to share a bedroom with some old guy, I generally slept in the living room, out on the couch.

Listening to *Jonathan Livingston Seagull.*

Peter and I have been friends ever since. (After a distinguished career at *Fortune,* he went on to Booz, Allen, then J. P. Morgan, and now writes his own newsletter.)

Summers are the best. And I figured summer was my best time for meeting someone, too, because in the summer people are looking for someone to snuggle up with for the winter. And because in the summer I could take off my shirt.

I'm not saying I was any great shakes, but I did notice—perhaps because of all those years of swimming and soccer and wrestling in high school, and endless sit-ups in college, and some hard-running squash even after college—people were more interested in auto insurance in the summer.

Pretty soon I was not unpopular among the models and the others I longed to be accepted by. It was fine that people like Peter—brilliant, successful professionals—liked me, so long as they understood hugging was as far as it went. (I am a good hugger.) But what I really cared about, *deeply* shallow though I fully appreciated this to be, were the Zoli models and the cater-waiters and, in a pinch, the B-School students. Specifically, the ones who, at the outdoor sunset tea-dance, assembled on the stairs overlooking the crowd, like royalty.

It's not that anyone guarded the stairs and let only certain people up. And it's certainly not as if this kind of looks-based pecking-order instinct is one of the finer attributes of human nature, straight or gay. But everyone just knew.

The meek and the homely shall inherit the earth—I do believe that, or at least that they deserve to. But you would not find them on the stairs at tea.

I loved that some of the stair-people became friends and urged me up onto the stairs themselves. (That was quite different from presuming to claim the territory solo.) With a couple of them I became close. I even had a magical fling or two. Anything that brings a smile to your face a quarter century later has to have been pretty magical.

But for the most part, I would throw myself at the few people I liked with such enthusiasm that I immediately ruled myself out as someone they might want in the same way. I had neither the patience nor the temperament to play it cool. I *wasn't* cool. Adorably neurotic in the right light—maybe. Cocky—certainly. But not cool. And about as "hip" at twenty-six or twenty-seven as I am at fifty—which, Charles will tell you with some glee, is not very hip at all. (You will not find *Jonathan Livingston Seagull* in *his* CD collection.)

I had by 1974 moved from Sullivan Street up to a giant old apartment complex in Chelsea called London Terrace. It encompasses thousands of apartments and extends all the way from Ninth Avenue to Tenth Avenue and from 23rd Street to 24th Street, with a courtyard in the middle. My $365-a-month tenth-floor one-bedroom looked north from my office/bedroom and into the courtyard from the living room. A tiny kitchen, good bathroom, thick walls—it was great.

Yet another summer had ended, everyone had his shirt back on, and I was still single. I was twenty-seven, for crying out loud, and had been at this now—the bar and dating thing—for quite some time. At the end of particularly bleak and loveless weekends I would sometimes slink self-consciously over to the baths, which is where you went for wild, uninhibited, multiple-partner glorious sex. Except that, being neither wild nor uninhibited, I found that the very same people who would have looked great out on the street in jeans, or behind their desks in jackets and ties, looked completely unsexy walking around in towels. So invariably I would skulk around for an hour or two until the horniness had turned into more like a self-loathing ache—loathing myself not particularly for being gay but for wasting so much time and in such a (to me) distasteful setting—and I'd go home.

If I were religious I would say this was God saving my life—except that the kind of things I would have done at the baths, even if I *had* done things, were not the kinds of things that would have put me most seriously at risk. Also, I can't believe that God favors the death penalty, or that, if He does, He would apply it to an offense so relatively innocuous as a couple of horny guys getting their rocks off.

The only time I can recall ever participating in something

sexual at the baths was when an older guy begged me to let him just touch my stomach and chest while he jerked off. It was so sad and embarrassing, and he was so persistent, that I went into his little cubicle and a minute later it was done. *What can it hurt?* I remember his pleading as he tried to persuade me. I can remember leaving the baths that night even more depressed than usual. Would I be desperately trying to sell the same concept when I reached his age?

And then something miraculous happened.

The sun had just set one Sunday evening in late September and I was getting ready to give up for the weekend. I had been in the Village at some bar with a couple of friends—one of them is now a banker in Chicago; I can't remember who the others were—and they were driving up the West Side Highway to an uptown bar. I couldn't go into yet another bar, waste yet another hour. *What was the point?* So they were going to take a quick detour and drop me off, but then I figured, well, no need to take me home—just drop me here, at 21st Street. It was a bar called the Eagles Nest, a sort of "leather bar lite" back then, especially on Sunday evenings, and such a short walk to London Terrace that, I figured, having invested so much time already, I could scope out another three hundred faces in all of a four-minute walk around the bar, and then go home to bed.

About two thirds of the way around the bar—what's this?— my eyes widened, chest tightened—it even looked as if he was alone and had looked back at me. Naturally, I immediately looked away and kept walking. There were several reasons for this. One, it was almost surely too good to be true. Remember, it's dark in those places and I'm nearsighted. Two, if you show interest, you're sunk. Three, what would I say? Four, what would I say?

So, like a pilot waved off for a second approach, I did another circle around the bar, and when I got back to the same spot—quickly, because my patience for all this really had worn thin, and it had been a long weekend—he was still there, still alone, still heart-stopping . . . and he smiled at me.

Forgive all the detail, but I could walk you over to that bar *today* and show you the exact spot.

He was a dentist in the Coast Guard. And guess where it turned out he lived? London Terrace! Different entrance, fifteenth floor.

We bolted from the bar, and as we did, I was still quite sure it was too good to be true. I knew that when I got a really good look outside under the streetlight there would be a certain nelliness or affectation or *something* that, while it would in no way reduce his worth as a human being, would burst the attraction for me. Yet under the streetlight, and seeing a little more of his manner, and hearing a little more of him talking, it was better and better. *Don't blow it,* I was shouting to myself, as we walked—fast—back to London Terrace.

Upstairs in his apartment—not unlike my apartment, but so immeasurably more cool—he wasted no time (he was kind of excited, too), and I realized . . . *wait*. A guy like this must have sex all the time. How do I make it clear to him that I'm not just anybody and that this isn't just one more night?

"Wait," I said.

We didn't wait. But I remember grabbing him by the shoulders and looking straight at him and saying, in effect: "Listen. *This is different.* We both trick around. But this isn't like that. You're special. *I'm* special. This is special."

And it was. I had met Mr. Right. At last.

6

In my eyes, Ed was perfect in every way—and perfect for *me*. A kind of lanky, aw-shucks Tom Sawyer Jewish dentist (how often do you come across one of those?), really smart, strong, Southern (well, Orlando), with a huge heart and a knack for making people O on their A's, as he liked to say (oscillate on their anxieties), that made them putty in his hands. He'd zero in on your foibles or insecurities and kid you just enough to throw you off balance, but not so much as to hurt—and in a manner that made you realize he understood and *liked* you.

Ed was actually six months my senior, about to turn twenty-eight—but that was all right—that was great, in fact. I loved that his advanced age didn't matter to me. And in any event he *looked* younger than me, if anyone would even notice me when the two of us were together. But that was okay, too, because I was not without my self-confidence in other areas. I had my little list of strengths and accomplishments—and I had Ed!

Here was a guy I could take home to Mom and Dad—my boyfriend the dentist. Just as soon as I found the right moment to tell them I was gay.

I was crazy about Ed.

So much so, I feel it's time to burst into another song. Not that these songs fit my life perfectly—for one thing, all the songs are written for men and women. But if you know the music from *Fiorello!,* you know that Marie has been searching and searching for Mr. Right—"Waiting for ships/that never come in," she sings dolefully—and has finally decided, "I'm gonna marry the very next man!"

Then there's a break and her secret love says, "Marie, will you marry me? I know it's kinda sudden." (I'm not sure who her secret love *is;* I guess it's Fiorello La Guardia or one of the secondary characters—I never actually *saw* the show, just grew up with the albums from all the shows my parents saw.)

"Sudden?!" Marie asks, ironically, catching herself as she decides to play along: "Why, yes, it is."

"But I think you could learn to love me."

"Well, yes," she says. "I've been practicing for fifteen years."

Music swells: "Waiting for ships/that never come in . . ." It's the second-to-last track on the album. Beautiful.

My ship had come in.

It was so great.

By day, I'd be writing for *New York* or working on my biography of Charles Revson, the man who founded Revlon. Maybe I'd break away for a game of squash. Ed—the young Coast Guard lieutenant commander (commanding a complement of one dental assistant, as he jokes about it now)—would be down on Governors Island drilling young Coast Guardsmen's teeth and, later, at the U.S. Public Health Hospital on Staten Island—possibly the only gay man on Staten Island—drilling the teeth of the officers' wives.

We spent almost every night together, usually at his place, though mine was just two elevator rides and a long jagged walk through the halls of London Terrace away. Ed made me great dinners. We met each other's friends. We jumped around on Ed's foldout bed and sang sappy songs. (I can see my career as a financial writer going down the tubes as I write this.) We knew *Mack and Mabel* by heart (Ed had actually *seen* it). We would wrestle until I pinned Ed, which was pretty easy to do because of my very modest experience in high school. He was taller, but that's not an advantage when you're wrestling. Of course, emotionally he had me coming and going. And he was much better in bed.

On weekends we would go out with friends and then, when it got warmer, to Fire Island.

When we passed poles—and there are a lot of metal poles on the streets of New York—we would grab them at waist level with both hands, extend our legs straight out horizontally from the pole, and see how long we could hold them like that. (We would do this separately, first Ed and then me, or me and then Ed, and not, thankfully, with *every* pole.) We were young. We were bursting with energy.

We never argued, never fought, never bickered—why would we?

I thought Ed was perfect. One of the problems we ultimately had was that Ed did not. He had more than a few self-doubts and needed a lot of reassurance. What's more, he didn't want to be "just a dentist"—though he was a damn good one—he wanted to be a star. And why not?

Any number of photographers were hot to take his picture, so he got a modeling composite together, took some acting lessons—you may actually have seen him in a toothpaste commercial. (I have another friend you have surely seen sneeze for Dristan. The spot ran so often, I began to fear for his health.) I suppose Ed could have said, "I am a real dentist, I don't just play one on TV," but actually he got the spot purely on charisma. He was playing somebody's older brother.

Another problem we had was Ed's aforementioned talent in bed. I can joke about it now, but at the time this little problem was most vexing. I loved Ed, but there were some things I just wasn't comfortable doing—some of them fairly basic.

Not that I didn't try. But even those that I could master it was obvious to Ed I didn't enjoy—so, loving me, he didn't enjoy them either.

We coped. It's not as if he didn't enjoy our sex (I *loved* it), but it left some things that he desired.

There was another problem. I had a book to write. By the time I met Ed, I had interviewed more than a hundred people who had known Charles Revson, some of them more than once and for hours at a time. I had endless tapes and a million words of typewritten transcripts. This was in the days before word processors, so cutting and pasting and searching and organizing were a great deal more difficult—I had files and Scotch tape and snippets everywhere—and I really had to get this done. My advance came to better than $15,000 after taxes, enough to pay forty-one months' rent. What's more, Revson had died, which I took to be a sign that I should quit stalling and *write the book*.

I won't say I was getting tired of Ed's constant need for reassurance—"This guy was looking at me in the showers at the Y this afternoon, rubbing himself; do you think that means he thought I was attractive?"—yes, Ed, that's what it means. But when he said he was thinking of taking July and August to bum around Europe and do a little soul-searching, I thought: Good. First off, I shouldn't smother him. Second, it might help him figure out what he wants to do with his life. Third, I'll get the book done while he's gone.

By now I was in a Fire Island house with a clean pool and elaborate glassware. Two of our housemates were a terrific young Harvard Law graduate who'd scored 800 on his LSATs and given me the crabs the summer before and his friend, an older semipro golfer–turned–full-time banker, who had organized rental of the house. There was some rich guy from Detroit—all I remember about him is that he was quite possibly the youngest man in America ever to have had cosmetic surgery. There was also one of my high school classmates, who would read scripts by the pool.

Ed came out with me, and I'll never forget his getting a little jealous when someone smiled at me. Was he out of his mind? Believe me, he had nothing to worry about.

Still, I liked it.

And when in the middle of July Fourth weekend we went back into the city to put him on the bus to Kennedy for his trip to Europe—both of us quiet and droopy at the impending separation—I was astonished that Ed cried a little when we hugged and said good-bye.

But I liked that, too.

About ten days later, big progress on my book already having been made—working day and night with Rosemary DeTore, Chris's old legal secretary, whom I had recruited to type and retype the drafts—Ed's first letter arrived. He was in Amsterdam watching his laundry slosh around at the laundromat, dejected. He missed me, he wrote—I still remember this—"to a googolplex." As you know, a googol is 1 followed by a hundred zeroes—10,000,000,000,000,000,000,000,000,000,000,000,000, 000,000,000,000,000,000,000,000,000,000,000,000,000,000, 000,000,000,000,000,000,000. Big. But it's nothing compared with a googolplex. A googolplex, the amount by which Ed missed me, is 1 followed by a *googol* of zeroes. It's almost enough to make infinity blush.

The thing that made our relationship so strong, and made it work, as best I could tell, is that each of us felt he was the lucky one. A movie poster I'd seen pasted to a construction-site wall—one gets one's wisdom where one can—had said something to the effect that "in any relationship, one loves the other MORE." I want to say it was for a movie called *More,* but *Cinemania* lists no such flick, so who knows what it was for? The point is, it rang true, or at least largely so. And yet in *this* relationship, it was equal, because *each* of us felt he had drawn the lucky straw.

I missed Ed, too, but went back to my writing. If I kept grinding away, I'd have the book done by the time he got home eight weeks later. After nine terrific months together, we could manage eight weeks apart while I blasted away on this thing.

It had been fun researching the book, except for my natural shyness—it's hard to call strangers and motivate yourself to meet with them—and except for the awkwardness I felt doing a book that was, after all, largely about women. What did I know about women? Or cosmetics, or fashion? Or life, even, really? One of my best sources, who was one of Revson's top female executives in her day, sharp and brassy, would make knowing comments that I was pretty sure I didn't understand but that I was too embarrassed to ask her to explain. Once she even asked me "which side I dressed on." Huh? "*You* know," she said. "Which side do you *dress* on?" And suddenly, to my horror, I deduced what she meant. *I* didn't know which side I "dressed on"—but I realized she was talking about *my dick,* in that swank Park Avenue dining room of hers, and that the fact that she asked this so casually must mean all *straight* men must be familiar with this concept and, more to the point, must "dress" on the left or the right.

Her point had something to do with where I should buy my suits, or how I should get them tailored better,* but the only thing I heard, and the thing that had reddened my cheeks—a

---

* Charles—my Charles—would have been delighted. Anything to spruce me up. But it would be many, many years before I would meet him and force him to shop with me for my $200 designer suits (I know this place on the second floor . . .). His suits cost $2,000, custom-tailored in London. Do you know what the $1,800 difference could grow to, in a deftly managed mutual fund, over thirty years?

sure giveaway, which made them redder still—was that this woman was thinking about my dick, which I just very much did not want to be discussing.

The next letter, a week or so later, was more chipper. Ed had run into this neat American—some sort of marine biologist or something—who was driving around Europe for a year in a VW van. Ed would be bumming a lift with him.

As innocent and open and more or less reasonable as this sounded—shouldn't this guy be floating around in a boat if he was a marine biologist?—something contracted in my chest when I read that. With hindsight, I would say it was my heart.

Again I went back to my work—what else could I do? There was no place to reach him, no cell phone, circa 1975, in the back of that van—but this time I was ill at ease.

It was also around this time that the FBI called to tell me I had been placed on an assassination list by a terrorist group in the Middle East. "But why not hang up and call me back at the FBI so you know this isn't a hoax," suggested the agent.

I did, it wasn't, and so I wondered what the FBI proposed to do about it. That, the agent said, was not their department. Their job was just to inform me. Don't be too concerned, he said—plots are forever coming out of the Middle East and are almost never executed. But it was their job to let me know. Along with me on the list were four or five other much-more-notables, including columnist Jack Anderson and Egyptian president Anwar Sadat (who *was* assassinated six years later).

A month or two earlier, I had written an article for *New York* entitled something like "Should We Really Kill for Oil?" It was back in the days of OPEC's stranglehold, and people were talking about sending in the marines. My article recounted all this and concluded: No, we should not kill for oil. But to illustrate the cover, Clay commissioned an Action Comics–like Kissinger and Ford in marine fatigues storming the beach, M-16s ablazing, with this balloon coming out of one of their mouths: "Are We Gonna Let These Wogs Kick Sand in Our Faces?" By Andrew Tobias. And this article—with this cover—had been reprinted in *Paris-Match*.

And now, very reasonably—for terrorists, anyway—they thought it might be a good idea to kill me.

I thought it might be a better idea for them to kill Clay Felker, but I didn't say anything.

So I was writing the book, but I was also worrying about what Ed was doing, exactly, in the back of that VW van. And worrying—a little, anyway, though I could hardly imagine terrorists actually bothering with someone so insignificant— whether that new guy running the elevator was *really* the new guy running the elevator.

I got another letter from Ed filled with excitement over their trip, and over what a great guy Todd was . . . signed with love, of course, but no more mathematical expressions. I called the American Express office I knew he would be checking in at and left a message for him to call me back. And shortly thereafter, very late at night, I was woken by a banging on my door.

Adrenaline reached my brain in about a tenth of a second— none of the groggy slow awakening you see when they do this on TV—and a second and a half later I had reached my front door, which was quite a feat since much of my brain stem had me running *away* from the door, but a little more of it was driving me *to* the door to look through the peephole—*quick,* to avoid poison knitting needles plunging at my eye—to assess the situation.

The door handle was turning slightly . . . no joke . . . although, being locked, it jiggled more than turned, and I heard a scratching around the lock area.

The one piece of good news was that, from the quick look of things and the modus operandi, this was an unlikely or, at least, an unprofessional assassin.

Still, someone was attempting to get into my apartment.

"Go away! I'm calling the police!" I said.

"Let me in," he shouted, banging some more.

"Someone's trying to break into my apartment!" I told 911. "And I'm on an assassination list!" (That latter tidbit, designed to convey special urgency, might well have caused my call to be shunted over to the loony queue on a busier night. Fortunately, the dispatcher ignored it.)

Oh, sure, one of my college roommates, or Tom Cruise, would have just opened the door, grabbed this guy by the collar, and punched his lights out.

I know that. And I really, really, want to be that tough and brave. But you are who you are, I guess, and who *I* was was very happy to hear the banging stop and look out that peephole to see an empty hallway.

A few minutes later the doorbell rang. Two of New York's finest had my assassin, who turned out to be some perfectly innocent drunk who, befuddled, had been trying to get into the wrong apartment.

Something told me this would be a good time to take a break. I called Icelandic Airlines (do you have *any* idea how much it costs to pick up and fly to Europe at short notice in peak season on a regular airline?) and reserved a ticket. Then, when Ed called in response to my message, I said, trying to be as nonchalant as possible, "Hey! Wanna have dinner Thursday?" It was Monday or Tuesday.

"*What* now?" he laughed. ("*What* now?" is Ed-speak for the Southern "Say, what?" or the much more stilted "Come again?" He also had this way of sort of talking out of the side of his mouth—literally, not figuratively—that was really cool, too.)

"Seriously. You've been gone a month, it's the midway point of your trip—I thought it would be fun to come take you to dinner and spend a few days together."

"Really?"

"Really! I've got a ticket to Luxembourg—I think that's only two or three hours from you. Want to pick me up and have dinner?"

There was some nervous hesitation. "What about Todd?"

"What *about* Todd?"

"Well—sure," Ed said as I read him my flight number. "Great!"

"Great!"

I called my folks, told them I was on an assassination list and was flying over to see my boyfriend Ed, the love of my life, to rescue my relationship.

Well, close. I told them I was going to interview the former head of Revlon's European operations.

Actually, I'm not sure what I told them—or that I told them anything at all. My vague recollection is that they may themselves have been away on vacation so I didn't have to tell anybody anything.

And off I flew to GPL—the Godforsaken Principalité of Luxembourg.

7

The Godforsaken Principalité of Luxembourg (which is actually a grand duchy, not a principalité, but I don't care) seemed to be populated by unpleasant people who lived to milk the tourists. This may be terribly unfair, but I had been flying all night, I was on an assassination list (actually, by now I was mostly just pretending to be upset about that—it made a good story), and, mainly, I had this terrible feeling that my lifelong happiness, so long in the attainment, was about to slip away. So the good people of Luxembourg should not take it personally that I truly hate them all.

When I broke free of customs and walked into the bright sunlight, there was Ed. *Huge* hug. And there was Todd.

The minute I saw Todd, I knew.

Ed loved me, yes. But Todd had one of those clefts in his chin, and all the lean, dark, masculine features that go with it. Where I was adorably neurotic in the right light, he was a strong, silent star in any light. Construction, scuba diving, engine blocks, titration. Didn't say much—ultimately would be nicknamed Yup, as "yup" was for him an average-length

speech—but you could count on what he *did* say. Manly handshake—the whole deal. To my delight, we discovered months
later that he didn't know who Katharine Hepburn was! But he
sure knew the principles of aerodynamics that would lift a plane.

What's more, I soon learned, he was easy and versatile in
bed, and head over heels in love with Ed.

"What, exactly, is the deal with Todd?" I asked about three
minutes after we'd sat for some godforsaken coffee in the blar-
ing midmorning sun overlooking some hideous river in the
shadow of some grotesque castle. Todd had gone off to put another franc in the meter or something.

"What do you mean?"

"Well, I mean, how do you picture this working out?"

"Well, I kind of thought maybe we could be like the Three
Musketeers," Ed said.

"Gee," I said. "I'm not sure three works very well."

Then, a few minutes later, Todd came back and Ed went
someplace—or maybe it was a little later that he got me aside,
but in any event Todd said, "Listen. I knew it was too good to
be true. I just want you to know I respect that."

"What do you mean?"

"Well, someone as great as Ed had to have a lover." Apparently, Ed had told Todd about me in general terms, but not until
I was flying over did he explain exactly who I was. "I just want
you to know I'm not going to mess it up."

Something like that. And he meant it, I think. The fact is,
we liked each other and, I guess, felt bad for each other.

It was the week from hell.

Ed's first thought was that, because he loved us both, we
should *all* get to love each other. And so that very afternoon we
found ourselves on a bed in a hotel room, and I found myself
doing something aggressive to Todd that Todd seemed quite
willing to have done—but which soon made me feel so weird I

stopped doing it (not that I didn't appreciate the gesture, or the symbolism), grabbed Ed, and said, Look, it's been a long day; I just want to take a shower with you.

The shower was somehow across the hall, out of earshot of Todd, and I remember clowning around with the hose and turning my armpit into a geyser—and just generally reminding Ed that it was *me*! And that we were *crazy* about each other! As it was evident that, in fact, we still were. The only problem being that Ed and Todd were crazy about each other, too.

One might think, if one were incredibly obtuse, that this was a terrific spot for Ed to be in—to have two guys crazy about him. Actually, of course, it was awful for all three of us.

Whenever I was alone with Ed, Todd got a hangdog look that tore your heart out. Whenever Todd was alone with Ed— one or two of the nights he slept in the van with Todd while I slept in the hotel room, not that I even have much recollection of what *cities* we visited (Switzerland, mostly, I think)—*I* was miserable.

And basically, because he loved us both and didn't want to hurt either of us, Ed was *constantly* miserable.

But I'm sorry. While I am usually an "After you," "No, after *you*" kind of guy, this was practically a matter of life or death. And, dammit, as great as their sex must have been since they'd met all of three weeks earlier, and despite the cleft in Todd's chin, and despite the fact that he was actually a very nice guy, this was one time it just had to be "No, pal—after *me*."

One day that week we decided to climb a small mountain. I am afraid of heights. (A lot of guys are afraid of heights. And Stallone, I hear, is afraid to fly at night. So just *give me a break,* would you?) But I was assured it was basically just a long steep walk, and, well, off we went.

After about twenty minutes Todd quickened his pace and was soon out of sight. I assumed it was to make me look bad. Later I learned it was because he was just so depressed that his time with Ed would be ending in a few weeks, when Ed went back to New York to me. Meanwhile, Ed and I kept climbing, except now the path was beginning to look all too much like a ledge, and the distance below—well, we had climbed pretty high. It was August and there were patches of *snow* below us, for crying out loud.

We went a little higher, and the ledge got a little narrower, and finally I stopped and laid my soul bare. I told Ed that I loved him but that I couldn't compete on this basis and—well, could we just go back down?

I was actually afraid he might ask me to wait there while he caught up with Todd and then, once they'd reached the top (the view from the top was supposed to be awesome), they'd hurry back down.

Instead, Ed was great about it. We went down to one of the snow patches, horsed around, and waited for Todd. A *long* time.

I was so happy to just be there with Ed, though it was a little embarrassing to see eight-year-old Swiss boys and their seventy-five-year-old granddads skipping down the mountain in their lederhosen, having not that long before passed us on the way up. We just looked at each other—Ed and I—and laughed.

"Did you get all the way to the top?" we asked Todd when he finally reappeared.

"Yup."

I won't even tell you about the night we crept across some Alpine pass in drizzle and fog and light snow on a winding one-and-a-half-lane road, with trucks lumbering slowly toward us from the other direction and no guardrail worthy of the name to protect us from the ten-thousand-foot drop. It sounds funny, and we did make it, of course, but quite a few people each year don't. If you ask me, we were out of our minds.

Todd, of course, did most of the driving and was unfazed.

On the last day, Todd drove us the three or four hours to the GPL International Airport. For the last hour or two, Ed and I were on the mattress in the back.

"I can't just leave this way," I told Ed. "I have to know how you feel."

Silence.

Again.

Silence.

"You must feel *something*."

Silence.

"Ed—"

"Will you hush *up,*" he laughed/cried. "I'm trying to figure out how to say it!"

More silence.

"It is an axiom of my existence," he finally said, slowly and deliberately, looking deep into my eyes, "that I cannot live without you."

Well. You can't do a whole lot better than that.

With that assurance, I got to the airport, said good-bye, went to the Icelandic departure lounge, sat down, and began to sob. My head knew what the words meant—"an axiom of my existence"—but my tear ducts knew better.

I'm not keen on being so candid, especially now that the John Reid jersey has been retired. For one thing, we all know real men don't cry when their hearts are breaking; they just clench their jaws and look off into the distance. For another, the last thing we need to reinforce is the image of a lot of wailing, miserable homosexuals. But truth is truth, and, though I wasn't noisy about it—I wasn't keening or waving my arms around, for crying out loud—the fact is, I was sobbing. I was grateful that Luxembourgers are as nasty and heartless as they are, because the last thing I would have wanted in that waiting room was to have one of them trying to come over to console me.

I flew back to New York with Ed's promise to write and call frequently.

I wrote about Charles Revson. (Being straight and a zillionaire is no guarantee of unalloyed happiness, either.)

I went about my other business.

And every second day or so, when no letter had come and when the sadness had become unbearable, I'd sob and sob and sob.

It was more or less like any other bodily rhythm. Wake/sleep, wake/sleep. Thirst/quench, thirst/quench. (I believe we have already covered want/sate, want/sate.) Crying is—you'll forgive me—emotional vomiting. It removes the toxins . . . and then they well up again . . . and then off you go again. For me, it was about a two-day cycle.

Plus, there was a constant pain in my chest.

I recognized that twenty-eight was too young for angina, whatever that is. But this wasn't some poetic metaphysical thing—this *really hurt*. So after putting it off a while, I scheduled an appointment with my doctor, who happened to be a cardiologist, and got myself X-rayed.

I was fine, he said.

And then a week or two later—no joke—I went back. I'm sorry, I said, but you must have missed something. Maybe it's something that doesn't show up on X rays, but *something's* wrong—this *really hurts*. It feels like someone's *standing on my chest*. And he's *heavy*.

And the answer was, though I'd always assumed it was merely a poetic condition, I was suffering from heartache. A real, constant physical pain. (I think it has something to do with the heart muscle being clenched so hard.)

Ed came back—with Todd, who was on his way home to Shreveport—and for a few weeks it was Switzerland all over again. Sometimes Ed would sleep at my apartment, most nights he would sleep with Todd. Basically, we would take turns singing "Time Heals Everything" from *Mack and Mabel*.

Ed, who had a dentist's prescription pad, began draining the nation's Valium supply.

Finally, one night Ed stayed over at my place and we talked long into the night, to the point that we were "vibrating." Do you know about vibrating? We had just gotten so keyed up and were so focused—and so excited and passionate—we decided, for real and for sure, that we would spend the rest of our lives together. And I remember Ed's saying he knew it was real because he was vibrating—and I remember knowing exactly what he meant, because I was vibrating, too. We were on nothing but endorphins, or whatever makes you vibrate.

The next day Ed told Todd. It was heartbreaking, but somebody had to get hurt here. Our triangle couldn't go on forever; it was ripping all three of us apart.

Ed and Todd stayed up all night together crying—even 40 milligrams of Valium couldn't doze them off, Ed told me after Todd had left. (For me, the few times I took it, 5 milligrams was the upper limit.) This was now October 1975, a year and a little after Ed and I had first met. Finally, Todd, poor guy, was gone.

By that Thanksgiving—the first Thanksgiving of the rest of our lives together—Ed was back with Todd. The attraction was just too strong.

I gave up.

It took a full two years to get over Ed—five, really, before I could be in the same room with him and not have all my wiring short out. Eventually I realized that he was just human, after all. (Ed's shrink had told him that he—Ed—was my fantasy and that therefore I didn't really love him, I only thought I did. Well, far be it from me to argue with a licensed psychiatrist who had never met or spoken with me, but I sure *thought* I loved Ed.) Time heals everything. The spell wore off. With hindsight, though Ed remains a great guy and a friend, I'd even say it probably worked out for the best.

For their part, Ed and Todd spent a sometimes good, and later increasingly rocky, thirteen years together, following which they had the Most Melodramatic, Longest-Running, Most Mutually Debilitating Breakup Since Time Began. Though it has finally petered out, let us pray, and Todd's wacko lawsuit over their brownstone was decided in Ed's favor, the Most Melodramatic, Longest-Running, Most Mutually Debilitating Breakup Since Time Began lasted nine years.

Such is the power of chemistry.

8

The sensible thing to do when someone breaks your heart is flee. I didn't really even begin to get over Ed until more than a year later, when I moved out of London Terrace to an apartment on the Upper West Side.

In the meantime, my Revson book, *Fire and Ice,* had come out. At twenty-nine, I had a *New York Times* best-seller. It seemed everyone in New York was interested in Charles Revson. He was a legend—and so fearsome that few had previously dared take him on.

I had not known when I boldly signed up for this assignment that Revson would die, but his passing did lessen—somewhat—my fear of how he would react to what I'd written.

The day in 1976 *Fire and Ice* debuted, the Doubleday store then at 57th Street and Fifth Avenue, two blocks from the GM Building, which housed both Revlon and Estée Lauder, sold five hundred copies. One store on Madison Avenue filled its entire window with the book. I went and took pictures. I knew this would never happen again and that I might as well enjoy it.

What's more, as spring turned to summer, I found that, because this book was, vaguely at least, about fashion and glamour, my stock on the stairs overlooking tea-dance had risen considerably. Models who had previously looked through me were waving and calling out to me by name. ("Up here, Andy! Tell us about auto insurance!")

Does the fact that I enjoyed this make me a rotten person? Why, of course! And I loved every minute of it.

So, yes, I shorted out when I thought Ed and Todd would be out on the Island or that I might run into them in town, but otherwise I was doing okay. My professional life was good. Unlike the paperback rights to *The Best Little Boy in the World,* the rights to *Fire and Ice* were vied over, and there was even a movie deal.* I was writing for *New York* and then, when *New York* was sold to Rupert Murdoch, followed Clay et al. to *Esquire.* There were offers to publish other books. One strong possibility: a biography of Lewis Rosenstiel, who had been to the liquor industry more or less what Revson had been to cosmetics. *Firewater and Ice Cubes,* I thought I might call it—especially when I realized I'd be writing a book about the insurance industry I could then title *Fire and Life.* Nordhoff and Hall, those bountiful mutineers, wouldn't be the only ones with a trilogy.[†]

As for my love life . . . or perhaps it was really my "yearn" life . . . I had begun palling around with, among others, David Sheehy. David was the kind of young man—I was now twenty-nine, he was twenty-five or so—everyone fell in love with. He liked me because I challenged him to do something more with his life. He was modeling—brought me back an urn from a

---

* Not to be confused with a movie.

† I collect "historic documents" and actually have a James Hall letter that leads me to suspect there may have been more to his relationship with Charles Nordhoff—the two of them living out in Tahiti all those years—than a simple writing partnership. I also have a James Dean letter—*James Dean*—which has nothing at all to do with his sexuality, but can you imagine how differently I might have felt about myself growing up if I had realized that James Dean, coolest young man on earth, felt at least somewhat the same way? But I digress.

fashion shoot in India—but soon also signed up with Catholic Big Brothers. He would have made a dazzlingly good friend to some youngster or maybe become a high school teacher or even a principal some day, like his dad.

One day he was helping a friend move, unloading furniture from a U-Haul on the Upper West Side, when a taxi ran a red light and slammed into a van, which slammed into David. At the hospital that night, they amputated his leg. A few hours later, a blood clot dislodged and he died.

He hadn't told his parents he was gay, but if they were surprised by the throng of tearful young men who came out from the city to his funeral, they seemed consoled to know that so many of us cared about him. I was a pallbearer.

This was pre-AIDS, when it was still unusual for handsome young men to die during peacetime.

One captain of industry *still* asks me, when he comes to town: "Who should I meet? Is there anyone like David Sheehy?"

For years I would send a contribution to Catholic Big Brothers in his memory.

I met Scot on Thursday, January 20, 1977, and with some anticipation. I'm not much for blind dates, but an acquaintance had called and said there was this senior at Yale he knew, really great—film critic for the *Yale Daily News*—and that we should get together.

Yale. Listen: I'm not *proud* of how shallow I am, but just the word *Yale,* let alone the phrase "a senior at Yale," catches my attention. "Have him give me a call."

He was coming down from New Haven for a screening of *The Late Show,* with Lily Tomlin and Art Carney, to write his review, so we agreed to meet for a drink at the Yale Club and then go to the movie.

First impressions are everything, and having been told how

handsome he was, and knowing that as a Yale man he must have the world around his finger, I was expecting—or certainly hoping—to go all gaga when I met him.

Instead, he had a mustache.

Oh, for crying out loud, why didn't you tell me he had a mustache! This could have saved a lot of time.

It was one of those Sundance Kid mustaches Robert Redford had that angle down around the mouth. And, like the rest of his hair, it was basically *red*.

So, obviously, this evening was going nowhere, and we hadn't even said two words to each other.

His handshake was okay, I guess, but just okay, and if I didn't notice it then, I can certainly tell you now: Scot's hands were really small. "Little Pig! Your hands are so little!" I would later say in mock surprise, as if noticing for the first time. (We called each other Mr. Pig or Little Pig or Piglet. In private, of course. When a collection of my magazine pieces came out in 1984 under the title *Money Angles,* it was dedicated, simply, to "L.P." Ours being the love that generally dared not speak its name, even in 1984, I went with initials.)

So we sat down and started to talk a little, which was awkward because I was disappointed and a little annoyed (well, it would not have been all that hard for our mutual acquaintance to mention the mustache, would it? I'm a busy guy! I have deadlines!) and because Scot was not, at this stage in his life, what you would call a confident conversationalist. Nor do I always make it easy. ("You have a mustache," I might well have begun by saying, though truthfully I no longer recall.)

The movie was all right,* and Scot (really just one *t*?) was

---

* Though a critical success, *The Late Show* is not one you need rush out and rent. Rent *Moonstruck*. Rent *The Ten Commandments*. Rent *Casablanca* and *The Maltese Falcon* and *Dr. Zhivago* and *Dr. Strangelove* and *Gone With the Wind* and *The Ruling Class* and *Z*—there are actually young people today who haven't seen these!

certainly a *nice* guy, if a disappointment. He had won a couple of
prizes at Yale for his fiction—had had a short story published in
Mademoiselle—and took his film reviews seriously. I like movies;
he liked films. And because he actually liked movies too, but felt
a little embarrassed to admit it, when he *did* see a terrific mid-
dlebrow movie, he would say, sort of apologetically, "It was actually quite wonderful"—as in "Well, you'd never expect it
from a piece so broadly accessible, but . . ."

Anyway, this was going nowhere.

If memory serves, he did come back to my place after the
movie rather than take the late train up to New Haven, and he
did join me in a Southern Comfort and orange juice, which I
needed to relax and get over the mustache, and he did doubtless
fall victim to the pinball machine hustle, at which I excelled
with a level of cocky glee that surely would have sent any sober
young man off to Grand Central, and—well, the rest is private
except to say I was probably fantasizing about David Sheehy,
who was still with us, and that Scot, in the raw, was a nice guy
with a college-film-critic's body. Nothing terrible in that, mind
you—and far better, to my eye, than one of those vein-popping
bodybuilders—but just nothing to write home about.

We were both a little awkward when he left the next morning. You know: the mild embarrassment two bright people feel
when they've basically used each other to satisfy physical "needs"
they know it's natural to have (straight or gay) yet are a little embarrassed about—my God, what are we, animals? well, yes, as a
matter of fact, we *are* animals—especially knowing that, in an
ideal world, we would be satisfying them with someone we loved.

So I was actually a little surprised when Scot called a week
or two later to say he had to come down for another movie.

I hadn't realized it at the time (and a good thing, too, or I
doubtless would have run the other way), but Scot had apparently decided, even before we met at the Yale Club, that we
would make a good team.

For me, this was quite a different thing from Ed. It was not, obviously, love at first sight, and I was not, obviously, putty in Scot's little hands. I was not helplessly in his thrall. He was *not* my fantasy, so in this sense maybe Ed's shrink was right; maybe the love that developed between Scot and me *was* more real, if for me the attraction was less magnetic.

I had it easy. I didn't have to worry about Scot's leaving me—Scot was almost as crazy about me as I had been about Ed. And I didn't have to worry about not being "versatile" in bed— Scot was a satisfied customer. And, perhaps most important to the secretary of defense who had taken charge of my heart, I didn't have to worry that if Scot ever *did* leave me it would be crushing. It would be sad—very sad—but not a mortal blow.

Perhaps I should have held out for another Ed or a David Sheehy. A fantasy to be worshiped and adored.

Instead, as the months went on and Scot continued to visit and then graduated from Yale, we built something I think is ultimately healthier. I may have largely missed the "in love" stage with Scot—I certainly skipped the "initial infatuation," which is so much fun—but the love part . . . well, that just grew and grew.

Scot was shy. We are all shy, of course, but I mean Scot was almost pathologically shy—so much so that I actually bought him books about overcoming it. He was shy in a way that was *so* extreme it was comical. Even he realized the illogic of it. Over the years, I took great pride in watching him gradually become a centered, caring man. I had to laugh as, near the end, running *People* magazine's Los Angeles bureau, he'd offhandedly juggle the phones—"I'll call Angie back. I'm working out the shoot with Dolly." (And damned if Angie Dickinson didn't show up at the funeral.)

Competitive though I am, it was easy to be supportive and take pleasure in Scot's accomplishments. For one thing, he was "art and fiction," I was "money and nonfiction." Different fields.

This is actually one of the things that works so well with Charles and me. Charles is graphics and style; I'm numbers and efficiency. The new federal budget is published and, as I like to describe it (neither of us has ever actually seen the federal budget), I'll be getting all excited over the figures—"Look what they've done with defense!"—and he'll be getting all excited over the binding—"Blue and gold! Someone in Washington's finally *getting* it!"

On top of that, I was older than Scot. There was not a reason in the world for us to be competitive. Of *course* I was further along with my career—I had a seven-year head start.

With Charles, it's much the same thing—a *ten*-year head start. (I hasten to point out this is actually a narrower age gap in relative terms, because we're older.) When the clothes Charles designs are on the cover of *Women's Wear* or appear on CNN, I'm entirely pleased. I had spent much of my life trying not to know anything about women's clothes—why would I feel competitive over this?

Of course, my benevolence toward Scot had its limits. At pinball—and also at gin, which Scot and I played endlessly those first few months as a way to just sort of stay home and get comfortable—I was merciless. And the wrestling—well, I had an even greater advantage over Scot than Ed because, at first, I was a lot stronger than Scot. So I don't mean any of this to suggest I had lost my cocky, competitive, obnoxious *edge*.

Shortly before graduation, Scot came down to look for apartments and snagged a small nineteenth-floor one-bedroom at 71st and Broadway. That put him just six blocks away—six blocks each of us walked happily and often over the years that followed. There was nothing official; we gradually just realized we were boyfriends.

They were great years.

At first, Scot was writing about culture and film for *Horizon*. I still have the August 1978 cover story he did on four rising young actresses with funny names: Jill Eikenberry, Swoosie Kurtz, Tovah Feldshuh, and Meryl Streep. I was writing about money and stocks and whatnot for *Esquire*. I'd also done a book my publishers had had the good sense to entitle *The Only Investment Guide You'll Ever Need* (never mind that I would later revise it), which, through avid promotion, they propelled to #4 on the *New York Times* list.

I even got to go on the *Tonight* show, with Johnny Carson. That was in the days when it was ninety minutes long and they'd often have an author on at the tail end.

To give you an idea how crazy I was, and how different the world still was, I should describe the experience. Anybody else flies out with his wife or his girlfriend, has a nice lunch at one-of-those-places, then watches the show from the greenroom until it's his turn to join in the fun. But I didn't have a wife or a girlfriend, and obviously couldn't bring a guy (it was 1978), so I would go out, borrow a friend's apartment, and lie on his balcony alone trying to prep myself but getting deeper and deeper into a sense of inadequacy and phoniness and, well, what if the guest before me got into a little innocent Rat Pack fag humor— you know, good clean kidding around of the type guys do? And what if Carson continued the kidding on into my segment? Should I just ignore it? Make a dramatic little speech?

Ridiculous things to be worried about, to be sure. But alone with my neuroses on that balcony in the cool Los Angeles winter haze, I would actually play through variations of that speech in my head, play through all the brilliant financial advice I could give . . . and what was I going to wear, anyway? And should I risk trying to put in my contacts? (I had, by now, finally gotten a pair of contact lenses. But—especially under pressure—I had a hell of a time putting them in.) Today, Charles would have or-

ganized all this for me easily (you'll wear your gray suit, blue
shirt, yellow tie) and I would not have been nervous because
times have changed. Back then, even though obviously no one
at the *Tonight* show cared whether I was straight or gay or came
to the greenroom alone or with a guy or a spouse, *I* was aware
of it. Irrational? Sure. They had gay entertainers on all the time.
But—well, also, what about my hair? I knew I should do *something* about it, because I tended to let it grow pretty long and
then just trim it myself at home with one of those razor-blade
doohickeys and a pair of scissors (saves time, saves money) or else
get a six-dollar haircut at the Harvard Club. But here I was out
in L.A. to do the *Tonight* show and *of course* I should get a professional TV-type haircut . . . but where? And, what—am I suddenly going to alter my appearance *the afternoon of the show*?
How risky and contrived is *that*? What I actually did was go into
my friend's medicine chest and find some hair gook—I never,
ever use that stuff—and, figuring that a little dab'd do me (if
you're too young to catch the reference, ask your dad), managed, an hour or so before the limo was to arrive to take me to
Burbank, to get my hair all gunky and matted.

Irrelevant to my story? No. I'm convinced it is all related. It
was just so obvious from my hair—both pre- and post-gook—
that I was a closeted homosexual.

So I got to Burbank in what was now the blazing late-afternoon sun, all suited and tied, while the other guests gradually
sauntered in with their suit bags casually slung over their arms,
husbands or wives in tow . . . and was shown into Makeup (noting the quizzical way the makeup artist and stylist regarded my
hair) and then into my dressing room, which I occupied alone,
which gave me *another* hour to vacillate over whether or not to
risk trying to put in the contact lenses (riskier still, should there
be a little fleck of dust between my eyeball and one of the lenses
and should I then want to get it *out*—a procedure that, under

pressure, could sometimes go awry, leaving me temporarily half-blinded with a scrunched contact in some remote recess of my profusely tearing, wildly blinking eye) . . . and now the show was about to begin (they begin taping around six) and I was ushered into the greenroom with Charles Grodin and his mother (he brought his *mother?*) and some other people I didn't know or was too traumatized to talk to (should I drink the coffee? the wine?) and I got sort of mesmerized watching the show, mouth shut, deep in my own terror, *for eighty minutes* until it was my turn to go on.

And guess what?

I did okay.

Skipping the obvious first question ("So *are* you a homosexual?") and the alternate ("Is it true you cut your own hair?"), Johnny and I got right into high finance—buying stuff in bulk, when it's on sale—I even made him laugh—and before you knew it we were out of time and he asked, on the air, in front of twenty billion people, whether I could come back, and I said I could.

Now, a quick word about television. *The only thing that matters is how you look.* I spoke with twenty-seven friends and relatives in the week after the show—I had made him laugh! I had gotten invited back!—and I am not exaggerating when I tell you that every one of them, without exception, told me just one thing: "You really should unbutton your jacket when you sit down." With hindsight, I realize that it was the jacket—flared out preposterously to either side of the button—that saved me from having people even notice my glasses or my hair.

Today, Charles finally has me buying clothes that fit (even then it's wise to unbutton your jacket when you sit down). "It doesn't cost more to get them in your size" finally clinched the argument (you mean the bigger sizes don't cost more?). But back then, well, I think I thought it was "gay" to care too much about clothes or to be all prim and proper. Not that I wasn't 100 percent gay; just that, I guess, it was important to me to be as-straight-as-the-next-guy gay.

A month or so later, having learned *nothing* from the experience, I repeated all the above steps almost exactly—except that I did unbutton my jacket.

By way of contrast, I got to do *Oprah* a couple of years ago. My suit more or less fit, my hair was short enough that gook was not required, and mainly I felt good about who I was, as I have for a long time now, so it was a thoroughly enjoyable experience. You don't get to speak with her before the show, but afterward, with the credits rolling, Oprah says something nice and shakes each guest's hand. When she came to me, I smiled and said, "You know, my boyfriend is angry with you."

"*Why?*" asked Oprah, genuinely concerned.

"Well, you know that Jackie Kennedy auction they had last month? He had his heart set on three pillows estimated at $150 to $200 and he bid $800 and *you* bought them out from under him for $26,000!"

"I didn't!" she protested. "I didn't buy *anything* at that auction."

"But it was in the paper!"

"I know! But they got it wrong. It was 'an anonymous Chicago woman' and the tabloids just assumed it was me. But tell your boyfriend it wasn't—really!"

She was grinning; I was grinning. (And Charles has forgiven her.) I can't see having had the same conversation with Johnny—or even Doc Severinsen—in 1978.

Between my modest success and Scot's film credentials, we got to go to a lot of openings. A mogul-even-then friend of ours, David Geffen, produced a show called *Dreamgirls*—great show; great party. Our friend Tom Moore, who had directed the original *Grease* on Broadway when he was twenty-six, had us to the opening of a succession of terrific plays and shows that our friend Frank Rich unfailingly closed the next day. ("Geez, Frank!" I kept thinking of appealing to him—"Didn't you hear the audience roar? They loved it!" I knew Frank was doubtless "right," but have always thought that film and theater reviews should have, at the end, some sort of easy ranking for the masses [me]—e.g., "While any even casual devotee of French farce will not fail to be offended by the awkward and obvious homage to Molière, the other 99 percent of the people there, being igno-ramuses, had a really great time. If you're not a theater critic, you will too.")

Scot and I didn't live together, but this is not to say we were not genuinely a team. Scot and Andy, Andy and Scot—you could tell the level of our commitment and affection, if nothing else, by the increasing piles of pigaphernalia that accumulated.

Of course, I have never actually touched a pig in my life, care nothing about pigs (except as bacon), and had previously thought about pigs only as characters of literary amusement. (What—you never read *Freddy the Pig*? Or *Freddy the Pig Goes to College*? What kind of childhood did you *have*? Reading Molière, no doubt, like Frank.) But we gave each other all sorts of great pig stuff—greeting cards, mostly—and to this day one of my favorite *New Yorker* cartoons, the original of which hangs in the hall, is Lee Lorenz's drawing of a pig behind his desk on the telephone. "Oh—you want Mr. *Big*," he's saying to the confused caller. "This is Mr. Pig."

As one does when one couples, I acquired a new family. In Charles's case, he being one of nine children, this has taxed my brain.* With Scot it was easier: a great mom and dad and two

---

* Go ahead, quiz me. I can do both Nolan parents, an aunt and uncle, all eight Nolan sib-lings, the siblings-in-law, *and* all eight adorable nieces and nephews.

wonderful younger twin sisters. Like Charles's family, Irish Catholic. And also like Charles's family, close and fiercely loyal.

This being still the late Seventies, early Eighties, however, Scot and I didn't entirely merge families on holidays, as Charles and I do now. Mom and Dad *certainly* had not been out to Fire Island—*are you out of your mind?*—as everyone in the Nolan/ Tobias clan has been, repeatedly, by now. But we were making progress.

"Look how the world has changed," I had been able to point out even back in August 1976, six months before I met Scot, in the Afterword to the paperback edition of *The Best Little Boy in the World.*

> Imagine: a six-part series on the sports pages of newspapers around the country about pro athletes who are gay; a front-page *Wall Street Journal* story about *The Advocate* (whose own circulation has doubled in the past year); a lead piece in the Sunday *New York Times* travel section on an all-gay cruise; a *Time* cover story on a much-decorated gay Army sergeant.

Though so few and far between you could more or less enumerate them in a paragraph, these were amazing things that would never have occurred even a few years earlier. "But not that much has changed," I continued.

> At a party in Beverly Hills recently, [a very famous writer] confided with disdain: "This is really fag city!" It was even worse than he thought, I told him—I was gay, too. Would he have called it "nigger city" if there had been a lot of blacks at the party? He said he saw my point—but I doubt he changed his mind. A week or two later, the Supreme Court (not mine, the real one) refused even to *consider* overturning state laws which ban consenting adults from doing what they want behind closed doors. And in Italy, a seventeen-year-old hustler

was becoming a national hero for having brutally murdered film-maker Pier Paolo Pasolini. The hustler had willingly drilled Pasolini for thirty dollars and a ride in his Alfa Romeo; but when Pasolini wanted to reverse positions, the hustler killed him. His father exuded a sort of confused pride when interviewed on Italian TV, hoping that in a similar situation he would have acted with equal courage.

The train had begun to move by the mid-to-late Seventies, but it was still very slow. It accelerated a bit in the Eighties. But it was not until Bill Clinton made gay rights an issue fit for open national discussion, in his first run for the presidency, that the movement toward acceptance really picked up steam—but I'll get to that.

The really brave people—and I was not among them—were the ones willing to speak up earlier, before it was the thing to do. People like astronomer Frank Kameny, who filed the world's first gay anti-discrimination lawsuit after the government fired him in 1957 simply for being gay. (Not until 1975 did the Civil Service drop its ban on gay employees.) He led the effort to have homosexuality removed from the American Psychological Association's list of psychiatric disorders. That was achieved in 1973—but not before, at one particularly dramatic point in the fight, at an APA annual meeting, Kameny recalls, honoree psychiatrists on the dais were beating gay activists over the head with their gold medals.*

People like Washington Redskin Dave Kopay and Barbara Gittings and Walter Lear and Tom Stoddard and Elaine Noble and countless others—but not so countless that, at any given

---

* "Whereas homosexuality per se implies no impairment in judgment, stability, reliability or general social or vocational capabilities," pronounced this group after further deliberation, "therefore, be it resolved that the American Psychiatric Association deplores all public and private discrimination against homosexuals."

time, you couldn't count them, in even the largest cities, on the fingers of a few hands.

I was "out" in a private sort of way, speaking up at editorial meetings, talking privately to friends, shaking hands with Mario Cuomo. But it would be quite some time before I got up the nerve to go much further. And Scot was pretty much the same way.

9

Straight people sometimes ask, or think of asking, "What exactly do gay men do?" (They may be even more baffled by what gay women do, but I leave that one to my esteemed colleague Rita Mae Brown.) I will make a deal with you. I promise not to tell you in detail what gay men do if you promise not to tell me in detail what straight men do. *I don't want to know.* The truth is, when the porn film goes into close-up, I'm not eager to look at the gay details, either. To me, this stuff is best left private, intimate, and in relative darkness. Moonlight. Or candlelight.

(Charles, bless his heart, likes *everything* in relative darkness. To him, the only acceptable rheostat position is: dim. He can never find things—"I can't find my keys"—and on rare occasion I summon the courage to point out it's because *the lights are off.* He's looking for them *in the dark.* To me, electric light was a great advance. Likewise, paper napkins. I need hardly tell you what Charles thinks of paper napkins.)

The point is, I can only give you a sample of the times Scot and I shared, and it will be rated G, but I do want to do that.

. . .

One New Year's Eve (I've had a fine time New Year's Eve ever since I came out) we celebrated as we always did: We went down the street to David Marlow's apartment at the Dakota, had champagne with friends, and all went up to the roof to watch the fireworks in Central Park. Only this time, during the champagne, Scot and I playfully disappeared into David's huge clothes closet, at one end of the apartment, and were marveling at David's wide assortment of sweaters—not a mail-order label in the bunch—and one thing led to another and, perhaps realizing I wouldn't be young and buff forever, and being, next to Scot, perhaps the youngest and buffest in the group, and just loving the notion of our freedom and camaraderie, I guess, I stripped down to my jock and ran to the far end of the apartment, gave David a hug—the party momentarily stopped, jaws dropped—and ran laughing back to Scot. I can't imagine now what possessed me to do this. Other than, perhaps, a desperate need for attention. I like to think it was during the days of "streaking"—i.e., it was vaguely related to the events of the day. And of course what made it so funny for me is that I was the sober you'll-never-get-*me*-to-dress-up-in-drag (and you won't) member of any group. So wouldn't *this* just shock 'em. Anyway, it was fun. Scot and I had a good time that New Year's Eve, and all the others. Charles's and my New Year's Eves are pretty spectacular also, but more grown-up.

Most nights, of course, were not remotely dramatic. Scot and I would meet for dinner or go to a screening or meet at Dobson's or Nanny Rose or the Cherry or one of the other Columbus Avenue restaurants that had sprouted and become institutions and have since passed on. We'd do what people *do*—talk about our work, talk about our friends, talk about our hopes. One of Scot's hopes was to write great fiction. Writing for *Horizon* and then for *People* was fun and he was terrific at it, but he was also a little embarrassed by it. Had John Updike written for *People*? Had John Cheever? So imagine my surprise—and delight— when Scot told me one evening at Dobson's, that, oh, incidentally, he had written a short story that would be published in *The New Yorker*. (Yes! *The New Yorker!*) *What?* I hadn't even known he was writing it. And this was no short short story, this was one *long* short story—it wound up occupying ten pages in the magazine. Well, he said, he hadn't wanted to jinx it by telling me before it was definite.

I decided we should celebrate. But I knew he was too shy and modest to want any of that, so I didn't tell him. Instead, I called around to find where I could get a custom cake baked and found that the most convenient place seemed to be the Erotic Bakery. I explained that I wanted a big sheet cake that looked like the famous annual *New Yorker* cover with bemonocled Eustace Tilley on the cover. Only, I wanted the date to be the date of Scot's story that coming week—August 11, 1980—and I wanted Eustace Tilley to have a red down-curving Sundance Kid mustache.

"Do you want a penis?" asked the clerk.

"*No,* I don't want a penis," I said. "But I want you to tape up the box really well. And I need it Friday."

Friday, I picked up the cake and told Scot I needed his help carrying "the cake for Bruce Stanwich's surprise birthday party" out on the bus with us to the ferry to the Island. By then we were in a wonderful house that had been previously christened Valmare (roll your tongue with Italian pronunciation, please—Val-MA-ray) and that became, for the four years we all rented it, a little bit of a landmark. (I may have overdone it when I ordered pens that read I'VE SLEPT AT VALMARE—WHO HASN'T, but remember, we were young, and penicillin had long since wiped away any serious threat from sexually transmitted disease.)

"What *is* this?" Scot asked when I put the cake on his lap in the bus.

"It is a grotesque penis cake," I told him, explaining that when I saw it at the store I couldn't *believe* that I, of all people—perhaps the only homosexual in the world who is not only embarrassed by talk of penises but who is actually not particularly fond of them—found myself carrying this disgusting cake out to the Island. What's more, to help David make it a surprise for Bruce, we'd have to keep the damn thing in our refrigerator until their party. Which was not 100 percent convenient, Scot pointed out (and I had to agree), because Valmare was having a little late-afternoon get-together of its own Saturday—we needed refrigerator space, too.

And so it was that Scot carried his own cake out to Fire Island. (And no, he could *not* look at the giant penis—the box was taped up within an inch of its life.)

A hundred-odd guys in shorts and sweatshirts came over at sunset that Saturday, and when Scot saw the cake and realized they had come over to congratulate him . . . well, wasn't I pleased with *my*self.

I loved surprising Scot. It's not as if he was living with a practical joker—remember, these stories are spread out over six or seven years. But one time, perhaps two or three years into our relationship, I can't remember quite why, I bought us two tickets to Fort Lauderdale and reserved a room at my old haunt-when-I-was-single, the then somewhat sleazy Marlin Beach Hotel (into which I used to check under an assumed name and pay cash, at least at first). It's not that I have an affinity for sleaze, just that virtually all gay establishments in the early days were more about sex and paying off the cops, or whatever, than many of us would have liked. Still, the rooms were decent, the pool was nice, and nobody said you *had* to pick up one of the sad teenage hustlers who hung out on the corner across the street. In fact, the Sunday tea-dance by the Marlin Beach pool was not bad—people came from all over—and it was cold in New York and I thought it would be fun to hoist Scot over my head and carry him into the Atlantic Ocean.

I thought it would be even more fun to surprise him.

So I got the tickets and I arranged for a busy schedule of—fake—events for Scot for that weekend in New York. We were having dinner with David and Arthur on Friday, he had been invited over to one of his sisters' Saturday (she was playing along), and so on.

Friday morning, after Scot left for work, I went over to his place and packed a bag.

Friday afternoon I reminded him he had agreed to sit in on a meeting with our friend Ira Barmak. But there was, in fact, no meeting that day with Ira.

Having adequately prepped the cabdriver and tossed our luggage in the trunk, I swung by Scot's apartment and off we went.

Scot was still in his tie and jacket from work because we were headed to Ira's and then some pretty nice place with David and Arthur.

"One sixty-one West Fifty-fourth," I told the cabdriver.

The cab turned right—north—on Amsterdam Avenue as I began asking Scot about his day. He didn't notice at first, but after we'd gone up a few blocks he said, "Where are we going?"

"Ira's," I said.

"But we're going north."

"Driver—Fifty-fourth Street," I said.

"I know. Broadway's all fucked up," the driver said.

"So did you hear from those people about the interview?" I continued to press Scot about his work.

Scot was now answering my questions with one side of his brain, nervously eyeing our circuitous route with the other.

"Where are we *going*?" Scot asked as the cab turned right—east—to go across town.

"Florida!" I beamed delightedly, raising my hands to either side of my head as if to catch a medicine ball.

"No, come on. Really. Where are we going?"

Scot, not unlike myself—and not unlike Charles—well, not unlike most of us, I guess—was a person who liked to be in control. This was beginning to make him really nervous, because we obviously were *not* going to Ira's.

"Really! We're going to Florida. Fort Lauderdale."

"What are you talking about! We have dinner tonight, we have—"

"No we don't, that's fake."

"I promised my sister—"

"That was fake too."

Scot paused for a moment, stunned.

"Well, but I don't *have* anything!" he resumed.

"Yes you do. It's in the trunk."

We were now halfway through the transverse to the East Side, and it crossed my mind that—possibly—we just might not be going to Florida after all. Scot had a hint of panic in his eyes.

"What about my blue shirt?" he protested. (In the summertime, it was his favorite shirt.)

"I packed it."

"What about my toothbrush?"

"Scot, I packed your toothbrush. But let me tell you something about Florida: It has stores. In an emergency we could *buy* a toothbrush."

"We're going to Florida?" Scot said, a hint of amusement and anticipation beginning to crowd out the panic. We were now between Madison and Park and I knew we were all but home free. I handed him his ticket, it rained the whole time we were there, and we had a wonderful time.

I had kidnapped my boyfriend. (A less serious journalist might say: pignapped.)

We had a lot of good times. One often doesn't realize that these *are* the good old days—one certainly could not have imagined that half our friends would die in the decade that followed—but there were lots of times when we both recognized how lucky and happy we were.

The best example of this for me was when we would be dancing (yes, I had more or less learned to dance, which is basically to say I had unwittingly invented aerobics long before the health clubs) and as one song began to fade, I'd hear the first hints of "If My Friends Could See Me Now."

I was alive. I was happy. I had made it. My ears would prick up when I heard that song start to play, my lungs would fill with freedom, my eyes would even get a little teary (or was that from the sweat?), and I would just grab Scot and squeeze really tight, and we'd dance and dance and dance.

Those summers. Those winters. If I was the best little boy in the world, I was also one of the most fortunate—and keenly aware of it.

We loved each other, but we were not entirely faithful to each other. It was the late Seventies, early Eighties, temptation was everywhere, and when you placed the pull of the temptation, on the one hand, against, on the other, the combined countervailing pulls of social opprobrium, the risk of pregnancy, the financial cost of divorce, the shame of violating vows you took in front of all those who mean most to you in the world *and* what it would do to the children, custody of whom you might even lose—the needle came out further to the left for gay men, on the TEMPTATION–FIDELITY meter, than it did for straight men. That's still largely true, but not as true as it was. Back then, on top of everything else, we were rejoicing with more than a little abandon in our liberation and in our young, healthy manhood.

AIDS has nudged the needle toward fidelity. But so has society's growing acceptance of gay people and its respect for gay relationships. I wouldn't have cheated on Ed, but if I had, I would only have been cheating on Ed. I hope never to cheat on

Charles. But not lost on me is the fact that if I did cheat on Charles, I would also be cheating, in a sense, on my mom and stepdad, who consider Charles part of the family, and on all manner of straight and gay friends who think of us as a couple and like us as a couple. Mom and Dad did meet Scot a few times, but it wasn't remotely the same.

One can talk about whether fidelity even matters in the gay world (it does!). One can talk about whether a single set of rules need apply to every couple and every life, especially where no children are involved (maybe not). Is there room in the world for serial monogamy? For open relationships? Can couples legitimately drift apart and start new lives? Must the rules brook no exceptions, or can they be understanding of slips and foibles? What about, dare I say it, the occasional *ménage à trois*? (You know those French. Not to mention their all having mistresses.) The answer to all these questions, I would say, is yes. But back when Scot and I were a team—and gay marriage, far from being actively outlawed as it is today, wasn't even imagined—there was even more tricking going on than there is today.

So from time to time one of us would slip. It was embarrassing, there were some hurt feelings—because we loved each other and wanted to be honest, we'd invariably fess up, being too young to realize *it's really stupid to ask* (and perhaps nearly as stupid to answer honestly)—but we recognized there was a world of difference between sex and love, between the crotch and the heart, and I guess the simple fact was that neither one of us was *so* chemically mesmerized by the other that we did not occasionally stray.

I strayed less often, I think, because (a) I'm such a prude; (b) I was older, even then (you may be relieved or horrified to know that one's sex drive diminishes somewhat as time goes by); and (c) I got to do pretty much what I wanted, sexually. Scot strayed more often, I think, and it was hard to blame him—

so I really didn't—because there were certain things he wanted sexually that I just couldn't do for him. At first, he didn't care. But as the years went on . . .

Anyway, this is a tremendously long lead-in to the time Joe Peckerman sent me a hustler for my birthday.

Joe, a Yale Law School graduate, lived in L.A. and led a pretty fast life. A few days before I was to turn thirty-three or thirty-four, he called and asked what I was doing for my birthday. For some reason, he knew Scot was going to be out of town. (Away for my birthday? The nerve! He must have been on assignment someplace.) From the tone of Joe's voice, I could tell something was up.

"I'm having dinner with my parents."

"What are you doing the night before?" he asked.

As I looked on my calendar, it came to me what Joe had in mind.

"Don't even *think* about it, Joe. I don't do that. I've never done that."

"Be home at nine," he said.

"No—really, Joe!" I said nervously, meaning it. Pretty much.

We went back and forth, he not admitting *exactly* what he had in mind but knowing that I knew.

"Don't argue with me," he said finally. "And don't spend all night talking about auto insurance, either." He was laughing, he was insistent, and I was pretty sure from his last comment that he was paying by the hour.

Thursday evening rolled around and I will not tell you I wasn't *very* nervous—I truly never *had* done anything like this. What would the doorman even think when he rang up to say this guy was here? And, mainly, what would this guy be like? And just how far, if at all, should I let my fantasies go? And what would I tell Scot? And what should I wear? I was wearing khakis and loafers and a white button-down shirt. *Please* let him *not* show up in the lobby all in leather.

The house phone rang, the elevator door opened, and in walked Troy. And I was instantly relieved. The tension just drained from my body. In less than a second I knew that this cute, enthusiastic, well-built youngster in his blue jeans, about my height,* was not someone I was going to touch.

It's not that he wasn't just swell. In fact, he let me know promptly, he was on the cover of that month's *Hot Studs* or some such. But I've told you I'm really choosy—a curse or a godsend, depending on your point of view (a little of each, really)—and he was not irresistible.

Well, *that* sure made things simpler! Except now I had to deal with not hurting his feelings. So I sat him down with a glass of wine and told him what I wanted to do.

"I'm going to get my Polaroid, and I want you to take your shirt off and let me take a picture of you so I can show my boyfriend what I turned down for him."

When I got back with the camera I was nonplussed to see— "I didn't ask you to take your *pants* off. Put those back on!"

He did, I took the photo, thanked him for being such a good sport, asked him a little about his life (although, having a friend who had hustled his tuition through Columbia Law School, I actually knew a fair amount about his life), and sent him back out into the night.

I still have the picture.

---

* Like Robert Redford, I'm not six-two, or even six, or, well, five-ten, either. In the last book I think I did make myself five-ten, and made myself just a little more athletic and self-assured than I probably was—not to deceive, and maybe just out of vanity—probably just out of vanity—but my rationale was that readers (remember, I envisioned mainly straight readers) would come in with a preconception that gay guys were all *here,* meaning pretty nelly, dweeby guys. So if I described myself a little more toward *here*—not a major distortion, but just a little shading, a touch more testosterone or whatever—the two distortions might at least partly cancel each other out: Readers might actually get a *more* accurate picture of me. Plus, I've always wanted to be five-ten.

I then waited three or four hours, until I was about to go to sleep, and called Joe Peckerman in California.

"Oh, *Joe!*" I said excitedly. "This is sooooooo great! I can't thank you enough. I know it's expensive, but—just another couple of hours?"

I could hear Joe nervously adding and subtracting the three-hour time difference in his head—when we're flustered, it's easy to get confused—and when I was sure he had multiplied by the right number of hours and was getting a small pain in his chest, I laughed that Troy had left hours ago—I was just pulling his leg—but, thanks, it was great.

And it was, because when Scot got back a few days later I was able to tell him the whole story, show him the picture, and go to bed with him instead.

Much nicer.

The only really memorable time I strayed was early in our relationship.

It was a weekday in July out on Fire Island. Being a writer, I could sometimes stay out there while Scot was stuck going into the office. I was working—I love working—but with a phone and a typewriter there was a lot I could do.

Fire Island, I should explain, is the barrier island—sandbar, really—that protects Long Island, which in turn protects Connecticut. So you'd better vote for our beach-replenishment projects if you don't want this country to be gradually just eaten away from the right edge.

There are eighteen communities on Fire Island, of which two—the Pines and Cherry Grove—are largely (the Pines) or almost entirely (the Grove) gay. There are no roads, just boardwalks. Each community has its own adorable little golf-cart-like fire trucks (as well as a couple of real ones that can run along the sand in an emergency) and, in the Grove especially, which is more largely lesbian than the Pines, a truly kick-ass volunteer fire department. From one end of the Pines to the other is just over a mile—about six hundred houses and, in the center on the bay, where the ferry docks, a small "commercial district." Population in the winter: about five. Population on July Fourth weekend: about five thousand. (The Grove is a little smaller. There is quite a bit of traffic back and forth between the less-than-a-mile of beach and forested dune that separates them. Some of that traffic, I have heard, takes the scenic route, with a considerable amount of spontaneous carpooling and rubber-necking. Putting my mosquitophobia far ahead of any interest I might have in sandy semipublic sex, I have always just walked or jogged along the beach.)

Our house—Valmare—was on Nautilus Walk, on a high dune. The landlords, whose sensibility was somewhat different from ours, rented it complete with platters in the shape of giant fish and vegetables. All I cared about in that department was that the refrigerator worked. What made the house special was that from its top deck you could see ferries coming out from Sayville across the bay and a carpet of treetops stretching the length of the island. You couldn't quite see the ocean, but sometimes you could hear it—the whole island is less than half a mile wide in most places.

(I'm told that a century ago there was actually an even slimmer wisp of a sandbar a few hundred yards out protecting *our* island. Now it's gone, and we may be next. Are you listening, Long Island? Do you catch my littoral drift, Connecticut?)

On weekends, we were a full complement. Three bedrooms in the main house (one had its own bathroom!), a tiny self-contained unit down by the pool, and an even tinier sort of spillover structure across the pool just big enough for all the cushions we were supposed to take off the outdoor furniture each night. (Yeah, right.) Only rarely did anyone sleep in the cushion shed, but most weekends the other beds were all filled.

We were, variously, in our mid-twenties to early thirties, not exactly just starting out, but still very much on the make—a Harvard Law associate at one of the major Wall Street law firms; the film critic from a major national newsweekly; a wunderkind Yale Drama grad director; an entertainment lawyer who had previously been president of *The Harvard Crimson;* his boyfriend of several (and now twenty-four) years, who had been *editor* of the *Crimson* (i.e., the smart one); an ICM agent with his own Harvard Law degree; a twenty-nine-year-old from Princeton who'd left the Bain consulting firm for Morgan Stanley; a rising young producer with Paramount Pictures; Scot; me; a college classmate of mine; one token young hedonist who would use his unemployment check for the seaplane to the beach (I disapproved)—and several others, depending on the summer and the weekend, who were only slightly less central to the cast. Wonderful guys, all. (The hedonist eventually straightened out and now works for *The New York Times*.)

On weekdays, I had the house all to myself. The quiet of it . . . the birds . . . the wind . . . the sky. I have always liked spending time alone, and no place on earth is more beautiful, or accepting, than Fire Island Pines.

So I'd work during the day, go for a jog, and then, typically, saunter down to "tea" around seven. Not looking for trouble— I was very happy with Scot—but just to say hi to whoever else was around and enjoy the sunset.

This particular night, a minor movie mogul type was there—one of the rich old guys, as, I guess, I lumped them all together, unflattering as that sounds now that I would myself have to be included in the lump—and he invited me to come join him and a few others for dinner. He had rented one of the really primo bayfront houses, and the sunset that night, combined with the crisp, cool summer sea air, was magnificent. What's more, the dozen people he had collected for dinner seemed to be an interesting mix. There was a really fun curly-haired guy I knew named Tommy, and then a whole bunch of guys, including a youngish Olympic gold medalist (no, not Greg Louganis) I did not know.

There was *one* guy there, Tony—he had come with the gold medalist—to whom I took an instant, visceral dislike. I saw him out on the deck and immediately shut off to him for the rest of the night. Wouldn't even look at him. He was tall, blond (a model, obviously), the kind of person people could not resist admiring . . . *and I resented that.* What had he done to have this hold over everybody? My experience with Ed had made me angry at people who had that power: people you wanted—everybody wanted—but couldn't have. *Forget it.* If I can't have it, I don't want to deal with it—and I especially don't want to give it the satisfaction of *fawning.* Or so my feelings ran back then, still raw from having had my life ruined by a cleft chin.

The dinner was great, I was feeling my oats and adorably neurotic—the light was right—holding forth on whatever aspect of auto insurance reform mesmerized the group that night, but shutting out Tony totally.

This turned Tony on.

It was not my intention. And thinking back on it, I think I may be overdoing the anger part. It may have been more simple shyness, or some combination of the two. Then, also, there was the fact that, handsome as he was, I wasn't really *drawn* to Tony—he was too tall, and maybe a little too blond (yes, you can definitely be too blond)—so in truth, it wasn't all that big a deal. Just a reflex, really: Don't look at the model.

After we had left the dinner table and were well into coffee-on-couches, Tommy came over, leaned down, and whispered, "Why are you being so mean to Tony?"

"What?"

I was completely surprised. I know the way I've told the story it's apparent that I actually was a little mean to Tony—and intentionally, on some subconscious level. But I wasn't aware of it at the time. My various defense mechanisms just had me on autopilot: Ignore him.

"He thinks you don't like him."

"Huh? I don't even know him."

"You should go over and talk with him."

"Why?"

"He likes you."

"Oh, that's ridiculous. And he's with somebody."

"Go ahead," Tommy laughed. "Talk to him."

So after a minute or two, I sauntered over, feeling as if I were participating in a Psych 101 experiment ("but the students who thought they couldn't *have* the butter pecan expressed a preference for it six times as often as the students it was being thrust upon"), and I talked to Tony.

"You're a writer," Tony marveled.

Well, after a fashion—not exactly Tolstoy.

"I love to read!"

Really.

Which led, naturally enough, to Tony's finding out the location of my house and asking me to wait up for him. He'd walk the Olympic medalist home and then come up for a glass of wine.

He would?

The party broke up, I walked home alone, and wondered whether Tony would actually show. Fire Island has one rule above all others, I'm afraid—and certainly did back in 1979—and that is: The normal rules of responsibility do not apply. It would not have been even remotely unusual for Tony, having asked me to wait up, never to have appeared. By the same token, it would not have been even remotely unusual for Tony, the houseguest, to ditch his obviously adoring Olympic medalist host and come over to my place.

Which he did.

My recollection of the sex, there on the couch at Valmare, was that I was not into it so much as watching it. Yes, I was fucking Tony. (Sorry! That will conclude the explicit sex scenes of this book!) But far from being lost in the passion of the moment, I was . . . well, bemused. Here I was at the very top of the mountain. Tony was the kind of sixty-foot-tall person you look up at on a billboard in Times Square or lust after on TV.

(You may have looked or lusted yourself. Years later, he played Samson in a TV movie and then starred in a weekly network drama.)

And yet, to my great delight, really—my huge relief— . . . *so what?* Yes, I got a huge charge out of his being attracted to me. And, yes, if the picture I was watching hadn't been so preposterous—Woody Allen fucking Marilyn Monroe—I might even have been able to get into it enough to stop "watching" and start really enjoying (except I was also thinking about Scot, which didn't help me relax, either). But the fact is, I had been to the top of the mountain and, well, so what?

Tony left.

The next day, vaguely guilty, vaguely smug, I went about my normal routine, researching the intricacies of title insurance,* and I hear, from way down at the foot of the stairs—I was up with my typewriter at the dining room table, looking out across the bay—a sort of androgynous Australian "Annnndrew? Are you up there?"

Okay. I'm not keen about being interrupted, but this was all still quite new—I barely knew Tony at all—so I took a break and lay out with him down by the pool. He had brought a book. He was an orphan. He was actually very nice, but, as I ex-

---

* The one line of insurance where it's not a rip-off that the loss ratios are so low—and yet wouldn't you think computers could by now have revolutionized our archaic, expensive system for registering title to real estate?

plained, if I hadn't earlier (and I probably had), I had a boyfriend. I enjoyed what we had done, but that was it.

This made Tony like and respect me all the more. Which was flattering, though a clear indication to me that Tony was not quite the impossible catch I had imagined anyone who looked like that would be.

After a little while, I explained that I had to go back to work and thanked him for coming by—"I'll see you at tea." (On Fire Island, this is the universally accepted exit line. It can mean anything from, on occasion, "I'll see you at tea" to "Though I'll see you at tea, I will make every attempt to steer clear of any contact whatsoever.")

The next afternoon, it was "Annnn-drew" once more, and I found myself thinking, Oh God—it's Tony again. And then I thought—*listen to yourself! "Oh God—it's Tony again."* And I realized I should always try to remember, all my life, from this excellent experience, how shallow looks alone are. Hardly news to any of you, I'm sure. But even looks combined with a nice personality—Tony was gracious, Tony read—well, the earth had *not* moved. Angels had *not* begun to dance from the ceiling. The stereo had *not* spontaneously skipped to that aria in *Madame Butterfly* where you feel you will simply burst with emotion.

Oh God. It's Tony again.

It was a good lesson (not so painfully learned, I am tempted to add), and it left me feeling all the more fortunate to have Scot.

For weeks afterward, Tony would pull me aside at one place or another and profess to love me.

"Oh, Tony," I would cut him off. "Don't be ridiculous. In the first place, you *don't* love me. In the second place, I have a boyfriend and I wouldn't think of leaving him."

Tony would smile and give me a wistful look (he was not just a model but an actor, after all), yet it was anything but intense or melodramatic—*he* knew he didn't love me; he was just unused to rejection.

I forget how Scot discovered this. I may have, well, told him. In any event, it led to Scot's carrying Tony's picture with him for several years (I was amazed to discover it one day when he asked me to grab something out of his wallet)—his motivation to do an *extraordinary* number of sit-ups, lift an extraordinary number of weights. With time, Scot developed one of those really great bodies (but not *too* built up) and—wasn't this a switch?—was actually stronger than his boyfriend. Hmmm. Didn't know exactly what I thought about *that*.

10

Scot and I didn't argue and we didn't fight. No, wait—we did argue. We didn't fight. He never got mad at me, or if he did, he didn't show it. To me, an argument is a load of fun, like being an amateur lawyer and attempting to persuade your fellow discussant of the logic—nay, the incontestability—of your position. I suppose this can become a bit overbearing.

"Just because you can argue better," Scot once told me in a particularly endearing moment, "doesn't make you right."

Charles has a different way of handling it when I become annoying or argumentative (or, if he's in a bad mood, when I merely disagree with him). He gets mad.

Charles and I don't argue, because I'm scared to.

I come from a nonconfrontational background. The Supreme Court sometimes rendered divided opinions (Dad occasionally voted Republican), but the only time Mom ever *shouted* at Dad was when he was way back in the woods, or down in the dark-room, and lunch was ready. And Dad never really lost his temper with Mom, except out of some humorous frustration. (There was the famous icy morning when all rational efforts to start the car failed until Mom tried it, started it right up, and Dad pronounced it, testily—though still not shouting—"the triumph of black magic over science.")

Charles, being one of nine kids, apparently had to fight for his rights—and he is Irish. Ireland. Land of . . . *ire.* There's really something to this.

So I was quite shaken when Charles first got mad at me—and only slightly less shaken when, periodically thereafter, he would get mad at me again. Particularly because the anger was generally over things that I either genuinely had not done (honest!) or else had done inadvertently and would be happy to make right the moment they were revealed. How could someone get so angry at that?

The best little boy in the world grew up getting praised, not shouted at, except for one time, at age five, with the paint that Kippy had spread over the lawn with his tail but that Dad assumed I must have messed with—and thus assumed *I was lying*—until Kippy reappeared, too late to keep me from getting spanked and yelled at in a way I would never forget and that sent me sobbing to my room bawling—wailing!—at the supreme injustice of it all . . . which is probably what kept my dad, horrified by his mistake, from ever yelling at me again. This trick did not work with Charles. If he decided I had been falsely accused at all, it would generally be the next day, when we made up. And though he could see I seemed far more shaken by these episodes than any of his siblings or employees ever were when he got mad at *them,* he couldn't imagine this was really a big deal. People fight! They get mad! They forget about it! And in any event, he wasn't *really* mad.

I know this because once, fairly early in our relationship (I'll get back to Scot in a minute), Charles was upset over the *littlest* thing, it seemed to me, and I just had to go to sleep. It was past midnight, I was exhausted—my battery had just run out.

So while he was padding around outside the bedroom, fuming, with me already in bed, I just sort of gave up, turned off the light, and hit the pillow. I knew that in the morning he might even agree his peeve was trivial but that, either way, we'd make up.

Seconds later there was an *enormous* crash—Charles had slammed the bedroom door with such force you'd almost expect the whole house to just sort of come unhinged and collapse, as in a cartoon—and he announced, "Now I'm *really* mad."

It is something I had never seen before and something that, I am happy to say, and to his credit, I have never seen since. In fact, it's something we joke about, as we've largely—not entirely—managed to work all this out. (I'm more sensitive to his feelings; he's more secure that I love him and wouldn't possibly have done whatever it was *intentionally*. And Saint-John's-wort, the poor man's Prozac, is one fine herb.) We even once tried choosing a name for these periodic flare-ups—"a Herbert," we decided to call them—with the thought that it could be a useful shorthand to head them off. "It's a Herbert!" I could say to remind Charles that we had been through this before and that in the morning he had almost always regretted the severity of his reaction.

Of course, when a Herbert *was* forming in Charles's eyes, I was always too flustered to remember the magic word. And when, often just seconds later, a Herbert was *here*, there was no turning it back. So just forget about those laminated cards Charles gave me to carry in my wallet. "To whom it may concern," reads one he composed. "I, Charles C. Nolan, promise to make the bearer of this card, Andrew P. Tobias, the happiest guy in the world." And he generally does! But do you think I have the presence of mind to reach for my wallet, shuffling desperately through Visa and AmEx and Costco in search of these special cards, when Godzilla is only *half a block away*? Hardly. I panic like everybody else. Cars get overturned and fly through the streets, people get crushed or half eaten—Charles is a man who at one time or another has made virtually all his assistants at work cry, who once made a 200-pound (straight) *personal trainer* cry. He knows how things should be done (he really does), and, well, when they're not done properly, it makes him cross.

Scot was Irish Catholic, too, but there was more of the Catholic guilt than the Irish wrath. What little arguing we did do, especially in the early days, was generally over money. I wanted to give him some; he didn't want to take it.

I didn't want, literally, to *give* him money. I just didn't want to charge him for half of everything we were doing, for crying out loud. And yet he found this imbalance hard to accept.

"Come on," I'd say, getting ready to hail a cab to go wherever we were going.

"I can't afford a cab!" he'd say, trying to angle me away from the curb and head toward the subway.

"I know you can't afford a cab," I would say. "When I first moved to New York and was just starting out, I couldn't afford cabs either. But consider the situation. I am going to take a cab anyway. I love you and enjoy your company. If you come with me, it won't cost a dime more. If we both take the subway, it will only cost a few dimes less [two subway fares versus one cab fare]. If I take the cab and you take the subway, it will cost even more. Please—get in the cab."

Sometimes I could persuade him. There were at least a couple of times, early on, that Scot would take the subway and meet me there.

So we had a few arguments over money, although not that many, because extravagance was not exactly in my nature, either. Scot was careful with money out of pride and necessity; I was careful with money because I was careful with money.

Happily, Scot got more comfortable with this as time went

on, and prospered in his own right, so the issue largely faded away.

We also had more than a few arguments over where to eat. I wanted to go where Scot wanted to go; Scot wanted to go where I wanted to go. You would think this might not lead to undue conflict, but Scot would suspect I was just *saying* I wanted to go to such-and-such a place, thinking that's where *he* wanted to go . . . and around and around. What dazzled me then and continues to baffle me now is that he could actually get upset— genuinely upset—over this.

It was a wonderful friendship, even if Scot was not one to get all mushy—which, of course, I appreciated. There was, for example, the day I went down to the beach and decided to surprise him by sprinting to catch up—but still had my sneakers on, which is a bad way to run on soft sand, and so split my plantaris (picture your calf muscle; now picture broken strands of spaghetti). Scot refused to play into my pain. Everybody else was running around like crazy getting me ice packs and hot compresses (one or the other was bound to help) and eventually getting me crutches, which I'd be on for a couple of weeks—but Scot was basically saying things like "Oh, you whine about everything."

Well, of course, I do whine about everything; but that *particular* afternoon I actually could have used a bit more sympathy. Fortunately, the rest of Valmare pitched in, and I knew Scot was concerned, just not one to pander.

That was also the summer of the Most Amazing Party Since Time Began. Yes, the White Party at Vizcaya in Miami each year is a pretty amazing party, too—I'll get to that. But this one was at a house in the Pines nicknamed Utopia, with hundreds of people around the pool and on every deck, *just* before the AIDS crisis hit, enjoying the late-afternoon sun and the amazing energy and, yes, the three sky divers who, as had been rumored they would, did in fact jump out of an airplane and land in the pool. (Well, two of them; the third got stuck in a tree.)

Remember, this wasn't some Paramount Pictures opening-night extravaganza, this was an afternoon pool party on Fire Island Pines.

Looking back, several of my friends mark this party as the peak. I remember being there on crutches (a whole *new* set of people seemed to find me interesting) and just shaking my head in wonder at the sky divers. It will be a long time before the level of carefree festivity reaches the peak it did that summer. It may never.

By now *Esquire* had been bought by someone else and I would be moving on to write a column for *Playboy.* I would have preferred a more dignified venue, and hoped I wasn't contributing to the exploitation of women. But I liked having as much space as I wanted each month to write about whatever I wanted and I was amused by the irony—me, one of the eighty-three out of ten million readers who *didn't* read it for the pictures, writing for *Playboy.* Also, the money was good.

But most of my time while I was Scot's boyfriend had been spent not writing columns for *Esquire* or *Playboy* but rather researching and writing a book about insurance. And not just auto insurance—that was only two chapters—but the whole thing. (Except health insurance. That mess, I could never get my head around.) And because the insurance game is actually a lot more interesting than you would imagine (Really! I'm not just coming on to you!), I had a book, yet again, on *The New York Times* best-seller list.

The life insurance people hated it. The property-casualty people also hated it, but in a much more reasonable way. With the life insurance guys, it was a matter of religion. No *way* did they ever want to have anything to do with me (though they privately agreed with my criticisms of the property/casualty side of the business). The p/c guys found it threatening and wrong in many ways (though they privately agreed with my criticisms of the *life* side of the business), but they were more than eager to discuss it. I respected that.

And so it was that for a year or two I would actually get paid, mostly by local associations of independent insurance agents, to go around from time to time to insult them (in a good-natured, constructive way). It's been well over a decade since I've accepted any fees to speak before insurance groups; for reasons too tedious to recount, I now even pay my own expenses when I go insult them.* But I raise all this because my opposition at many of these debates was, in a sense, Raymond Burr. You know—Perry Mason. Ironsides. He didn't literally debate me; it was usually an officer of that state's chartered property/casualty underwriters' association. But Raymond Burr, as national spokesman for the Independent Insurance Agents of America, would often precede me or follow me at these events.

I never actually met him, but I was fascinated when I learned, somewhere along the way, of his requirements: In addition to whatever fee he charged, and his first-class travel, of course, he required an adjoining room for his young blond valet.

And I just thought, this being still largely the Emperor Has No Clothes stage of my life, *Isn't this wild* (in a trivial yet interesting sort of way). Here is this industry's biggest public critic—*secretly a homosexual*—and here is this industry's biggest public

---

* If this sort of thing actually does interest you, please see *My Vast Fortune: The Money Adventures of a Quixotic Capitalist*. The original book, *The Invisible Bankers: Everything the Insurance Industry Never Wanted You to Know*, is out of print—though they still don't want you to know most of it.

defender—*secretly a homosexual, too.* These poor people are *surrounded* by us.

I like to think that many, if not most, of them wouldn't have cared either way. But in 1982, few of us would have been brave enough to find out.

Barney Frank had been elected to Congress in 1980, but it would be 1987 before even he would come out publicly—and he is one brave, tough cookie. ("It's too bad, Barney," Tip O'Neill told him at the time. "You would have made a great Speaker of the House." Who knows—he still might.)

One of the things that was great about the years Scot and I spent together was the . . . how to make this sound manly? how would Sean Connery deliver this line? . . . well: the brunches.

I had certainly not planned to become any sort of regular party giver. In the last book, I think I recounted the time, that first summer, that I invited all seven gay people I knew to a party in my apartment in Cambridge—urging them to bring all their friends—bought a load of dip and beer, and then watched as they all came, but generally without friends, and at different times. One would show up, *see that there was no one there,* and leave as quickly as possible. (This was one of Steve Rubell's great insights at Studio 54 years later: Don't open the doors until there's a huge crowd outside *begging* to get in to the imagined pandemonium inside.)

Well, that disaster was in the summer of 1970. These little parties were different.

The first one—back in 1976, when I was still in London Terrace and trying to get over Ed—was small and tentative, yet a big success. A friend came and made eggs; I'd bought plenty of OJ and Bloody Mary stuff. (That's one thing I'm good at. I like to make the mix; I get a kick out of the celery-stick tassels. I pour them really light, so I can have more than one.) But having established the *premise* of Sunday brunch in what had inad-

vertently served as a sort of not-so-dry run . . . and having
moved up to a larger apartment on Central Park West that, because it lacked all but the most cursory furnishings, had plenty
of room for guests . . . and having had a little professional success . . . I grew more confident. I began thinking bigger. I went
to one of those T-shirt stores that had begun to sprout, where
you could custom-design your own shirt, and negotiated a
really, really low price for 125 T-shirts, in sizes based on the
guest list, that read: HOT BRUNCH. That set me back a good
$400, if memory serves, because I had not yet realized the fun-
damental truth of party giving: *All that matters is the people.* Soon
I dispensed with gimmicks and settled into my basic $1,200
brunch. That included all the food, drink, and labor (I'd get a
couple of people to help)—and none of the 125 guests ever left
hungry or thirsty.

I had this whole routine—once each fall, once each
spring—of buying cases and cases of OJ and V-8 and beer, grabbing three clumps of celery, bringing home gallons of cheap
vodka to be funneled into my two Stolichnaya bottles (Charles
made me *promise* not to tell you this, but the fact is, when it
comes to mixed drinks, vodka is vodka), going around to Miss
Grimble's on Columbus Avenue for a dozen frozen quiches and
a few cheesecakes. I remember carrying home the fifty or sixty
pounds of stuff from Miss Grimble's each time and having those
little bakery strings cut deeply into my hands. But, hey, I was
young, I was tough, and I was saving the cost of delivery.

To say Charles and I entertain differently now would be an
understatement. I find some of the change a little silly, or worse.
If I told you how much we spend to rent dainty little gold-leaf
chairs—*can't we just buy some folding chairs at Office Depot?*—you
would be horrified. But I love the fact that our parties are now
co-ed, and generally mixed. Some of that is the changing times,
but some is Charles's good influence. He *likes* women. Well, I
like them, too, but I mean he's *easy* with women. He works

with women and dresses women and sketches women all day
long. He has four sisters who are women! So now when we
have people over, it will often even include our parents (imagine!) and straight couples, straight singles, and, if we're lucky,
even a few lesbians. My thought is to get our building to buy
twenty-four of these dainty gold-leaf chairs and make them
available for parties the way they do with the communal coat
racks. This would save us enough money to build and staff a
hospital in Burundi. But otherwise I'm happy. The kind of party
it's appropriate for a twenty-nine-year-old to throw is different,
I have come reluctantly to acknowledge, from the kind of party
you throw when you're older. But, oh, were those Seventies
brunches ever fun. I'd load quarters into the jukebox and hope
for rain. (When it rained, people would linger; on sunny days
they'd want to get out into the park.) There was so much energy in the air we probably could have sold some of it back to
Con Ed.

At some point—perhaps around the time *Real Men Don't
Eat Quiche* was published, though that would have been purely
coincidental*—I discovered Manganaro's six-foot hero sandwiches, which simplified my life greatly. Out went the quiches
and any issues of how to light the oven; in came these two preposterous sandwiches on six-foot-long planks, complete with
knife.

The sandwiches were actually quite good, but as long as
there was enough ice, it made no difference. It was the people.
Everyone there was either attractive or successful or very, very
nice. Some were all three. Moguls, models, medical students,
bankers, lawyers (lots of lawyers)—"You know what I like about
your parties?" David Geffen liked to say. "Everyone's employed."

Scot and I knew a lot of great people in New York, and

---

* April 1982, and it wasn't coincidental.

sometimes friends would even come from Washington or Boston or North Carolina or California. We were, for the most part, decent, productive tax-paying professionals. And even though some of these same people might have been found in less than savory locations at 4 or 5 A.M. the night before, I think most enjoyed the wholesome respectability of it all. Some even wore ties. Can you imagine? On a Sunday afternoon?

Then people started to get sick.

11

My first thought was that it wouldn't hit Jews. Not because God would intervene—come on, if God were interested, this plague wouldn't be here in the first place—but because it just didn't seem to be hitting us. The people I knew who had it all had WASPy names like Glover and Stanwich and Hibbard.

All right, sure, there was Henry. But he had done so many drugs and lived such a sleazy, decadent life—not that he *deserved* this, Lord knows. Neither he nor the hemophiliacs nor the millions of heterosexual Africans suffering from it *deserved* this. (So please don't tell me this was God's vengeance on homosexuals unless it was also God's vengeance on Africans—or that Legionnaires' disease was God's vengeance on veterans.) But whatever was causing it, I only knew one Jewish guy who had it, and my lifestyle was so different from his, I figured that unless we were *all* going to die, I was probably safe.

We *are* all going to die, my doctor explained a year or two into it as he drew a little curve on the back of a scrap of paper to illustrate the trajectory of an invariably fatal, infectious disease. Okay, he said, not *all*—but this thing is going to take huge numbers of our friends.

Scot and I were fine. Everyone in Valmare was fine. But from the day one of our housemates first read that *New York Times* news item aloud over breakfast, July 3, 1981, there had been worries.

Some of us felt it more than others—at first, I couldn't imagine this affecting me, given my relatively prudish life—but with each month it became more real.

And then Bruce Weintraub, my funny, vibrant—Jewish—terrific buddy Bruce, got sick. Bruce, a few years my junior, who had worked in the art department at *New York* magazine. Bruce, who whenever I saw him on Fire Island would be the spark plug of whatever group he was with . . . who when he moved to L.A. to do set design (did you see *Pretty in Pink?*) would say, "Annnnndy!" when I called from the airport to find out what was up and would always have something "up" for us to do that night, or a pool party the next day. One of those nights he told me to meet him up in the Hollywood Hills at a famous director's house—the director was in London—for a little dinner. It turned out to be Julie Christie cooking dinner for Bruce and me, for a married couple who were teachers, if I remember right from so many years ago, and for one other woman, sitting next to me, whose voice was so breathy and whose diction was so . . . theATrical . . . I actually got up the nerve to say (remember, I'm still not as easy as I'd like to be with women until I get to know them, to say nothing of how awkward I was back then): "I'll bet you're an actress." "Why, yes," replied a somewhat startled Brenda Vaccaro. "I ammmm."

So I loved Bruce as a buddy, and now, early in the epidemic, *he* was sick, and we were talking on the phone—he from L.A., I in shorts with my feet up, sitting in that twenty-dollar swivel chair on Central Park West—and I was asking him how he first knew, and so forth, and he said it all began with a purple spot on his calf.

My cheeks flushed. I regarded the purple spot on *my* calf, somehow forgetting—one is not always rational or composed when sentenced to death—that it had been there since I was about sixteen. And for a week or so I realized *I* had it.

And then I gradually calmed down and realized I probably didn't have it—though poor Bruce sure did, and died after an amazing, oddly upbeat struggle.

And then I was watching the Academy Awards like a billion other people, and there was the first Oscar, which is always for Best Supporting Actress, going to Anjelica Huston for *Prizzi's Honor* (so this would have been March 1986), and she concludes her list of thank-yous with a gulp, looking skyward: "And to my guardian angel, Bruce Weintraub." It was so unexpected that, watching alone in Miami, I burst into tears.

"Annnnndy!" Bruce would say whenever I called, however many months it had been.

Eventually, AIDS would take four of my Valmare housemates; friends like Randy Green, the photographer, and Joe Peckerman, the lawyer; David, who had gotten 800 on his law boards and given me the crabs, Bruce, his semipro golfer lover from Bankers Trust; brilliant, funny, Russian-speaking, concert-piano-playing, movie-producing Ira Barmak;* and, well, about half the brunch list.

My mother's mother was also dying by 1983, which even at her age was naturally very sad and trying for my mother, especially because *Dad* was dying—which at *his* age, barely sixty-

---

* Ira ran a company called Filmways for a while, then went out on his own. You probably didn't see his horror spoof *Santa Goes Psycho,* but I have to tell you, in Ira's defense, that Phil Donahue and his audience took it *much* too seriously when they had him on—*it was a joke!* Ira loved Santa as much as anyone else.

four, and given the complete and utter oneness of their relationship—was far worse.

(His death from lung cancer at sixty-four and his mother's
death from lung cancer at fifty-nine a generation earlier are actually not the reasons I got so deeply into fighting the tobacco
companies. But their deaths certainly confirmed at first hand
what everybody knew yet the fine men and women of the tobacco industry consistently denied.)

Friends were beginning to get sick and die. Nana died on
April 28, 1983; Dad, exactly one month later.

My dad had been one of those wonderful men of the generation
that braved the Depression, fought Hitler, and built much of
modern America. He was a man of tremendous integrity and
intelligence. He wasn't all chatty and social, as one of his sons—
amazingly—turned out to be. That was Mom's department. But
when he was down making furniture in the cellar or developing
his photographs in the darkroom or fiddling with an audiotape
to make a radio commercial *just right* or rewriting one of his
prizewinning ads for clients who were sometimes too thick to
get it—but they were the clients and that was the business—he
was a craftsman of the first order.

I remember how exciting it was to be able to go down the
back elevator—alone! myself! seven!—with thirty-five cents to
buy Dad a pack of Chesterfields from the vending machine in
the basement of our apartment building. I remember his letting
me drive the Gravely, a small tractor, the day one of the advertising industry publications came to profile him—and nearly
driving it into the brook. (And didn't *that* make it obvious that
this fourteen-year-old was a homosexual!) I remember his sitting in the big chair up in Bedford watching Goliath and Mom
and me open presents Christmas morning, in his khaki pants
and flannel shirt. I remember his astonishment that I could hear

from my bedroom—it was all *mine* once Goliath went off to Harvard—what he and Mom were whispering at the dining room table (none of it about my secret, thank God, and I didn't want to eavesdrop anyway, so I'd just shout in some pointed comment that inevitably led to a little scurrying and "*You can hear us?*"). I remember telling Dad I was gay and Dad's telling me Scot was a fine young man and the doctor's telling Mom that Dad's lung cancer was inoperable and that he had only six months to live. I remember Dad's determination to live until he had seen Goliath graduate from law school (a midcareer switch from anthropology) and until he had gotten his business sold and Mom adequately provided for—nearly three years, not six months. I remember saying good-bye.

Mom coped with losing her mother, and then her husband of forty-one years, as well as anyone possibly could. It was without question macabre—having to arrange for *two* cremations, *two* funeral services at almost the same time.

Goliath and I did what we could to help, and we all agreed that one day we'd scatter Dad's ashes up in Bedford, under one of the beloved trees he'd transplanted and seen grow with the family. But that could wait—we'd been through enough for a while.

The place in Bedford was sold last year (with three quarters of it deeded to the Westchester Land Trust as the Seth Tobias Family Preserve). Nana and Dad remain in urns in cartons in a shopping bag in our—Charles's and my—front hall closet. Charles finds this unusual, but every family has its own ways of dealing with loss, and in our family, burials and headstones— meaning no disrespect—just don't loom large.

This was not such an easy time for Scot and me, either. Scot had secretly begun seeing a utility-rate lawyer with huge arms who was much more sexually compatible with him than I was.

I *hate* sex. Not having it—I like having it. But the way it screws everything up. Ed and I loved each other! But because there were some things I could not bring myself to do, that was that. Scot and I loved each other! And I would have been perfectly willing not to have done to others—him—what I would not want done to myself. But it wasn't that Scot didn't like my doing it—he just needed to do it, too.

Am I getting too graphic here? I apologize.

What's more, I hadn't even asked Scot to move in with me. Well, who knew he wanted to?

So while Nana and Dad were dying, Scot's situation surfaced. I ran *into* Scot's situation in the elevator of his building, actually, and from Scot's situation's instant look of having been caught in the act of rigging utility rates or something, even I, dense as I am, realized what was up.

And Scot had to figure out what to do.

It wasn't anything like what had happened with Ed. I loved Scot, but I wasn't helplessly in his magnetic field. Scot really liked the lawyer—why not? good guy—but the lawyer's big arms alone were not like Todd's cleft chin. No, if I had been more versatile, more domestic, Scot would likely not have retained this lawyer.

So Scot was in Hawaii with his lawyer when Dad died. When he got back, we actually did try living together for a few weeks. One of the reasons we hadn't previously is that I was not yet a living-together kind of guy. Another is that I am an *incredibly* light sleeper. Maybe a little less so now, but back then . . . well, for starters I couldn't *possibly* sleep with someone I didn't totally know and trust. What if he got up in the middle of the night to kill me? Worse, and more realistically, what if he woke and looked over and I looked dorky? How much control over your appearance—or anything else—can you have when you're asleep? So sleeping with strangers (as in, literally sleeping) had always been out. But even sleeping *alone* I was impossible. The slightest unusual noise . . . *boing!* And Scot was, for all his wonderful attributes, a terrible sleeper. Apart from tossing and turning and occasional nightmares, some of which even involved a little sleep-talking (*that,* at least, I found sort of interesting), he had this unusual way of lifting his leg—with his knee on the mattress raising his foot—and then letting it fall back down on the mattress. *Boing!*

Now, isn't that a ridiculous reason for two people who clearly love each other—and who continued to love each other after they broke up—to break up?

Alone, yes.* But added into the mix, particularly the Big Problem (which for all the grief it's caused me may well also have saved my life), it all just sort of added up to Scot's leaving me for the utility-rate lawyer.

It was sad, it was mopey—I even cried a little up on the bed in his apartment as we looked out from the nineteenth floor imagining what our friendship and futures would be like— Little Pig! how can this be happening?—and from his look of surprise that I had actually lowered my guard and showed some emotion, I guess maybe I should have done that sort of thing more often. Maybe our six years together would have become sixteen, the Big Problem notwithstanding.

But that was that, and life moves on. I couldn't—and didn't—blame either one of them. Scot and I remained great friends, and the lawyer and I got on fine. If I caused him to oscillate on his anxieties a bit from time to time, well, wasn't I entitled to a *little* fun?

.   .   .

---

* We could, for one thing, have gotten a bed like Mom and Dad's. I don't know what kind of sleepers Mom and Dad were, but in the city, they had this enormous king-size bed that was actually two singles latched together. Now wasn't *that* a smart idea, I came to realize. Plenty of room to play—not that I can or would want to imagine any such thing—but once under the separate blankets, on the separate though adjoining mattresses, one person's bounce would be one's own; one person's blanket grab—likewise. Why don't they teach this stuff in school?

Everyone's different, but basically it seems to take me about two years between relationships.

Of course, when you're coupled, you can't help thinking how much fun it would be to be free to date—not least because when you're coupled, you're more attractive and thus the recipient of more longing stares. You are unattainable—always a plus. You obviously have your life together—which any single person respects and longs for. You apparently know how to make a guy happy. *Ah,* thinks the single person, *if only that happy guy could be me.* For your part, you imagine how incredible the other person might be—except, fortunately, I could always remember having been to the mountaintop with Tony, and that, on a rational level, at least, did help.

When you do break up and you are single, of course all this changes. You're very much attainable, clearly can't sustain a relationship, doubtless needy—the object of sympathy, not desire. Well, okay, maybe some desire, too, but basically you're now just single and desperate like everyone else, and being free to date whomever you want doesn't seem like such a fantasy anymore; it seems . . . well, draining. The whole thing with not being too enthusiastic on the first date, having to *have* all those dates before you even know whether the guy really *likes* you or merely likes you. And since, if you're me, you assume anyone younger than you may certainly and genuinely like you but almost surely wouldn't *like* you, any more than you would like someone five or ten years *your* senior—well, the whole single thing is really not all it's cracked up to be.

And if it was not great fun for me, in 1983, when I was all of thirty-six and more fortunate than most, what must it have been like for my mother, coming off a forty-one-year marriage?

For me things were basically fine. Sure, I got lonely sometimes, and frustrated by the ridiculous games we all play. (No, I'm not into games, either, but the fact is that *everybody* is into games, even though almost none of us wants to be.) But most of the time I was happy in my work and surrounded by my amazing family of friends, which by now extended far and wide.

And Mom?

You might think Mom would have sold the apartment in New York and moved to Miami with the old folks.

That's a laugh!

She did sell the apartment—all those years of memories were just too crushing—and moved to a sunny apartment across the park. But I was the one who moved to Florida. She was still running around by subway arranging benefits and attending board meetings.

No one believes this, but my moving to Florida wasn't about money. I had always known I could save a fortune in taxes moving from New York to Connecticut or New Jersey like everybody else (or pretending to, like many of them), but that wasn't what I wanted to do. I was happy to pay New York City and New York State income taxes on my income. But when the New York City Department of Finance came after me for "unincorporated business" tax, saying that if I gave a speech in Utah I owed, also, this third tax "for the privilege of doing business in New York"—and wanting to go back ten years, with interest and penalties, even though they agreed that any reasonable person reading the tax booklet instructions would have concluded as I did, etc.—well, this became 2,500 words in *The New York Times Magazine,* so I won't inflict it on you here. The bottom line is that the whole experience was so incredibly frustrating I decided to *leave.* I paid the tax bill, but I left. That was 1985.

And in truth it's not all that awful spending seven cold months of the year in Miami.

More on Miami in a minute.

Goliath was out in California, so I wouldn't have been as comfortable leaving New York for much of the year if Mom had been lonely and miserable. But for starters, Mom is not the miserable type, and for clinchers, there was Lew.

Personally, I had not imagined Mom could ever be with anyone but Dad. Not only did *I* find the thought repellent; I was quite sure she would. Yet the most remarkable thing happened.

It seems that when Mom was seventeen, some old guy—twenty-four—had asked her to marry him. Well, Mom was flattered, and was apparently getting more than a few such offers as a teenager, but she naturally dismissed them out of hand. At seventeen? What would her mother have said?! Ridiculous.

A few years passed, Mom met Dad, they got married, and they had the kind of storybook life together that most people only dream about. If Mom felt a little constrained—Dad wouldn't have dreamed of allowing her to get a job, husband/ wife roles being very clearly defined in the Forties and Fifties and Sixties, during most of their life together—she made up for it with charity work and all the stuff moms at home do. I don't think it's any secret that being a homemaker can be as taxing as any other full-time job (though since Goliath and I were the best little boys in the world—especially me—we did make it relatively easy).

Anyway, one day—after four and a half decades—with Dad already diagnosed with lung cancer, Mom ran into Lew on the street—on crutches, no less. He had broken something. She gave him a lift downtown. Soon the four of them—Mom, Dad, Lew, and Mrs. Lew—began double-dating. When Dad died, Lew and his wife took Mom to lunch that very next day. Then sometime later just Lew took her to lunch to discuss renovation of the apartment she was buying. Well, before you know it, Lew was saying things that made Mom very nervous (being the best little girl in the world), suggesting that he liked his wife very much—terrific person—but that he really wished he'd married Mom.

Years passed, and the bottom line is, well, he fell in love with her at seventeen, waited fifty years or so, got a divorce, and married her after all.

And it's so interesting, because you should just see them together. To you or me they look to be about twenty years younger than they actually are. But even at that, given their age, you wouldn't challenge them if they asked for the discounted movie tickets. Yet in each other's eyes, they're still kids.

One day many summers ago now, even before I knew Charles, they came out to Fire Island to inspect. They came midweek, because I was more than a little afraid, even midweek, what embarrassments they might encounter on the ferry or as we walked to the house—and because on a weekend, I guess, I would have felt a little embarrassed about being a child. Did James Dean ever bring his mom to the drag race? How would George feel if Mr. and Mrs. Costanza came down to the coffee shop one day?

Not for a moment to put Mom and Lew in that category— no son/stepson could be prouder or more fortunate. Maybe the only thing that annoys me about them at all is that they whip through the Sunday *Times* crossword puzzle every week as if it were easy.

Still, Fire Island, land of fantasies and . . . well, I'm pretty much over that by now (one of Charles's first official acts was to convert the hot tub into a planter), but the first time Mom and Lew came to the beach, I was happy they came on a Wednesday.

It was one of those really hot summer days—the kind of day you're really glad to have a pool—and I suggested that Mom and Lew, hot from the walk to the house, hop in.

No thanks.

Why not?

Well, it seems these crossword puzzle whizzes, for all their wit and wisdom, had not brought bathing suits. To the beach. In the summer.

My mother keeps out of the sun. And Lew—well, maybe at his age he was a little shy about peeling down to a pair of shorts, or maybe he'd just forgotten.

In any event, Lew wasn't about to fit into a pair of my shorts, so—case closed.

And then it occurred to me. "You know," I said. "No one's around today, and I can stand guard . . . why don't you go skinny-dipping?"

Which, after suitable modest hesitation, is exactly what they did. Like a couple of teenagers.

12

I first met Peter Burns on Fire Island in the mid-Seventies, at tea. He was being much too friendly, with a very large drink in his hand. (They made these drinks that turned your tongue blue.) I took Peter for a loud, fat drunk.

First impressions being what they are, it's all the more a tribute that I so grew to love and admire him that I'm now in the midst of building a scholarship fund in his name at Harvard. (I already finished one for Scot.) Peter went to Columbia (and Scot went to Yale), but what few dollars I can muster for the Ivy League, I'm sorry, are going to Harvard.

When Peter moved south to join his dad's Palm Beach law firm, Palm Beach became my destination for the occasional midwinter weekend. Not the fancy "society" Palm Beach—though Peter himself was comfortable in that (or any) setting—but the Palm Beach of his little house, some warm weather, and a gay bar.

It was at that house, one rainy evening, that Peter taught me to put in my contact lenses. "Oh, you pathetic fool," he would have said, or words to that effect, as he told this normally very much in-control guy to stop moaning and obsessing and just focus—watch: see what I'm doing—and *get over it* like everybody else and just do it. "No, Andy, you wash your hands *before* you put them in."

As with Ed—though in this case it was entirely platonic—I grew to love Peter in part because he knew me so well and made fun of me so well and I felt completely confident in his competence. When Ed was drilling on my teeth . . . even when he was getting close to what he called the You Know What . . . I felt completely secure. I might tear up a little, but not from any pain in my mouth. (Eventually I wised up and switched to a Miami dentist.) When Peter was instructing me to shut up and put in my contacts, I knew I could finally do it—and I've basically had no trouble with them since. Although I still often wash my hands *after* putting them in, which you need no degree in ophthalmology to realize is pretty damn stupid.

When Peter moved to his law firm's Fort Lauderdale office, Fort Lauderdale became my winter destination. The *first* time I took Scot to Fort Lauderdale, we stayed at the Marlin Beach Hotel, as you know. But other times we stayed at Peter's.

Scot's and my big winter trips were to Hawaii—we went two or three times—but even that was ground I had first broken with Peter. I had been offered a free trip for two to Australia in return for giving a speech to some business guys. I took Peter. We saw kangaroos and koala bears; Peter took pictures of me in conversation with the cockatoos. ("HELL-o," I said, enthusiastically, not expecting a response. "HELL-o," twenty-odd cockatoos startled me in unison, as if it were a twelve-step meeting of some kind. They didn't say, "Hello, *Andy*," which, I admit, would have been more impressive—they were not psychic cockatoos or Uri Geller cockatoos—but I spent a good fifteen minutes talking with them—"HELL-o," "HELL-o"—which seemed to amuse both Peter and the cockatoos, as it obviously amused me.)

Where the rubber meets the road in a friendship is when you travel together. Peter was the perfect traveling companion. So smart—happily reading his novels on the long flight at a hundred pages an hour as I struggled along "hearing" each word in my head at one fifth the speed, constantly distracted by the hors d'oeuvres (they flew us first-class!). So enthusiastic and creative and adventuresome. When we stopped in Hawaii on the way back, my first visit ever to that magical place, we wound up getting stuck in the sand "off road," where you're not supposed to drive (we thought we were okay because we had a Jeep). We were rescued by a bunch of navy guys. And after snorkeling at God's own aquarium, Hanauma Bay (another source of amusement to Peter, who had to show me how to snorkel) . . . and after chasing little fish around with the underwater Instamatics we had brought (I became almost as engaged with some of the fish as I had been with the cockatoos) . . . we stopped at some particularly scenic cliff, from which Peter insisted on having his picture taken. "You stay here," Peter said, knowing that this instruction was hardly necessary—no *way* was TBLBITW going down *there*—"and take a picture of me down on that rock." "No, Peter!" I said, wondering whether I could find my way back to where we were staying after Peter had been swept out to sea. But Peter had to do it. He went down the cliff and onto the surf-sprayed outcropping, beaming there in his swim trunks and T-shirt and sunglasses-with-the-string-around-the-back-to-keep-from-losing-them, *so happy* and triumphant, and then an unusually large wave smashed into and up and over the rock, knocking him off his feet. I still believe that if he had been swept over, he would have died. There was no way he could have gotten out of the water. No ladders, no beaches—just sharp, jagged rock and choppy, turbulent water smashing in every direction because it had no place to go.

Peter made it to his feet, made it back up to me—"Did you get a picture?"—and when I told him how reckless and stupid he had been, he just laughed at me and said, "You are *such* a wuss." Which I am.

Later, as my gift for taking him on the trip—though as you can tell, his company was gift enough—he sent an elaborate photo album documenting the whole thing, with scurrilous captions that *were so untrue* but very funny.

So when Peter's dad's firm was swallowed by a bigger one and he moved yet further south, to Miami, Miami became the occasional winter weekend destination.

I met his friends there, who became my friends; I eventually bought a condo as an investment; and then, what with the tax dispute and all, one thing led to another and I became a Miamian seven months a year, a New Yorker and Fire Island guy five months a year.

Not a bad life.

In an earlier era, this would have been less feasible for a working stiff. But with FedEx and faxes, not to mention personal computers and then *laptops,* working out of multiple locations became relatively easy.

And speaking of computers, it was around the time everyone had begun dying—1983—and around the time I began staying in my *own* Miami condo on occasional winter weekends that I was offered the chance to produce what would come to be called *Andrew Tobias's Managing Your Money.* This was software that would pay your bills, track your stocks and bonds, calculate your life expectancy and insurance needs, track your appointments, maintain your Rolodex, estimate your taxes, print out your mortgage amortization—even starch your shirts. (Well, not that, but I did rig it to provide optional financial insults, to keep you humble.) Since it was the only software I was ever likely to be involved with (knowing, as I did, *nothing* about programming or software) and since in the early days of personal computers it was extremely tedious to switch among programs (you had to close one, then launch another, then close it and relaunch the first), it was basically my thought that this should be *The Only Software You'll Ever Need*. We even built in a word processor. It is a mere twist of fate that Bill Gates is the richest man in the world, not me. I still use this incredible (obsolete, orphaned, DOS) software and entrust my entire life to it.

The *Managing Your Money* era of my life—a decade, basically—was enormous fun, and I got an amazing ride on the brains of the kids (and even a few adults) who programmed the thing and actually made it work. ("How about putting in a word processor?" I would say. They would then spend night and day developing a word processor. "Hey, neat!" I would say.)

So I had a great deal of fun working with these brilliant, marvelous people, and even developed crushes on one or two of them (not that I ever expressed, let alone acted on, any of them—this notion that gay men attack their prey is no more accurate than the notion that fathers all pinch the butts of their daughters' teenage friends). But the only reason I mention *Managing Your Money* at all, really—other than to give you some sense of what occupied much of my time from 1983 to 1993 and what ultimately paid for the rental of these ridiculous dainty gold-leaf chairs Charles feels we must have if more than twelve people are coming to dinner—is so that I can impart one small, delicious (to me) irony. Namely, that TBLBITW, who had pretended in the last book he worked for IBM—to show, I guess, how straight he was and how establishment he could be, or whatever—actually became IBM Part Number 6024301 and had his face beside the IBM logo on the PCjr version of *Managing Your Money*. Never mind that the PCjr was a disaster and that the billions I expected to earn from this never materialized. Who cared? There I was *in IBM ads*.

Today, IBM is one of the many forward-looking companies that recognize the worth and talent of their gay employees—and don't want to lose them to the competition. Along with such other stalwart names as J. P. Morgan, Disney, American Express, Mobil, and Chevron, to name just a few, IBM not only explicitly proscribes in its personnel policies discrimination based on sexual orientation, it also provides domestic partnership benefits—i.e., health insurance for gay and lesbian partners.

It's just good business, and it's wonderfully American.* This is the one country where, in theory at least, you can make it no matter what minority you belong to, so long as you work hard.

So there I was in New York and Fire Island and soon to be Miami, and there was Scot moving out to L.A. with the utility-rate lawyer, and Chris in San Francisco, and Ed and Todd in New York (though I was happy to see them from time to time, I was finally over *that*), and in most respects things for me were "peachy," as Peter would have said: good health, good software, great friends. But I wasn't getting any younger, and would I *ever* find the right guy? At my age—by then I was well into my mid-thirties, for crying out loud—would I even be attractive to anybody?

At which point, repainting my apartment hallway could be delayed no longer—even I recognized that a couple of hundred dollars had to be spent on this—and Matt arrived to paint it.

Let me back up to tell you what Dr. Larry Harmon says about relationships. I met Larry on Fire Island when he was about twenty-three and a graphologist—handwriting voodoo. Now he is a well-established psychologist with a thriving practice in Miami. I don't know him well, but I know more than a few of his clients, and from them I have heard about Larry's

---

* "Our workforce has changed, and our benefits need to reflect that," Mobil spokesman Dave Dickson told *The Boston Gobe* in 1998. "We also believe it will help us attract and keep top-level employees." In 1990, only six national companies provided some type of domestic partnership benefits; by 1997, more than 350 did—including 23 percent of the Fortune 500—and the number was rising fast.

"four A's." For a relationship to work, he suggests, the other party must be: ATTRACTIVE to you; AFFLUENT, not necessarily in the sense that he's rich, but in the sense that between you the economics will work out; APPROPRIATE—as in, how will you feel introducing him at the office Christmas party; and AVAILABLE—as in, is there even a chance in hell he'd ever consider being *your* boyfriend?

Charles is all four of these things. Scot and Ed basically were, too, except, ultimately, for the last (and then only because of what I like to think of as "technical difficulties").

Matty—whom I would not be analyzing in this way if I were not still very fond of him—was, to begin with, perfect in the ATTRACTIVE department. To most people, he is an immediate knockout. To me, oddly, it took a little while to realize just how good-looking he is. Which was great, because it meant that this wasn't one of those awful chemical magnetism in-his-thrall *Ed* kinds of things. Yet it also meant, wow—look at me! A guy like Matt looking out for me? A guy like Matt, whom everybody else was instantly head over heels with? I might have been embarrassed if I had been sixty-five. But the age difference—my then thirty-eight or so to his twenty-six—while wide, wasn't beyond the pale, and while I was clearly not in his league myself, I didn't have a hump. So this part of it worked fine.

More important, he was, in private, ADORABLE—which is not one of the four official A's, but the thing that was nicest about our relationship: how comfortable and relaxed we were together. He enjoyed taking care of me; I enjoyed taking care of him. No arguments, no bickering. The one time in two years I actually shouted at him (because I was afraid the house was going to burn down and it was really important that he pick up the hose, only he didn't realize why I wanted him to and so kept asking questions as the ember grew brighter and I finally just shouted: "*Matt! Pick up the fucking hose!*"), it was so out of character and unlike me, or us, that even though I apologized and explained profusely immediately thereafter, I could see it had left a wound.

But the exception proving the rule, the point is we were always nice to each other.

As for AFFLUENCE, Matt had his own little painting business—sometimes just him, sometimes a few helpers—and was very serious about working and contributing. We didn't count who paid for what, but I had no sense he was freeloading, which he wasn't.

APPROPRIATE? Well, it never would have occurred to me to take Matt to what I still thought of as "grown-up"—i.e., straight—business or social events, and I don't think he minded in the least. What on earth would he do while I was in Phoenix giving a speech about auto insurance? (I hope I won't embarrass him too much by telling you I don't think he even much *cared* about auto insurance.) No, he was busy working; my professional life was my own. He met "Mrs. Tobias" a few times, and I guess all that was okay. He even came to Bermuda with me and my friends Paul and Renee for our fortieth birthday (Paul and I are two days apart), and *that* was okay. But Paul and Renee are very close friends of very long standing. So the fact that I was comfortable with that didn't totally count, because I knew they would look beyond any superficialities (he's a young housepainter?) and see that Matt and I made each other happy.

The thing that was so funny about Matt is that . . . well, I can only think that someone lost a grip when he was an infant and dropped him on his head. He is such an odd combination of smart and less smart. With numbers especially, he can be really slow. And as part of his shtick—having learned, I guess, that some guys find the tough, dumb tradesman type attractive—*he actually played this up.* "Huh?" he would say, screwing his face into an almost over-the-top question mark. "*What's* six times three?" "Shakespeare *who?*"

And yet he wrote very gracious, grammatical letters—the

kind all too many high school English teachers today cannot
themselves write. And when pressed (and after a couple of
wrong answers I think he faked for effect), he usually could
come up with the product of six times three after all. So maybe
a lot of this was an act. Who knows? Except for that time with
the hose, it was a playful part of the relationship.

I'll say this: When Matt asked me what I thought of his
writing a book—well, he had been around writers now, and he
liked the idea of writing a book and seeing it in stores and getting some money for that—it was *so* preposterous that, rather
than encourage him, I thought I should help steer him away
from disappointment. "Nah," I explained. "You have many talents and you're a wonderful person, but . . . well, writing a
book?"

True, his idea was not to write *Ulysses;* it was to write a do-
it-yourself house-painting guide. And he had been encouraged
in this by an editor at some publishing house. But Matt was encouraged to do a *lot* of things by a *lot* of people who wanted to
keep him interested in them. So it seemed my responsibility, as
jovially as I could, to give it to him straight.

I told him how hard it is to write a book, I told him how
much harder still it is to get a book *published,* and then—you
have to just trust me this was done in a funny way that didn't
hurt his feelings—I told him I would *eat my hat* if he ever actually managed to pull it off.

You will find Matt's book, *Grand Finishes,* with his picture
on the cover, at your neighborhood bookstore. At least I found
it at mine. And you will find on Matt's wall in San Francisco—
he now lives with a terrific Yale-grad partner of nearly ten
years—a framed certificate I designed and had notarized, testify-
ing that I had, in fact, eaten my hat.

(One moment with Matt I'll never forget involved an older,
unctuous fellow in Miami who always made me uncomfortable.
He pressed too hard, he drank too much, he leered too much. I

wished him well but could never bring myself to be around him for long. And it didn't help that he always somehow arrived uninvited at our parties. So one day he stopped by our house to invite us to one of *his* parties. "Gosh! Love to, but I'll be in New York," I said. He turned to Matt. "Well then, Maaaaaaattt, can you come?" "No," said Matt. "Why not?!" trilled this fellow, pushing too hard as usual and forcing some sort of polite excuse. "*Because I don't want to,*" said Matt. Loved that.)

And then you have AVAILABLE, which Matt thoroughly was.

And then one day, after two years, was not.

He wasn't being mean when he told me this, just straightforward. He had enjoyed the physical side of our relationship for two years—or at least most of two years—but he didn't enjoy it anymore. That simple.

Ugh.

I couldn't blame Matt—we feel what we feel. If he didn't want to have sex with me, I certainly didn't want to have sex with him—not out of pique, but because I hate the notion of forcing myself on someone not interested.

I was sad and so was he. He didn't want to lose the emotional side of the relationship (which was 99 percent of it—we were not exactly sex fiends).

So after a time, with me unwilling to be condemned to celibacy, and perhaps a little restless myself, truth to tell, we parted friends and after a while he moved out west. This was long before he got the notion to write that book—the book came several years later—but not before I turned forty. We were basically still breaking up when I turned forty.

When they used to say "Life begins at forty," I did the same "yeah, right" that you, if you're under forty, still do. But of course if you play your cards right (study hard! work hard! buy in bulk! live beneath your means!) and if you have your share of good luck—*it's true*. For straight couples who married young, maybe it meant that the two kids were about to go off to college and you could finally start having noisy sex again. For me, I didn't know what it would mean. As it turned out, forty was great. But I will admit to having had a certain amount of trepidation.

After all, everyone makes such a big deal about it.

Which was part of the uneasiness I felt. Here I was breaking up with Matt, here I was not yet really having integrated my gay life with my straight life—it was the spring of 1987—here I was going off to a Very Straight Thing called Renaissance Weekend the week between Christmas and New Year's each year, but cutting it short each year to get back just in time to give my Big Gay New Year's Eve Party—and here I was, I guess, feeling just a *little* bit sorry for myself.

I made a point of saying I didn't want any parties or anything, that it really wasn't a big deal. We'd go to Bermuda with Paul and Renee and the baby for our birthdays and it would be fine. That's always a good plan—flee the country.

On the eve of that trip, Matt took me over to a friend's house and—SURPRISE! They had a cake and some gifts and warm feeling and . . . well, it was not one of those epic fortieth birthday parties where you charter a plane and fly everyone you know to France. But they cared enough about me to do something, and it was nice.

And Bermuda was nice.

All right, I'll admit it. I felt somewhat deflated. I had gotten cards and calls and it was fine—really! it was fine!—and, well, hey: If this was the worst disappointment I had to deal with, I'd be a lucky man. Maybe my fiftieth would be one of those amazing things.

So being the glass-half-full type, I bounced back quickly. Plus, the following weekend a friend of mine, Very Big Deal from California, called to see if I wanted to go yacht shopping with him. He was in Miami, on his way up to Fort Lauderdale the next morning—Sunday—to meet a broker who was flying down from Toronto to show him some yachts.

Cool!

Not being a Very Big Deal myself but enjoying the chance to chide this one on how *extravagant* yacht ownership is and on how many starving *villages* he could rescue with the money he would be spending merely on *caulk,* and always excited to be with him—he's been a steadfast friend for twenty-five years now—I said sure. Love to.

No limos for this guy. Into the slums he drives the next morning—with the top down—to pick me up, and off we go to Fort Lauderdale.

I like inspecting yachts. I like counseling centimillionaires on the money they could save not buying them (but hoping, of course, that they do). And this particular yacht was an old classic.

How does this work? Is he going to pull out his checkbook?

"I'll let you know," said the Very Big Deal as he waved the yacht broker back up to Toronto and we went off to a Denny's or someplace for a sandwich. (I was buying.)

And then, fun over, he drove me home. "Can you come in for a little while?" My house in Miami cost only $120,000, but in my neighborhood, you get a lot for $120,000—it has a tall concrete wall around the property and King Kong doors at the entrance. (Well, little ones.) It looked to me from the cars out front as though a couple of friends had dropped by—friends I knew the Very Big Deal would like. But the Very Big Deal said no, he had to get out to his Very Expensive Plane to go back to L.A.

"It's *your plane,*" I explained to him, knowing it would wait. "Come in for ten minutes."

"Okay," he reluctantly agreed.

I opened the King Kong doors and almost had a heart attack.

The photos from all this show my jaw dropped so low that even then, at forty, I appeared to have three chins. My eyes were so wide I may have sprained a facial muscle.

There, in what a few hours before had been my empty courtyard with its little fountain and $29.95 stone "pineapple" out of which the water shoots (no way was I going with the $395 cherub)—and a full week after my birthday, about which by now I had truly forgotten—ancient history—were a hundred of my closest friends. Jane and Fred had come down from New York! Scot had come from Los Angeles! Appropriately, perhaps, the first to throw a lei over my head and give me a big kiss was an incredible young medical student I had a crush on, followed by just about everybody else I knew in Miami and a load of people from out of town.

To the bottom edge of the wide awning that overhangs the front of the house they had clipped a parade of *Parade* covers— for a while there, I was an annual *Parade* cover boy (YOU CAN FEEL SECURE ABOUT YOUR MONEY)—a whole box of which Matty had apparently obtained from the publisher. There were little ego monuments everywhere. There were bartenders. There was a cake.

"Did you *know* about this?" I asked the Very Big Deal, astonished.

It was such a stupid question, and he suffers fools so ungladly, that the Very Big Deal just gave me a look as if to say, "That is *such* a stupid question"—but it was my birthday party, so he was nice—and to this day, as far as I know, that poor yacht broker flew all the way from Toronto—on his own dime, no less—unwittingly to be part of the ruse. ("Well, I *was* thinking about buying a yacht," said the Very Big Deal when questioned on this point later.)

.   .   .

So it turned out to be a sensational fortieth birthday after all—without question one of the happiest days of my life, possibly *the* happiest—and a great way to kick off a decade that has proved, all in all, to be pretty great itself.

Matt, with help from Peter Burns and some of my other friends, had outdone himself—proving yet again that there's a world of difference between sex and love.

13

Oh, Little Pig. It's not that I wanted to *sleep* with you more—you were a terrible sleeper and I was glad that you were happy with your lawyer, thrilled that you were thriving in L.A., proud as a big brother when (a couple of months *before* my fortieth birthday, actually) *People* featured you on the "Publisher's Page"—just you—standing in your tux with an uncorked champagne bottle overflowing in front of the HOLLYWOOD sign. Look at you, Little Pig! I just so wish we hadn't lost you.

Because, like so many people in 1987, Scot was sick. Coping bravely, and not yet *sick* sick; but HIV-positive, low on T cells, and frightened.

By May 1990, this well-muscled thirty-five-year-old—about Robert Redford's height—was truly old, stick-thin, and haggard. Even so, he led the *People* crew that went out to cover the eruption of Mt. Kilauea on the Big Island of Hawaii. Well, what else can you do? Just sit around waiting to die? You had to keep your hopes up, continue working, and hang on—hang on—until they found the cure. Because they would find the cure. Or at least ways to cope. One day people would be dying "with" AIDS rather than from it.

In June, Scot was in Sherman Oaks Community Hospital. His wonderful mother and both his sisters had long since moved out to L.A. to be near him and help. And his dad was very much on call. The lawyer had been as fine and stalwart a partner as anyone could have, and I was more than grateful to him for that—I can't imagine having had to cope with this myself. And not just the emotion, frankly. Emotion, though sad, can in its way be sweet. The *details*. You don't want to know the details of AIDS. The pills and the sweats and the lesions and . . . well, it just gets worse and worse.

One builds defenses—certainly if one is as egocentric as I am ("It's all about *you!*" reads one of the laminated cards Charles gave me for my wallet, though in truth I think we have the mutual-respect thing down pretty well)—and early in the epidemic I had shut myself off to a lot of it. My God, otherwise you'd spend your entire life nursing friends, grieving, and attending funerals. It seemed to me that those of us lucky enough to be healthy had an obligation *not* to be miserable and unhappy all the time. It would almost be disrespectful of the horrible stuff our friends were going through. Not to be rejoicing in our own great good fortune? This amazing gift *we* had been given of good health and energy and comfort—and time? That was it: the time. To waste this precious, precious resource being miserable—what right did we have to be miserable? We were *so fortunate!*

I do and did believe all that, though I also recognized it was a convenient rationalization for not getting nearly as involved in the hands-on caregiving as many of my friends did.

I did what I could, and I picked my shots. One shot I picked was Scot. The other, a few years later, was Peter.

I did go to other funerals, of course; I did make some hospital visits and a lot of phone calls. I sent Randy Green to

Switzerland for some miracle cure we both certainly knew wouldn't work. I flew out to visit Joe Peckerman near the end—if sheer force of will could have kept anyone alive, it would have been he. You never saw anyone fight so hard in your life.

But with Scot, and then Peter, it was family.

Not that there was anything I could actually do.

Yet fearing it might be serious now—who knew? some people had these near-death nightmares and then recovered for six months until the next one—I headed for Los Angeles, to the hospital.

"Hey, Little Pig!" I grinned when I walked in. His mom was there.

He was a little startled and, predictably, frightened—who would be next, the priest?

Not meaning to alarm him, I told a story I had concocted for this purpose—that I was out in L.A. anyway on some kind of business and heard he was in the hospital so I figured I'd come by and buck him up. How're you feeling?

He was feeling so-so, but he was yellow and his stomach was bloated. I was anxious not to say anything that would upset him. I mentioned that a friend of ours was going to the *Total Recall* screening—Arnold Schwarzenegger's movie—figuring this was harmless enough. Scot bolted upright—"Is that tonight?" he said. "Oh my God, I thought that was next week." I said, "Scot, it's okay. We'll get it for you on videotape. It's not that important." He said, "No! No! No! No! They get very mad if you don't cancel. Get me my briefcase. Hand me the phone." He called the office. "Is Jack there? No? All right, is Tina there? No?" He finally got someone. "Listen: Call Tristar and tell them Scot Haller unfortunately won't be coming to the screening— very sorry—but put him on the list for the next one."

He was on a lot of medication, but not so much as to dull his sense of responsibility.

His mom and I kidded him about that, we talked awhile, got the medical scoop—they were going to try doing this and that to relieve the bloating and balance the whatevers—but the thing that never ceases to confound me about death, not that it always works this way, but it often does, is that the *brain* is all there. The *person* is all there. Scot was fine! It was Scooter (we also called him Scooter), with the same memories and anxieties, the same sense of humor, as always. Scot was fine! It's just that some damn chemistry things were out of whack. Receptors were being fooled into turning off when they should turn on or turn on when they should turn off—I've never learned the science, always just tried to raise some money for the scientists.

"Hey, if I get time tomorrow I'll come back."

(Well, of course I would come back—that's why I was there.)

A day or two later Scot had to be intubated. My own feeling about this was, basically, dread. Talk about a loss of control. Not being able to talk? I would find this *very* constraining. But with luck they'd just do the things that needed doing, remove the tube a day or two later, and continue to fight the disease.

So in went the tube, up started the machines, and that was the last we were ever able to talk to Scot.

We talked *to* him, of course. His dad and mom and sisters and Jerry (the utility-rate lawyer)—we all took turns sitting by the bed in the ICU, holding his hand, watching the monitors, talking to him. The nurses—who had all come to love Scooter, too—waived the visiting hours rules.

But what do you say?

On the one hand, you want to say things you may never have a chance to say again. On the other hand, the monitor told you that he actually *heard* a lot of this stuff, despite the morphine, even though he couldn't respond: The numbers, which it was our "job" to keep nice and low and steady, would spike up. And since we all felt incredibly helpless, having a job—feeling we could help in some way by keeping those numbers nice and low—was at least something to focus on.

But in fairly short order it became clear that, hope and good intentions notwithstanding, this was not going to work.

The funeral, on a hot sunny summer afternoon in L.A., was open-casket.

I don't want to be disrespectful, so I won't tell you what I think about that.

Then there was a memorial service I did not attend in Cincinnati, Scot's hometown.

Then there was a memorial service in New York. Scot would have been amused, I think, by all the hoopla—what is this, out-of-town tryouts coming to Broadway?—but that is in fact more or less what we did. David Geffen, bless his heart, got us a small Broadway theater. Scot had died on June 24, 1990. On July 2 a few hundred of us, and a huge contingent from *People,* gathered with Scot's family and Jerry for a program entitled "One Singular Sensation."

Mack and Mabel was Ed's and mine. *A Chorus Line* was Scot's. We had wanted the Shubert Theatre, where *A Chorus Line* had played, but that was being renovated, so the Shubert Organization let us use its sister theater, the Booth.

Everyone got a box of fudge sticks—Scot loved fudge sticks—and a sixty-four-page booklet I'd had printed up that chronicled his life. I was very fortunate to be able to do this, because in such situations we are always asking, "Is there anything I can do?"—and here was something I could do. What's more, it was easy, because of the nature of Scot's life. In addition to the childhood pictures almost any family has,* there were his résumé and his *New Yorker* short story and that great *Horizon* cover and some of his *People* stories (one of them a 1985 cover story:

---

* Take pictures!

AIDS IN THE FAMILY: What Happens When a Son Comes Home to Say He's Gay—and Dying). Because of his work at *People,* I had shots of him with Travolta, with Dolly Parton, with Bette Davis, with Angie Dickinson. And of course there was Scot with his friends from Valmare, with Jane, with his sisters and family, with Jerry—I felt as if I were editing my high school yearbook again, only this was a little shorter and had only one graduate.

On the cover was the champagne-popping, smiling black-tie photo in front of the HOLLYWOOD sign—SCOT HALLER 1954–1990. On the last page, a shot of Scot from behind, on a kayak, raising his paddle triumphantly to salute the sunset.

The thing to say about all this, apart from how embarrassed Scot would have been to be the subject of so much attention, is that Scot was just one of so many. Yes, he stands out from the crowd more than most. But so *many* young men died, and are still dying, albeit less regularly: good sons, good brothers, good employees, good citizens, good friends, even if few happened to work at a job that provided so many great photographs and articles to fill a memorial booklet. So . . . needless to say, I guess . . . this is not just about Scot. It's about the friend you lost, too.

At one service I attended, for Doug, who'd been Jason's boyfriend (whose own memorial service a year or two earlier had also been gut-wrenching), it became quickly apparent that Doug's dad, a cop from the Midwest, had basically known almost nothing about Doug's adult life until just days before. I remember his tearful words, urging sons and parents to *talk* to each other. And I remember the wine on the roof of the building afterward and the sweet, sad music—"Don't give up" was its soft refrain—and each of us releasing a balloon up into the sunset.

So many balloons.

. . .

Scot's obit in the *Times*—we got an obit in the *Times!*—listed
the cause of death as something other than what it was. Some of
us argued strenuously against that—I *knew* Scot would want to
be honest about this—but even in 1990, and even with as loving and genuinely good a family as Scot's, there were those who
felt it would be wrong. Shameful, basically. And so their wishes
were respected.

Peter's passing was even more personal to me in a way, because,
while not really shouldering much of the load—his friend Keith
did that (never was there a better friend than Keith was to
Peter)—I was a little more central to the process than I had been
with Scot. There was not quite the same family infrastructure as
there'd been in Los Angeles. And, well, I was here, in Miami.
So when I could take Peter to the hospital for an eye treatment
(cytomegalovirus largely took his eyesight, and this was a man
who lived to read) or when I could read him the latest Dave
Barry column (for years we would read these out loud to each
other and howl) or do other small things for him, I was more
than eager.

    We had had so much fun together, in one place and another.
Peter worked hard and was a brilliant, responsible trusts-and-
estates attorney, a partner, ultimately, with Steel, Hector &
Davis, one of Miami's most prominent firms. And he played an
active role in the Episcopal church. But—more than me—he
knew how to have fun. The Catholic or Jewish guilt thing that
underlies so much of a personality like mine or Scot's or
Charles's? Not an issue with Peter. Fat-free cooking? Oh, puh-
lease—you should have seen the pounds of butter and quarts of
cream he'd pour in with the chunks of beef and then serve to
his little family of eager friends. (He'd make merciless fun of me
when, after all my fat-free whining, I wound up eating more

than anyone else and contrived ways to get the leftovers home.) His waterskiing and his sailboarding and his *Star Trek* and *Golden Girls* obsessions . . . his trusty retriever, Nate . . . Peter got only half the years he was entitled to, if that. But he *enjoyed* those years.

And he had some pretty wild friends in his earlier years. One, Tom Fortuin, would come visit the Fire Island house Peter had taken a share in while he still lived in New York. The "solar house," it was called, because it had solar panels and waterless compost-heap toilets (which in a half-million-dollar house may have been environmentalism run a little mad). Tom would do drugs, dance all night, make a quick stop at the meat rack, change into a suit, take the "bucket of blood" sunrise-Monday-morning ferry back to Sayville, a cab to Islip, a flight to Washington, a cab to the Capitol—arriving just in time to take his seat as one of the lead counsel in the Koreagate investigation. "And *so*, Mr. Park—can you explain to this committee . . ."

Tom had already died by the time Peter got really sick.

One of the last things I got to do with Peter was go see *Henry V,* the Kenneth Branagh movie. I still savor that afternoon, because Peter *loved* it. Shakespeare's magnificent language, the richness of it, the look of it, that extraordinary rallying cry to the king's beleaguered troops on St. Crispin's Day.

Did you know, by the way, that Richard the Lion-Hearted was *gay*? That he had a passionate affair with the king of *France*? This has nothing to do with the movie, but I, myself, found the movie a little hard to follow, and my mind wandering. It had no subtitles—and I ordinarily take "no subtitles" to be a plus in choosing a movie—but I sort of felt it needed subtitles.

Or so I told Peter, egging him on a bit as we left the theater. "Oh, you are *such* a moron," Peter wailed. I loved that he loved it so much—I did grasp the passion of it and his passion *for* it— and I loved the fact that in Peter I had a soul mate who was so smart, and in his friendship with me so completely honest and steadfast and loyal. If I had been dying, he is surely one of the few people I would have felt comfortable having help me.

But I was not dying. Way back in the *Managing Your Money* days, my fellow software "celebrity," Jim Fixx, the "running" expert, died while jogging. This naturally knocked the oomph out of the sales of his celebrity-fitness software. Now the publisher was afraid *I* might die, although, as I repeatedly noted, it was not my death that would hurt sales—mine was not fitness software—it was my bankruptcy (so pay me more!). Even so, they wanted to buy a life insurance policy, which meant my having to go for a physical, which also meant, especially for a single, never-married male, an AIDS test.

I didn't want to get an AIDS test. What good would it do? I was pretty sure I was okay. And if I wasn't—then what? This was back in the days when all you could do was worry (which itself couldn't be great for your immune system).

I put it off as long as I could, feeling in part—not rationally, but in my gut—that since there were only two ways it could turn out, positive or negative, there was sort of a fifty-fifty chance. Yes or no, live or die, heads or tails . . . and I also did have this purple thing on my calf (could my memory have been playing tricks about how long I'd had it?), and I certainly had been with enough guys, albeit not doing the kinds of things that seemed most likely to be its main form of transmission between males. Nor had Scot gotten sick yet. So I was pretty sure I was okay, but *oh* was that a long week waiting for the results.

Because I didn't really know for certain.

And because an *awful* lot of my friends had tested positive.

I was in Connecticut, working on *Managing Your Money,* when I called the doctor and got my results. I was fine. They could get all the insurance they wanted.

I took a few minutes to have one of those little cosmic talks with myself that I have had periodically through my life, and went back to work.

Peter had not been so fortunate. I don't know when he first found out, but by the time we saw *Henry V,* it had been two or three years and things had begun to accelerate.

I have since gone back and played the video of this great movie and made a little more sense of it (except *why* were they invading France? and *what* did Falstaff have to do with all this?*). What I loved on second viewing was what Peter loved: The passion. The soaring spirit of the thing. The *meaning* it gave to lives.

There was no intubation for Peter, thankfully. He died where and as he wanted to—at home on his big bed with the soft Miami breezes blowing through the big windows, the sound track to *Henry V* and a few of Peter's other favorites cycling over and over, Nate and Keith beside him (and Daisy—Nate's young golden retriever princess bride), an ample morphine drip, and Peter's able sister to administer it. If you have to die, it helps greatly to have a loving sister who is a registered nurse.

I remember the bishop coming—the bishop!—and asking: "Peter, where do you want the funeral?" I was taken aback. Is this what you would call comforting bedside manner? Is this what you learn in bishop school? And either Peter was thinking the same thing or else he hadn't heard him, because he didn't answer. So now this tall, dignified man leaned over close to Peter and shouted: "*Peter! Where do you want the FUNERAL?*"

At which point Keith confirmed what the bishop had suspected: Peter wanted the funeral at the big church down by the *Miami Herald*. And then the bishop left.

---

* Note to Horace Mann School: Don't even *think* about revoking the B+ I got in junior-year English. I got it somehow, and that's that. You can't do a thing about it.

The afternoon wore on. The morphine level was set high enough to make it easy.

But not breathing is not something most of us, let alone those of us as bright as Peter, readily do. "I know where *that* leads," I can imagine him chortling.

And so after a quiet, peaceful while longer, his sister gently leaned down and softly said, "Peter, it's okay. It's *okay.* You've done enough. You can go now."

And he did.

He was forty.

Not one but *three* bishops came to the funeral, two of them from New York. The place was packed (and it is a big place); the "smells and bells"—incense and pageantry—were things I knew Peter really liked. One of the bishops said something particularly poignant. He said that a man's mind is like a library. And when a man dies, especially a man like Peter, it is like a great library burning to the ground.

14

After Matt came the couple-of-years-in-between and then Stevie—or "Stevie Fabulous," as he would come to be known, which tells you already that, though he had many wonderful qualities, this was perhaps not the most appropriate relationship for me. Someday he'll write his book about it (he was a sedulous student and poet) and maybe I'll write mine, and both will be largely positive and affectionate and that's that. People think it's hard getting dumped—look what it was like for me with Ed. But it's also hard being the one saying no.

That was 1993, and as Stevie had pointed out to me more than once as I was trying to say no, "You're not getting any younger." I was forty-six. Ugh.

"I wouldn't have *liked* you when you were younger," Charles insists, somehow imagining that I was brash, obnoxious, and cocky. (Well, sure I was—but how did *he* know?)

As Charles tells it—and I am not one lightly to contradict him—we first met at Fire Island at my Fourth of July party. I had long since abandoned brunches, being in Miami in the fall and spring, and had more or less fallen into the rhythm of giving a couple of parties in Miami each year and then that one at the beach on July Fourth. But I was cocky and obnoxious and he doesn't like lobster, anyway—will never eat anything remotely fishy (which is great; I get all his shrimp)—and that's what this party is each summer: a clambake. Specifically: 25 quarts of clam chowder, 150 lobsters, 35 pounds of peel-your-own-damn shrimp, 600 steamed littleneck clams, 4 bushels of corn, and 2 watermelons (of which 1½ are always left over), a keg of beer by the pool, a keg up on the roof deck. All that, plus the cups and plates and staff, for so much less money than you'd expect that I consider it a trade secret.

Except for the corn, Charles must have hated it.

(Now when we give the party, he still eschews the food, still allows me to do the whole thing on the cheap—but it is so much nicer-looking!)

One of my favorite things about the party in the early years was inviting people—can you come for a lobster at six on July Fourth?—and then just sort of easing into my story of how, to cook so many lobsters, "we toss them into the hot tub—obviously, there's no pot big enough for 150 lobsters—and switch off the safety on the heater." Eyes widen; heads tilt skeptically. "It takes a while, because we can only crank it up to a hundred fifty, a hundred sixty degrees—" "Are you serious?" they interrupt. "Well, there's just a *very* faint chlorine taste," I continue, as if to acknowledge what I take to be their objection. "But you don't notice it with the melted butter"—eyes are now very wide—"and then we basically give everybody a turn with the pitchfork grabbing one of the lobsters from the tub. It's a great party. Come!"

A silent "but" would be forming on their lips, to which I invariably replied, "I know, I know—the noise they make. But we have the music up pretty high, and they lose consciousness pretty fast anyway, so I don't think it's really any worse than boiling them the regular way."

Instead, of course, the guys from The Fish Store (that's what it's called: The Fish Store, in Patchogue) bring over some giant pots and propane cookers. There are no pitchforks, just little plastic ones.

I have no recollection of meeting Charles that July Fourth. I do remember meeting him a few times thereafter and getting the sense that this was someone people treated with respect. I wasn't clear on exactly what he did; something having to do with clothing design—and I wasn't quite sure at first which Nolan was which—I would see Charles with his brother Kenneth, who also did something with clothes. *Which* one is Charles and *which* one is Kenneth? (Little did I know how many more siblings I would later have to internalize.) And *why* would a guy go by Charles when he could be Chuck or Chaz or Charlie—or Craig, Charles's middle name, which he went by as a kid? I was, after all, on record in *The Best Little Boy in the World* as having explained all that. A *guy* ought to go by his *guy's* name, not by the name he's called when his mother has him all dressed up for church. (Sure, I'm Andrew—*in print.* That's different.)

So I was aware of Charles, as he was of me, and as I ran into him at one thing or another over a couple of years I began to get clearer who was who . . . I can be very slow with this . . . but it would never have occurred to either one of us that we'd ever think of each other *that* way.

And then in the summer of 1994 I was walking to the Fire Island grocery store with a friend and encountered Charles. I had had my one Diet Coke with a splash of Myers's rum, and the cool dusk air was so invigorating, and I felt so great—and so proud of myself that I finally remembered who Charles was!— that as we met I gave him a big hug and said whatever stupid, hyperbolic things I say. ("I thought you were a lunatic," Charles told me later.)

What I do remember clearly is seeing Charles a weekend or two later in the store* and thinking, *Oh gosh. Not him, too.*

I mean, it was so obvious to anyone who had had any experience with this; and by 1994, I had had all too much. He had lost so much weight, he had a dark little spot on his lip . . . why did this thing have to hit all the best people?

Anxious to do what little I could—what can one do?—I went straight over, gave him a huge hug and smile, and asked why in all this time we hadn't even ever had dinner. We should have dinner.

Sure, he said, a little surprised by my enthusiasm. Call me. He gave me his number.

Of course, Charles had had that little thing on his lip since the day he was born, and as for the weight, he'd decided a few months earlier it was time to drop twenty pounds. So, given my enthusiasm, Charles may have assumed I was interested . . . *that* way. (Well, he actually was looking pretty good with the weight loss—isn't *that* an ironic side effect of the disease, I thought bleakly.)

So, being the kind of guy who calls when he says he'll call (and also the kind of guy who likes to prove he can remember phone numbers), I called. And I left a *long,* detailed, funny message . . . the kind of message that betrayed not even a hint of sympathy, let alone pity, but that would make a guy with problems forget those problems and feel *good.* As for dinner—why not? It would just be dinner . . . obviously, he would know I didn't mean it *that* way. But it would be perfectly fine to get to know him, and the least I could do for a dying man.

He didn't call back.

---

* When I was younger, I would go out of my *mind* at the store's monopoly pricing, but do you know what? The service and warmth of the wonderful (straight) people who run it, plus my good fortune in the years since, have totally washed that away.

A couple of weeks later I again ran into him at the store.

"I'm *cross* with you," he said, before I could say anything, a little fire flashing from his blue eyes (unless that was just the reflection from the oranges).

"You are?" I said, much as Oprah would, a few years later. *"Why?"*

"You didn't call."

"What do you mean I didn't call? Of course I called."

"I got no message."

"No message? I left an *endless, brilliant* message!"

"Oh yeah?" asked Charles skeptically. "What did the recording on my machine say?"

"The recording on your machine was one of those stupid mechanical voices."

"What *number* did you call?"

"The number you *gave* me—two one two, eight seven four . . ."

Apparently, I had misremembered a digit, or else—equally plausible, if you ask me, given Charles's head for numbers—he gave it to me wrong. Later, he apparently called the number I said I had called and found that, sure enough, it played a tape of the type I had described. He decided I was telling the truth.

There was some benefit dinner that weekend and I figured, You know what? There are a dozen twenty-six-year-olds I could ask, take, lust over, and then not get to sleep with, but why not actually go with an adult? There's a novel idea! So Charles and I went. For his part, he was assuming I must have an interest in him or why would I be gushing and hugging and leaving—according to me—brilliant messages and now inviting him to dinner?

The dinner was boring. We left in the middle, went back to his place, listened to music, and—now, *this* surprised me, but it seemed like it couldn't hurt—we cuddled.

There I go again getting graphic.

.   .   .

Charles lived just a few blocks away in the city, as Scot had. Charles was Irish Catholic, as Scot had been. And Charles was vaguely the same age Scot would have been if he had lived. What's more, just as it had taken me quite a while to realize how uncannily Scot looked like Robert Redford in the poster from *The Candidate* that hung over his bed (only with a mustache, and even a little better-looking), so it would take me quite a while to realize . . . *oh my gosh! Kevin Bacon!* Only, again, a little better looking.

This is not to say anything spooky was going on or that I even really thought about it at the time. But I do think Scot would be pleased I found a man of talent and substance to share my life with, much as he and I might have done if things had worked out differently.

My mother was certainly pleased.

Before you know it, there were flowers everywhere. And then window seats and built-in bookshelves in the living room (which I was all prepared to fill with *books* but which are filled, as well, with all manner of interesting or whimsical *things**). And a gallery of my *New Yorker* cartoons in the oval dining area, but with special frames Charles designed that cost more than the cartoons. And track lighting and then . . . all this over a period of years, as Charles felt my heart could take it . . . a dining room table he designed with *incredibly* beautiful legs that he keeps the apartment too dark to see. "But, Charles," I begged, "we already *have* a dining room table," thinking of the $300 it had cost me. But the new one was handcrafted, hand-sanded over and over, hand-stained, and looks really great, like everything Charles does.

Within a couple of years, we had a grown-up apartment.

---

* What books there are, Charles arranged by size and color while I was down in Miami. After much negotiation, I got the go-ahead to rearrange them by subject.

This left me with mixed feelings, but I am one who, although he complains a lot, basically sees the bright side.

Here's our routine. Thanksgiving morning, the Nolans all come over, with the nieces and nephews, to watch the parade from our window. One great advantage of being on a low floor is that we get to see Barney eyeball to eyeball.

Then Charles and I go over for Thanksgiving dinner at Mom and Lew's, with the other side of the family.

Then we fly down to Miami for the White Party. The White Party is an AIDS benefit held out under the stars at Vizcaya, Miami's own small Versailles, the Sunday after Thanksgiving each year. It begins at six and ends by midnight. My kind of party.

Vizcaya, the brochures explain, was built on 180 acres (since trimmed to 28) purchased in 1912 by James Deering, heir to the International Harvester fortune. The population of Miami at the time was just over 10,000. For three years, close to 10 percent of it worked on Vizcaya. While they labored, Deering himself, a never-married man in his mid-fifties, was touring Europe with his designer—coupla bachelors in Europe—buying the art and antiques to furnish Vizcaya's seventy rooms. The staff of thirty made him and his guests comfortable the four months each winter he came down, but in fairly short order he died. The brochures don't say it, but presumably Deering was gay. And here is my point: As we mill around Vizcaya's gardens and waterfront, 3,000 or 4,000 of us, mostly youngish gay guys dressed in white, enjoying the evening, Deering, looking down, must feel as if he's died and gone to heaven (as indeed he may have). *Yes!* he must be thinking. *That was my fantasy!* Sure, he probably had a few special young men come to enjoy his home and yacht. Maybe the staff even looked the other way if they held hands. But this? In a million years he would never have imagined it could happen.

So that's Thanksgiving Sunday. The night before, we often

give a party of our own. And the next day Charles goes back up
to New York—he works, after all—and I get to enjoy Miami.

We still haven't entirely worked out the Miami/New York
thing. The five months a year I'm up there are easy, of course;
the seven months a year down here . . . we negotiate as best we
can.

Shortly before Christmas, I go back up for Charles's—now
our—famous Christmas party, which brings together everyone
from his folks and mine to a lot of our straight friends to a lot of
our gay friends. Given that we don't have seventy rooms ourselves, we have the party as close to Christmas as possible so
most people won't be able to make it. That way, we can invite
everybody we know and not have the walls burst.

Christmas Eve, Charles cooks an amazing dinner for family-
members-with-no-small-kids, as well as a couple of friends with
no ready access to families of their own. This dinner is followed
by a game whose rules are too complex to describe. It involves
mostly hideous presents that one takes, wrapped, from the pile,
unwraps, and then attempts, through negotiation and the mechanisms of the game, to unload on someone else.

Christmas morning, Charles and I exchange gifts. Big computer jock that I am, I once gave him a hand-me-down laptop.
He had never had a computer. You should see him *now,* with a
system for sketching and color printing that makes anything I
have look lame. Then we drive out to Long Island to his folks'
place for the Nolan family Christmas. No small event. It's fun
watching these kids grow up. One of them (I won't embarrass
him by saying which) is always four. Charles says I'm nuts, but I
tell you: From the first year I met him through this past Christmas, he is always . . . four. One day, suddenly, he will be nine—
pop, just like that. But the rest, as I get to see them on holidays,
or sometimes in the summer if they come out to the beach, are
growing up just as little people ought to. Not having to deal

with any of the hard part of it, it is, naturally, very fun and easy. Uncle Andy has a good time.

Then we flee back into the city, hopefully in time for a movie. That's where I'm *really* happy—in the fourth row of a movie theater slunk way, way, way down in the chair with my knees up on the chair in front of me, Charles-the-popcorn-dispenser by my side.

Then back down to Miami for a couple of days.

Then up to Hilton Head, South Carolina, for New Year's and the aforementioned Renaissance Weekend that only inadvertently became a big deal when one of its regular participants went and got himself elected president.

15

The first few times I was invited to Renaissance Weekend, in the early Eighties, when Phil and Linda Lader started it, I was too chicken to accept. It was billed as this wonderful chance for families to get together over the holidays and basically have something wholesome and interesting to do New Year's Eve (while everyone else was out getting drunk, was the subtext). Well, I didn't *have* a wife and kids, and I obviously couldn't bring a guy, and going alone to a group that, according to Phil's letter, included a former astronaut, a famous admiral, and several governors, congressmen, and federal judges—yeah, *right*. Like I'm really going to fit in to *that*.

It was flattering, if mystifying, to be invited year after year. Yet each time, knowing that *of course* I should go—what an opportunity!—I found some excuse not to.

But then my friends Paul and Renee began going—they are the couple Matt and I would later go to Bermuda with for my fortieth birthday—and I got an idea. They were such good friends, I figured I might be able to summon the nerve for this if I went, more or less, as their third child. Paul is two days older than I am. He was already screaming his head off up at Mt. Auburn Hospital in Cambridge, getting ready to go home to Belmont, while I was just beginning to think about making an appearance at Lenox Hill Hospital in New York. So the notion that he could have three kids—a few months, one-and-a-few-months, and thirty-nine—was not entirely implausible. And thus, after another couple of years' chickening out, I finally went as one of their children—in my own mind, if not officially—and stayed in their bungalow.

The Laders could not have been warmer, and the same could be said of virtually everyone else who attended this very informal, very unofficial, albeit to me very grown-up gathering. Just a lot of casual conversation, good meals, amazing speakers at some of those meals, bike rides, maybe some touch football on the beach if the weather was good.

Uh-oh. Touch football. By now, at fifty, it's not so unusual that I don't play. Plus, I'm no longer trying to hide anything. But at thirty-nine, I felt the same gut-churning, cheeks-burning horror at not being able to play as I had felt growing up. *Oh* how I dreaded situations like that.

Everyone at Renaissance wore enormous name tags on strings around their necks, so even the not-young Supreme Court justice could cheerfully say "Hello, Andy!" without having to squint—it was that informal, that unpretentious—and yet I felt as if my name tag said, ANDY, NO WIFE, NO KIDS, HOMOSEXUAL.

Is this rational? No. By and large, people back then certainly weren't thinking about that, though of course they'd ask, "Are you married?" Or "Do you have children?" It's as natural and friendly a question as can be, but a minefield for the closeted homosexual.

By then I was open with all my friends. But when a stranger asked a question like that, I wasn't ready to say "No I'm not allowed to get married." Or "No, my state considers me unfit to adopt." Or even just "No, I'm gay." (Although how is that directly responsive? I could still have been married, coupled, or a dad.) So I'd just say "No," and "No" again if they had a follow-up ("Are you seeing someone?") and "Gee, no thanks" if they offered to fix me up. (You can't say "Thanks, but I'm seeing someone," because that just opens you up to "Oh—who is she?")

The first few years, I would actually cut out early, on the morning of New Year's Eve. One night I would be telling the three hundred assembled at dinner about my various pet peeves (until Al Franken started coming, I was considered funny), and the next night I would be serving champagne in plastic cups to two hundred guys and encouraging them to use the hot tub. Not that a few of those two hundred weren't amply accomplished in their own right; but it was, let's face it, a boy party.

The stuff that goes on at Renaissance Weekend has always been "off the record" not because anyone much cared before participants Bill, Hillary, and Chelsea became our First Family, but just so everyone could relax and freely say whatever they liked, including some rather personal family things, without worrying that some of the writers who attended—me, for example—might wind up quoting them in print. There was nothing remotely sinister in this policy, and there was certainly nothing "secret" going on, à la the Republicans' famous all-male Bohemian Grove event in California, where for years the country's true power elite would gather as boys, get naked, piss on trees, fix prices, and who knows what.

Yes, the group does have a liberal bias, though some very good-natured conservatives have come every year. (This past year, my friend Arianna Huffington was one of them and was both a good sport and a big hit.) But it also had a Southern tilt, because it had always been held at Hilton Head and because Phil and Linda had built a base there—he nearly became governor of

South Carolina—and it also had a religious tilt, because Phil and Linda are people of faith.

Oh great: hundreds of Southern Baptist families and me.

But actually, as I say, these were wonderful people, mostly oblivious to my insecurities, and with each passing year I relaxed a bit more. Plus, presumably, many of them knew my story, as I either told those I got closer to or they heard it from others. And yet they still seemed quite genuinely happy to see me, as I was to see them.

To give you an idea how relaxed and easy it all was, I remember one time at lunch, in 1989 or 1990, going over to one of the more popular regular attendees—knowing that important people actually like to be kidded a little—tapping him on the shoulder, and saying, "Now, Bill, forgive me, but *where* is Arkansas again?" I still remember that he didn't laugh.

I had actually heard rumors that this guy was thinking about running for president, but I didn't take them seriously because, after all, he was just a guy. And no older (well, only a little older) than me. Presidents were . . . well, huge national figures, larger than life. They weren't any of *us.* The closest I had ever come to meeting a president was the time I was invited to Disney World's twentieth anniversary and actually got within about fifteen feet of President Bush at a press conference. (There was also the time as a teenager I stood in a crowd across the street from the Carlyle Hotel in New York, looking up in hope of catching a glimpse of President Kennedy, but catching only a glimpse of his hotel room window.)

I'll get back to Bill Clinton's campaign and how I came to realize he is head and shoulders above almost anyone else I have ever known. But let me stick for now with Renaissance Weekend.

It is December 31, 1992. In three weeks, Bill Clinton will be sworn in as the forty-second president. There are Secret Ser-

vice agents everywhere. As people mill around with their cocktails, a close friend of the president-elect grabs my arm and asks
whether I have an interest in working for the administration.
"No!" I say without hesitation. What do I know about working? If I can do any good at all, it's through writing, not working. "Good," he says. "Follow me." He led me over to one of
the tables as the crowd was beginning to stream in. "You sit
here." And so it came to pass that at the stroke of midnight,
1992–1993, I was sitting directly across the table from Bill Clinton, and my dinner companion, Hillary, squeezed my hand.

Apparently, the Clintons didn't want to sit all night with
people who'd be—charmingly, to be sure—lobbying for a job. I
just happened to be in the right place at the right time.

A couple of days later, I was one of twenty-three people on a
lunch program in the ballroom called "What I'd Tell the Next
President Over a Brown Bag Lunch (2 minutes maximum)."
We didn't know whether the next president would be there, but
we knew he might.

What would I say?

I had spoken to this group quite a few times by now, but this
was clearly different. For one thing, an audience that used to be
three hundred was more like twelve hundred, inasmuch as all
the folks who used to be invited but had something better to do
all coincidentally found themselves free this year. For another,
my hunch was that the president-elect *would* be there.

I never write my speeches, but this one I did. Because, I realized when I got the assignment sheet and started thinking
about it, there was really only one thing I *could* say—and I
wanted to say it right.

"If I had just two minutes with the next president over a
brown bag lunch," I began, heart pounding, "the first thing I
would say is—Here! Have anything you want! My tuna salad,
my Twinkie, an apple? Anything!

"And the second thing I would say is:

"*Thank you.* You haven't even taken office and yet—at absolutely no cost to the taxpayer—through simple courage, leadership, and goodwill, you have already dramatically improved my life and the lives of millions of other gay Americans.

"You have signaled America that people who happen to be gay—just like people who happen to be black or Jewish or female or anything else—should be accorded respect and judged on their contributions and conduct, like anyone else.

"You have signaled the parents of gay children that they need not be ashamed of their children, or of themselves. You have signaled other leaders and opinion makers that it's okay to speak out on this issue.

"You have saved lives. Thirty percent of teenage suicides are ascribed to gay kids who would rather *die* than face a lifetime of not being accepted. Because of you, some of those kids, at least, will feel they have a place in the world.

"Pat Buchanan says AIDS is God's retribution on gays—and presumably on Africans and hemophiliacs as well. Dan Quayle says that being straight or gay is a choice—and perhaps for him it is. Perhaps he'd *like* to sleep with men but believes it's wrong and so chooses not to. But most people are not strongly attracted to both men and women. For most of us, it's not a choice. We are who we are.

"Thank you, Bill and Hillary, for accepting us. Thank you for standing up for us, and for including us in your vision of America.

"For most of America, it doesn't much matter. But for ten or fifteen million of us, it has made all the difference in the world."

To cut the tension, I looked straight at him—his head was bowed—wagged my finger, and concluded: "But if I *ever* catch you with another cigar in your mouth, there's going to be *big* trouble."

And let me tell *you* something. If you *ever* think Bill and Hillary Clinton have not done more than anyone in the history of the world for gay and lesbian people, even including Bette Midler and a few others who come close, you're just dead wrong.

There was a little laugh at the cigar line and then a moment of silence as I looked down to grab my script, then louder applause than I have ever gotten for anything in my life.

I beat a hasty retreat.

16

It was not the first time I'd "come out" and it wouldn't be the last. Unlike losing your virginity, coming out is something you can do over and over. Not because you want to bore the world to tears, but because there always seems to be a new audience to whom it remains, even today, unexpected.

Which inspires this question: *Why must everyone keep shouting about this stuff in the first place? It's private. Live and let live. Just don't shove it in my face.*

Four problems:

First, until you do shout about it for a decade or two, nothing changes. That's the paradox: In order to *get* these things to become ho-hum, who-cares, you have to call attention to them.

Second, how else do you change laws? For example, I am not one who likes to talk about oral sex. But if two guys indulge in it in Maryland or Oklahoma, the laws there say they can be imprisoned for ten years, while if a man and a woman do, it's perfectly legal. That should be changed. Three years would be a much more reasonable sentence, and it should be applied equally to people of whatever sexual orientation.

(Oh, all right—make it legal for everybody. But for heaven's sake *gargle*.)

Third, if no one talks about it, and you never see it on TV, who is today's repressed, suicidal gay teenager supposed to model his or her life after? How is he supposed to see a future for himself?

Fourth, what *am* I supposed to do when someone on an airplane asks me if I'm married? Lie? I can just say no, which is technically true. But then what do I say if they ask about my ring? If invited for dinner, must I come solo?

So I do shout about it from time to time, but have tried to shout . . . quietly. If you threaten people, they run away.

It started very small. Piping up respectfully at a *New York* editorial meeting or two, way back in the early Seventies, when it seemed to me a story on "single New Yorkers" should include a few gay singles as well as straight ones . . . showing up in a suit to meet the future governor of New York, Mr. Cuomo . . . letting people I worked with know who I was. Like that.

Then AIDS came along and we all got more involved. It raised our profile, raised our need to get serious and seriously organized, raised our need to interact with the straight world to gain the support needed to fight the disease and care for people who were dying.

It was a terrible price to pay for visibility, of course, but that's what AIDS thrust upon us—visibility and, ultimately, from many Americans, a measure of sympathy.

AIDS is just a virus, naturally, not a gay virus. Most of the world's infected are heterosexual. So coming out against AIDS is only coincidentally about being gay.

Still, in the mid-Eighties, we were becoming a lot more visible. And truly courageous people like my friend Tom Stoddard, the longtime leader of the Lambda Legal Defense and Education

Fund . . . and not too long after that Barney Frank (with whom I'd become closer since his days as a tutor in Winthrop House) . . . were presenting the public a side of "gayness" many had not considered before.

This is why the gays-in-the-military debate a few years later, despite being a complete failure on the most immediate level, would prove to be a tremendous success: Night after night America saw on CNN and *Nightline* and the evening news people of extraordinary character and accomplishment like Colonel Margarethe Cammermeyer, West Pointer Joe Steffan, fighter pilot Tracy Thorne, and soldier-of-the-year Jose Zuniga. And America could see that the Ted Koppels of the world regarded these people and their points of view with respect.

The thing I found so remarkable about Barney and Tom and other public pioneers was their ability to keep their cool. In their place I would have been overcome with sarcasm, with sputtering, with—well, with all the things that turn off TV audiences. I also would doubtless have betrayed a certain self-consciousness, and that doesn't help, either.

One day sometime during the Bush years I had occasion to fly down to Washington—an auto insurance meeting, presumably—and when I got off the shuttle (at that point the 18 billionth 621 millionth who-knows-what shuttle passenger of the decade), who should be leaning against a pillar with his jacket slung over his shoulder but Barney Frank.

"Barney!" I said delightedly. "How nice of you to meet me!"

Actually, he said, Herb was on the plane and he was there to meet him. Had I met Herb? Wait. We'll give you a lift to your hotel. (Anyone who thinks congresspersons get chauffeured around in limos should have seen Barney and Herb's car.)

Herb—who has been Barney's better half for eleven years now—was then finishing up his MBA at Dartmouth on his way to becoming a success in the mortgage industry.

So Barney and I are talking, waiting for Herb, who's one of the last off the plane, and then I see Barney brighten as he spots Herb—a big bear of a guy not unlike Barney, very manly, button-down shirtsleeves rolled up a couple of notches. They give each other a quick kiss on the lips, and off we go.

Hello? They *kissed?* Leaving aside for a moment TBLBITW's feelings about cowboys and kissing in general, *they kissed right there in the crowd at the airport?*

But the thing that was so interesting and instructive about it was the complete *un*self-consciousness with which they did it— as any other committed couple would. Spouse meets spouse at the station, quick kiss, into the car. As natural as could be.

And that's when I realized that how we are perceived depends in large part on how we perceive ourselves. If Barney and Herb had first looked furtively to see if they could get away with it, and then, a little embarrassed, given each other a kiss, anyone who did see it would have realized instantly there was something wrong with it. But there *was* nothing wrong with it.

Of course, it's one thing to know you shouldn't be self-conscious and another thing not to *be* self-conscious—trying to force yourself not to be self-conscious is about as effective as forcing yourself to fall asleep. And when you know a certain proportion of the folks out there have been conditioned to believe you are *filth* (in Russia, I would soon learn, one survey showed a third of those polled thought homosexuals should be put to death—which was good, because the number had been higher in the previous poll, a few years earlier), it takes more confidence than I sometimes have to smile calmly and say, "I'm gay."

It gets easier. One day in 1986 *The New York Times* actually used the word *gay* for the first time, and began covering our lives and our rights far more sympathetically than it ever had. And look at this! A cover story in *Fortune.*

By the time it appeared, I was writing a column for *Time*. *Fortune*'s story gave me a hook to write something of my own. I titled my March 1992 column "Three Dollar Bills." As follows:

How times change. First we freed the slaves (good move), then we gave women the vote (jury still out), and now we seem to be saying gays are okay, too. A recent *Fortune* cover story was titled "Gay in Corporate America—What it's like, and how business attitudes are changing." The Episcopal Church has seriously considered sanctioning gay marriages. And as if that weren't enough, Harvard Business School (*Harvard Business School!*) now has a gay hotline.

Of course, whenever such sea changes are occurring there's lots of controversy, sometimes even Civil War. But with time, we adapt. Racial prejudice lives on, but few Americans today believe in slavery—or even segregated drinking fountains. Not every man is comfortable working for a woman, but relatively few believe women should be denied the right to vote—or even the right to run a small country (Britain comes to mind) or join the Army.

Hatred of any type is rarely justified or productive, not even the good old-fashioned hatred of one religious group by another. But when an idea is young (gay lib began in 1969, after police harassment sparked a riot in New York's Greenwich Village), there's usually tremendous resistance. It's just the way the world works. Even automated-teller machines took a while to catch on. Can you imagine?

So it's noteworthy that a mere generation after someone got the notion it isn't right to persecute people for their sexual orientation—a thing no more easily changed, it turns out, than Martin Luther King's skin or Gloria Steinem's gender—there is quiet recognition among a large segment of the country, and even the conservative business world, that, hey, most people are straight, some people are gay, and it's really not that big a deal. Sometimes it's even pretty funny.

One New York printing firm, run by gay women, advertises, "We're Here, We're Queer, and We Do Quality Printing." Obviously, most people would just as soon know as little as possible about the sex lives of their printers. But as marketers have increasingly discovered, there's a large, affluent gay market, and gays like to patronize businesses where they feel welcome.

When I was at Harvard Business School, there wasn't a single openly gay student. Oh, at Harvard *College* maybe, but Harvard Business School? Please.

Yet there was *Fortune* this past December reporting on gay-employee organizations "at companies ranging from AT&T to Xerox" and on a gay corporate network in Chicago with 600 members (nicknamed "Fruits in Suits") . . . and on an openly gay second-year Harvard B-School student named Jonathan Rotenberg.

Rotenberg, 28, is a member of the Harvard Business School Gay & Lesbian Students Association. It was founded in 1979, around the same time, coincidentally, that Rotenberg, then 13, founded the Boston Computer Society. (He remains its chairman.) The Boston Computer Society—the most influential computer-users group in the world, with 32,000 dues-paying members in 45 countries—is larger than the Harvard Business School Gay & Lesbian Students Association, but since arriving at Harvard, Rotenberg has devoted more of his time to GLSA.

He created the GLSA Audiotext Hotline, "an automated service designed for people of all sexual orientations: straight, gay, bisexual and unsure." You dial up the GLSA computer and, in total anonymity, choose from a menu of more than 100 brief pre-recorded messages—everything from "What causes people to be gay?" and "Can a gay person be changed into a heterosexual?" to your choice of 12 "Common myths about homosexuality," a directory of counseling services and the policies of 11 different religious denominations toward gay issues.

Last semester Rotenberg and his cohort distributed a pamphlet to everyone on campus. "There's something a bunch of your classmates would like to tell you," read the front cover, continuing, inside, "It's not easy being gay at Harvard Business School." The pamphlet acknowledged that "sexual orientation is a topic that makes many people uncomfortable"—an understatement on a par with original estimates for bailing out the savings-and-loan industry. Yet Rotenberg says his classmates and colleagues have been almost uniformly positive, both before and after his appearance in *Fortune*. His hot line (not mentioned in *Fortune*) has logged more than 1,100 calls.

To those who are astonished that Liberace was gay (or Alexander the Great or Leonardo Da Vinci or numerous current power people whose right to privacy should be respected), as to those who wonder whether Ed Bradley of CBS's *60 Minutes* is black (this was actually a question some years ago in *Parade:* "My husband and I can't agree: Is Ed Bradley of CBS's *60 Minutes* black?" Yes, dear, he is), these must be strange and frightening times.

But it looks as if yet another scaffold of prejudice is in the early stages of dismantlement, and that's likely in the long run to make America stronger and more competitive. If the best man for a particular job happens to be a woman—or gay, or Catholic, or black—why waste that talent? It's inefficient. A nation whose citizens respect and get along with one another has an advantage. Good for Harvard Business School.

You will note that I said nothing about my own sexual orientation in this column. I assumed *Time* knew—it was hardly a secret that I was gay, and I may even have discussed it with my editor—but my own feelings were that (a) the message would be more effective if the people who assumed I'm straight continued to assume it; and that (b) this would be an odd way to make my print debut. I had been thinking something more along the lines of a book, say, than a footnote in a magazine column. I'm not sure *Time* was right in not having me identify myself as gay, any more than I'm sure publications are right not to have their black writers identify themselves as black or their Jewish writers identify themselves as Jewish when writing about civil rights or anti-Semitism. But I'm not sure they're wrong, either.

Anyway, I am happy belatedly to acknowledge that the author of that column was gay. (And that he was *joking* when he said the jury was still out on women's suffrage.) I am even more happy that after running the column I decided to go meet Jonathan.

I'd been so impressed—inspired, really—by the easy way he posed for *Fortune* and allowed it to use his story that I figured, since I was headed for Boston to address (of all things) the Boston Computer Society, what could be more apt? We met for breakfast and have been good friends since.

Today, the hot line behind him,* Jonathan works with one of the country's leading management consulting firms. His equally tall partner—these guys are *tall*—is also a management consultant. ("Two management consultants dating can be scary," he has told me. "We never argue; we just have facilitated conversations guided by conceptual frameworks.")

One of the things that amazed me about Jonathan's story, as it unfolded over breakfast, was just how new to all this he was. I would have assumed that anyone bright enough to start a computer society at thirteen would also be bright enough to recog-

---

* Now HBS's gay students have an Internet site.

nize that he was gay, though in fact I've come to know that for many people sexual orientation is *not* as clear and urgent as it was for me the moment I reached puberty. And I would have assumed that anyone brave enough to be featured in *Fortune* with regard to being gay, and who had gotten Harvard Business School to fund his gay hot line, for crying out loud, would prove to have been a veteran of many a gay-rights demonstration. Especially considering the fact that, as I learned, Jonathan's family had been good friends with Barney Frank for twenty years.

But no. At the age of twenty-six, the summer before he entered Harvard Business School, Jonathan had not done anything at all about this. He had *thought* about it a lot, always hoping the feelings would go away or that he'd meet the right girl. He had spent nine years in *therapy* about it. But he hadn't actually *done* anything about it. Following a twenty-six-day Outward Bound program in Maine that included a two-mile run followed by a thirty-foot jump into the forty-six-degree ocean ("you just turn off your mind and do it"), he dove into the B-School grind. And there, looking out at his peers, it struck him that first week how *old* everyone looked. He remembers wondering whether he'd still be alone, hoping for a miracle, when he was fifty. So then and there he decided, finally, to take action. He called the "student host" HBS had assigned to his visit the previous spring, who he knew was gay, and soon found himself nervously headed to a GLSA meeting. There he found about forty students, including three of his section mates. That night he went to Buddies, his first gay bar ever. That was October 1990. And now here he was, eighteen months later, having set up the Audiotext Hotline and been profiled in both *Fortune* and *Time*.

The thing was, Jonathan had thought a lot about this even before he did finally act—about how unfair and illogical homophobia was. And Harvard Business School was no stranger to it. In one of his classes, he remembers, they were split into five-person affinity groups and instructed to discuss what made them similar. It was part of some sort of exercise. Jonathan was in the Jewish-not-from-New-York group, but one of his closeted-gay classmates was in an all-male WASP group. What made them similar? After they had run through the most obvious attributes and begun looking for others, one of the five offered, "We're all heterosexual."

"How do you know?" asked Jonathan's closeted friend.

"Because," interjected another guy good-naturedly, "if there's a faggot in this group we'll kick his ass out!"

Jonathan's friend said nothing, overwhelmed by a feeling of powerlessness. Jonathan remembers hearing this story later and deciding to do something.

"I'd spent the previous thirteen years trying to help people overcome computerphobia," he told me, "and became increasingly struck by the similarities between computerphobia and homophobia. I decided to try to tackle that in some way."

So he did.

I took heart from his example.*

At each Renaissance Weekend since my 1992–93 little talk, I've tried to be visible—but casually, like Barney and Herb at the airport.

In one panel discussion, I was holding forth on personal finance, talking about how hard it is to get people to sit down and make a budget—"I can't even get my boyfriend to make a budget!" I interjected in amused exasperation—and by the time it was registering on people (did he say *boy*friend?), I was already well into their need to make a will.

---

* Another from the business world who sets a great example is Allan Gilmour. He rose in thirty-four years to be the number-two guy at Ford—one of the dozen largest industrial enterprises in the world. Two years after leaving, in 1995, he appeared on the cover of *Fortune* as a gay man to make the case for our equal rights. "Discrimination and intolerance," he told *Fortune,* "are never good business."

The following year I remember having to do a live CNN *Newsmaker Saturday* by satellite feed from Hilton Head. The other guests (by satellite from other cities) were deputy budget director Alice Rivlin, *Wall Street Journal* columnist Alan Murray, and Gail Fosler, chief economist of the Conference Board. "Expectations for the 1994 Economy" was our New Year's Eve topic. I mention this not because there was anything remotely gay about it—I did *not* take this occasion to announce to the world I was gay (or even to describe the economy as *"fabulous,"* which would have amounted to much the same thing), nor did I even consider it. That's the point. Much of my life, the context of this book notwithstanding, has had little to do with being gay—and even less so as more people knew it and I felt accepted for who I was. But after the CNN thing, or maybe it was before—I forget—I was on a panel with the open-ended title "If Only . . ." So I figured, *hmmm.* Why not tell the story of Eddy?

Eddy, I explained, was a young lawyer friend of mine in Miami—nice kid, clean-cut, lots of energy, but not exactly someone you'd confuse with John Wayne. And so a few months earlier, I told those Renaissancers who'd chosen to come hear our panel (other "If Only" panelists included the dean of the Harvard Divinity School and a U.S. senator), Eddy had called his law partner boss and asked for a meeting. He was nervous about this, but knew that with the publicity for an upcoming march he intended to participate in, it needed to be done.

"Jack," Eddy apparently said. "I . . ." and he went around and around the subject a few times, trying to prepare Jack and making clear his loyalty to the firm and yet the need he felt to be straightforward . . . and then he finally got to the point.

"I'm gay," Eddy said.

"Duh!" said Jack, with a how-thick-could-you-possibly-think-we-*are*? expression on his face.

And that said it all. Of course you're gay, we don't care that you're gay, you're Eddy, we love you, you do good work, get out there and march for your civil rights.

"If only everyone reacted this way," I concluded, to tie it in to the theme of the panel.

Nodding heads; thoughtful questions afterward.

In 1995, Charles began coming to these New Year's weekends with me, which may have been statement enough (and Phil and Linda, to their great credit, had by then invited several other openly gay and lesbian singles and couples). Charles was nervous the first year—who wouldn't be?—and found himself on his very first panel with four experts in worldwide terrorism. The topic of the panel was broader than that, but for some reason the other panelists all had connections to stuff they could tell us but would then have to have us killed. That kind of thing. Charles talked crisply and sensibly about the terrorizing influence of fashion, and said something like, "I know we're supposed to have a quote, so I offer you this from Coco Chanel." Actually, you didn't have to have a quote; I had just suggested to Charles that having a clever quote could be helpful. But the others on the panel, who were rookies too, didn't know that, and you should have seen these people—who could have had any one of us terminated like *that*—apologizing for not having their quotes. Charles was in charge. ("Fashion is designed obsolescence," Chanel had said.) Later, one of the terrorism experts asked if he could come to Charles's next fashion show.

So Charles did just fine, and as I had already discovered in other contexts, I was actually a good deal *more* comfortable attending this big grown-up event with Charles than I had been without him. Imagine that!

Much the same in 1996, only this time some of the participants were actively asking me what panels Charles was on or where he was or how our Christmas had been.

Then in 1997—last year—they forced me on to the Fun & Sizzle Committee. *Oh, no! Not Fun & Sizzle! Isn't there a panel on bonds?* I wound up having to crawl on my knees, pretending to be our newly minted ambassador, Phil Lader, to present my credentials to the queen of England (Arianna Huffington, for whom Charles had fashioned a more than creditable robe from a tablecloth, napkins, and tinfoil).

New Year's Eve, Charles and I gave each other a little unself-conscious kiss at midnight, then hung around sipping champagne and talking with amazing people. Around one-thirty (with the president still going strong, of course), we went to bed. I had to do another of those two-minute New Year's Day panels, so I wanted to get to sleep. This year's topic: "If These Were My Final Remarks."

The hotel wake-up call came promptly at ten. (By this time the president, who had doubtless been up until at least three, had also doubtless played eighteen holes of golf.) In the shower, I thought through what I was going to say. I had pretty much decided the essence of it over the course of the weekend, but now I had to actually try to get it straight in my head. Two minutes is much harder than ten.

By ten-thirty, Charles and I were down in the giant ballroom, where nearly fifteen hundred people were already seated and talking and eating, and I was sort of zoning past the buffet line.

"Good morning, Andy," some guy said from behind. The great thing about Renaissance, as I've said, are those huge name tags, so it's the easiest thing in the world—no matter how zonked out you are—to place a face.

I turned and—it was the president.

I told him my idea about smoking in the movies. As you know, one of the reasons kids smoke is that Hollywood makes it *so cool.* There's far more smoking in the movies than in real life. In almost every movie, the really cool characters smoke—be they Sandra Bullock, the liberal anti-death-penalty law student who in real life would never have been a smoker but who, in pursuing Matthew McConaughey in *A Time to Kill,* was (Message: Smoke, and Matthew will want you, too); or Matt Damon, who in *Good Will Hunting* was brilliant, sexy, and, naturally, a smoker. Watch for this and you'll see it in almost every movie. So here was my idea: What if, at the point when all the theaters show the NO SMOKING DURING THE MOVIE message, it were stronger? What if it were the famous photo that shows a healthy pink lung beside a smoker's lung, and someone saying . . . before the start of every movie . . . "Please don't smoke during the movie, even if the actors do"? It could really undercut the pro-smoking message that invariably follows. That grotesque black lung has caused more than one kid to think twice. And Hollywood actors and directors—who thus far have largely shrugged off suggestions that they voluntarily cut back the smoking—would see this message every time *they* went to the movies. They just might begin to *get* the message. Movie theaters don't sell cigarettes, so who knows? Maybe this could work.

The president seemed to like this idea, though you don't get to be president telling your supporters their ideas are terrible. But if you ever start seeing what I've just described, you'll know it emerged opposite the shirred eggs at Hilton Head on New Year's Day 1998.

And now it was time for us to take our seats. I was the fourth of thirty on the "If These Were My Final Remarks" roster. Soon Phil was introducing me, concluding with a mention of my tobacco obsession.

"I hope to live a long time," I began, "so if these *were* my final remarks, I actually hope they *wouldn't* be about tobacco. I like to think it would have become a fairly minor problem in this country by then. And I like to think they wouldn't be about gay marriage—that most folks by then would have decided it was a good thing, not a bad thing, to encourage people like Charles and me to form strong, committed relationships.

"No," I started to say, fully intending to get on to the good stuff before they realized I had slipped in my little plug—"if these were my final remarks, I suspect they would concern the *really* intractable issue, the *really* tough one that might *not* have been solved by then and that I know is on the mind of every person in this room—*auto insurance reform.*" Whereupon I did my one-minute pitch.

I will spare you that pitch (it's a good pitch; it's an outrage that the trial lawyers so rape consumers and accident victims on this issue), because what happened, to my great surprise, is that the room erupted in applause before I could get out my joke.

I don't want to make too much of this—obviously, there may have been people in the audience who were not thrilled. Nor was this in any way a typical group. We remain a much-disliked minority. ("I was *sickened* by your cover story," one good Harvard man wrote in to the alumni magazine a few months later, referring to an article I will tell you about shortly.) But it's still worth reporting, because while all of us got polite applause after our respective two minutes, this gay-marriage line was the only one I heard acknowledged in midstream.

"Stop, stop," I said, embarrassed. "You're cutting into my two minutes!" (And I really did want to tell them about auto insurance reform.) But it was another reason this book is something of a thank-you note to the many good Americans who, given a little time to get to know us, open their hearts and their minds.

17

None of this would have happened, or not nearly so quickly, I think, had it not been for Bill and Hillary Clinton.

I happen to think the Clinton administration will be seen by history as having been excellent in many other ways as well: free trade and the economy; investments in education, science, and research; issues of fairness and inclusion. One of the first things Bill Clinton did was hike my taxes 28 percent and use some of that money to provide the earned-income credit—actual cash—to the working poor. (Another thing he pushed for successfully was a hike in the minimum wage.) To me, much as I had enjoyed the largesse of the Reagan and Bush years, this was only fair. Clinton and Gore shrank government, took on the tobacco lobby, sparked the Irish peace process . . . and on and on and on.

Leadership does matter, government does matter, and even though I thought Bush was a perfectly decent man, and obviously more qualified for the job than most Americans (and that Reagan, for that matter, was actually the right man for his time), the Clintons are just extraordinary. Not perfect—who is? But extraordinary, and deeply committed to making the world better.

I didn't know much of that when, a week or so before he formally announced his candidacy, the phone rang and it was he. Even I was bright enough to realize that he must have been calling *hundreds* of friends and acquaintances—thousands, more like it—to let us all know that he would be announcing his candidacy, to make us feel special, and to enlist our support. But it sure worked for me.

It was not, as you will recall, a cakewalk. The first time he came to Miami, for a breakfast fund-raiser, maybe seventy-five people showed up. A good short speech—good luck, Governor. The next time was cocktails. I brought a friend—"Governor, I'd like you to meet my friend Andy Bernstein. Andy, the next president of the United States"—and I remember a woman coming up to me all excited, thrusting her camera at me and asking me to take a picture.

It doesn't take much to rattle me, and there, in front of the man who might actually become president, I went into quiz-show mode. (Quiz-show mode is when you are asked something you know perfectly well—the capital of Kentucky—but, because you are being watched by a hundred people in the studio audience and four million people at home, you stutter, "Louisville?")

The woman had a firm grasp around Governor Clinton. Both were smiling. But, conscious that dozens of others were eager for the moment to pass so they could have *their* moment, I was fumbling. The natural ergonomics of the camera, where your eye just more or less automatically finds and frames the subject and your finger just more or less automatically finds the button, were eluding me.

"Turn it around, Andy," said the next president of the United States. Even from a few feet away, he could see I was about to take a picture (if I could locate the button) of my cheek.

I knew at that moment I would never have to leave the private sector for government service.

(The capital of Kentucky, by the way, is Frankfort.)

. . .

And then he came to Miami a third time, and the scandals and poll numbers were so bad that attendance was sparse.

Which is part of the reason it was such a kick, in September 1992, to be part of the crowd at the final fund-raiser of the campaign—4,000 people at $1,000 a head at the New York Sheraton. It wasn't certain he would win, but it was looking more and more as if he would.

Before the dinner we had a couple of tickets for the exclusive reception with the candidate, which, as it turned out, seemed to exclude no one but the candidate himself.

Then, shortly before we were to go downstairs for dinner, in he walked.

"There's Bill!" said my friend Joanie Zofnass, who is a psychologist, beloved aunt to Paul and Renee's two daughters, and all-around swell gal—but without a pretentious or politically ambitious bone in her body. She was excited to see Bill because she *likes* Bill. Bill is her jogging partner.

Bill came straight over to Joanie and gave her, and then me, a big hug.

We talked for a few seconds and then I remembered that my friend David, who is the kind of guy who just radiates enthusiasm and excitement—no shrinking, jaded cynic he—was right behind me, just dying to shake hands with Governor Clinton.

"Governor, I'd like you to meet my friend David Durst. David, the next president . . ."

David stepped forward, shook the candidate's hand, paid him an enthusiastic compliment, and then—just as I was getting ready to step in again—he grinned: "And, Governor, I'd just like to be the first to nominate Andy Tobias to be secretary of the treasury."

I was so embarrassed I thought I was going to die. The only saving grace in this was that it was *so* preposterous, it couldn't possibly be taken seriously. (Trust me: I would be criminally inadequate to the task—though I could be deputy undersecretary for auto insurance.)* I grabbed David's arm and pulled him away, stage-whispering, *"David!* I said you could *meet* him. I didn't say you could *talk."*

Meanwhile, Joanie had resumed her conversation.

"Are we running tomorrow?"

"Yeah!" says Bill. "Meet me here at seven."

A Secret Service agent whispers something in his ear.

"We're not staying here. Meet me at the Waldorf. Andy"— he turns to me—"are you gonna run with us?"

I am, as I've mentioned, someone who needs his sleep. I also like warm weather, and even though summer had officially ended only a few days earlier, it was . . . nippy. The prospect of getting up three hours earlier than normal and then throwing my body into chaos—well, clearly there was no way I was going to do this.

"You bet, Governor," I said firmly.

Now, hang in there with me on this long story, because there's a point.

Governor Clinton disappears and we all begin to go down to the giant ballroom dinner.

Hours pass.

We've finished eating and we realize—oh, look at this. The candidate has apparently been going around the scarlet velvet "rope line" the Secret Service uses to keep him separate from the audience, shaking hands.

Our table is very near the end of this process. And it has been a long process.

My own feeling is that, well, we've gotten to say hi already and that's plenty. My main concern is getting home early and

---

* In California, nearly two thirds of the $7 billion paid annually for bodily injury liability insurance goes to lawyers and fraud. The most seriously injured recoup just 9 percent of their actual losses from that $7 billion pool.

forcing myself to go to sleep so I can get up at some truly insane hour to jog. But my mother hasn't gotten to say hi, and she is not one to miss a golden opportunity, so she gets up to go over to the rope line. Wanting to be sure he remembers her, I come along.

He does remember her, has a nice little chat, and then, looking over my shoulder, raises his index finger and says—to *David,* who I hadn't realized had gotten up from the table and was standing behind me—"No decision has been made yet, but it's under consideration." And moves on to the next well-wisher.

Do you see what I'm saying? Hours had passed. In the interim, he had met thousands of people, *every one of whom* had some important comment to make or amazing story to recount. "My *cousin* once stopped in Little Rock when his car broke down!" "My brother's *lawyer* actually went to Yale Law School—do you remember him?" And now he was looking at David, continuing the conversation.

The evening ended. I went home. I couldn't sleep. I arrived at the Waldorf in the frigid predawn air in sweatpants and my heavy, reversible *L.A. Law* jacket (like one of those high school varsity jackets that buckle in the front). There was Joanie, bright and cheery, ready to run. There was I, nervous and zonked and ready to die.

"Don't worry!" laughs Joanie. "The way it usually works, we all pile into his limo, they drive us up to the reservoir, he starts out pretty slow, and then halfway around he breaks into a walk and just talks."

Not *this* morning, September 25, 1992, he doesn't.

No, when he finally comes down a little after seven, he says hi to everybody and then off the five of us go—he, Joanie, I, Renee, and some young politico with a Greek name who wasn't George Stephanopoulos. Not that we were really just five. There were the Secret Service joggers, there was the CNN van and the camera crews . . . they would leapfrog ahead of us, stop, crouch, film, and then leapfrog again . . . there were the New York City police cars closing off each avenue as we went by (red lights didn't apply to us), there were some black cars that must have been Secret Service . . . but the core group were we five.

I will not lie and pretend it was unexciting. Wide awake now, and very eager to look properly nonchalant as we cut through the cold morning air, I was thinking, *Wow! Is this neat or what!* as we crossed from Park to Madison to Fifth—oops, red light, oh look at that! we get to cross anyway!—to Sixth—"Hey, Governor!" people going to work would grin and shout with a thumbs-up—"We're rootin' for ya!"—and then up Sixth and into Central Park.

Now, I am no stranger to the Central Park Reservoir. The Central Park Reservoir is 1.6 miles in circumference, with a nice level cinder track. Scot and I used to jog it quite frequently, and even in 1992, at forty-five, I would occasionally force myself around it. But contrary to what Joanie had led me to expect, we had *not* started out slowly, and by the time we got to the southern entrance of the park, we had already covered three quarters of a mile. And now we were running *to* the reservoir, another mile-and-some away. Uphill. And talking. Which is, naturally, a dumb thing to do if you're trying to preserve your wind, but you certainly don't want to miss the chance to talk to the candidate or appear too winded to talk. I had said some completely inane things, so was trying hard to recoup, trying hard to look nonchalant, and now, sweating a good bit from the run and with the rising sun, and having seen the candidate do the same thing a minute earlier, I too took off *my* jacket and handed it to one of the Secret Service guys—politely—asking if he could put mine, too, in the car that was trailing us. He looked at me as if I were out of my mind. I put the jacket back on.

(At a Renaissance Weekend a few years later, I was startled

when a huge Secret Service agent came up to me, shook my hand firmly, and said—remember the name tags—"I believe you wrote a book many years ago that really made a difference in my life, and I just wanted to say thank you." I was so surprised, and the crowd was so fluid, I did not have the presence of mind to say anything but "Thank you!" So I never could be sure. But my sense was that he didn't mean *The Only Investment Guide You'll Ever Need.* How do you like that? A gay Secret Service agent. Did you see the movie *My Fellow Americans?*)

So now I was sweating and panting and running uphill in the sun with my heavy jacket on and had covered pretty much the 1.6 miles my body had been programmed for—and still the reservoir was a few hundred yards up ahead. Oh. My. God. What if I actually, physically, can't make it?

Joanie was springing happily along chatting with Bill— Joanie jogs five hundred miles every morning—and I was now a couple of yards behind, feeling the weight of the jacket and the weight of a terrible shame if I couldn't keep up with a triple-burger-eating candidate a year older than me and with (forgive me) a *girl*. But I was in some trouble here.

My growing distress was relieved by a face-saving idea. I realized that Renee, bless her, bless her, was nowhere to be seen.

"Joanie! Bill!" I shouted, "I'm going to check on Renee. I'll catch up."

Not that either of them was likely fooled, but I felt I needed *some* excuse.

I turned around, found Renee, who had sensibly started walking, and together she and I walked up to the reservoir while Bill and Joanie and the Greek ran counterclockwise around it. They started at three o'clock, we walked over to six o'clock— which is to say, three quarters of the way around the reservoir from where they began. When they got to us, we picked up with them for the last little leg.

Only then did the candidate stop running, down by 90th

Street and Fifth Avenue, where there's sort of a grand stairway up to the jogging path. The cameras were there, some joggers and passersby were there, and so a brief impromptu press conference was held, following which the candidate asked whether anyone needed a lift back to the hotel. Joanie and Renee, not needing one, inexplicably said no. I, not needing one either, piled into a Lincoln Town Car with the next president of the United States—who has legs the size of trees—and the Greek guy.

When we got to the hotel, the candidate went upstairs, took a shower, gave a breakfast speech, went up to New Haven or Hartford, gave a lunch speech, went up to Boston, gave two more speeches, had dinner and drinks, talked with hundreds more people well into the night, went up to his room, did some work, and went to sleep.

My day was similar. I hailed a cab, went home, took a shower, and went to bed.

That was the fall of 1992.

In December, I went with Barney Frank and a dozen others supporting IGLHRC, the International Gay and Lesbian Human Rights Commission, to Russia. Barney's lover, Herb Moses, had helped found IGLHRC. Now it was sending over this delegation—the rest of us were basically just a pedestal for Barney—in hope of getting Russia to repeal Rule 121, Stalin's 1937 dictum that if two guys had sex, they were subject to five years in prison. (Two gals having sex was a notion that apparently had just not occurred to him—or perhaps it turned him on.) It was an awesome trip, thanks in large part to IGLHRC executive director Julie Dorf, whose Russian is pretty good, and the well-known writer Masha Gessen, whose Russian is so good she served as our simultaneous translator. My own Russian is terrible, but while we were there I looked into the camera earnestly anyway ("Excuse my pronunciation; I have something important to tell you") and made a series of antismoking TV commercials. I managed to annoy an entire country. (All Russians smoke.) Separately, I got the main Russian network to air *Longtime Companion* (at midnight, but still), and produced a couple of gruesomely somber AIDS warnings—stark text crawling up the screen against a black background, read by a famous Russian actor and actress.

It's hard to pinpoint cause and effect—who knows how these things get done?—but not long after our trip, Rule 121 was taken off the books. The typical Russian still hates us, just as does the typical rural Alabaman. But this was still progress.

In 1998, six states in America retain sodomy laws that apply only to same-sex couples; fifteen retain laws that apply to everyone but are more likely to be applied to gays and lesbians. "We're just one aggressive, misguided prosecutor away from arresting gay men and lesbians," writes Dorothy Foley, an attorney with the U.S. Department of Justice. "If we're prosecuted under the sodomy laws, we can serve jail time, be fined, lose our jobs, lose our children . . . in Idaho we can be sentenced to life in prison." In today's climate, such prosecutions are unlikely. But the laws are there, ready to be used. Not to mention "informal" law enforcement. In our nation's capital, while gay sex between consenting adults is not itself illegal, Lieutenant Jeffrey Stowe, commander of the police department's anti-extortion unit, was arrested in November 1997—for extortion. Specifically, he was arrested by the FBI for "fairy shaking"—blackmailing people seen entering a gay club who, it can be ascertained from license plates and in other ways, appear to be ripe targets. A rogue cop? There was strong reason to suspect that Stowe's silent partner was the chief of police.

18

In a way, it was almost fun getting older.

I got to spend five years writing columns for *Time*—they even let me do one decrying *Time* for accepting tobacco ads—and I had a great time with *Managing Your Money,* though I was sent packing, sadly, when its publisher was acquired. But not *that* sadly, because I got a fairly large check.

There are few luxuries greater than being able to say yes when asked to support a worthy cause. This fairly large check allowed me to say yes more often.

Charles and I have an "authors" dinner each year for the Goddard Riverside Community Center on the Upper West Side of New York. About thirty such dinners are held simultaneously, and last year we got Faye Wattleton, the longtime force behind Planned Parenthood and author of *Life on the Line,* to come as one of our authors, along with Roger Lowenstein, who writes brilliantly for *The Wall Street Journal.* As usual, our little band of contributors was black and white, straight and gay, young and less young. A straight centimillionaire and his wife, a black fashion model and her fiancé—the gamut. Back in

Leonard Bernstein's day, when he gave the very well inten-
tioned but perhaps slightly self-conscious party for Black Pan-
thers that became the subject of Tom Wolfe's delicious *Radical
Chic,* I imagine this kind of blend might have been more
strained. At our little dinner, everybody had just the best time.

The year before, it was Charles's turn to pick an author. (It's
not formalized, exactly, but basically we run down the list of
possibilities that Goddard Riverside sends, and I choose one and
he chooses one.)

"How about Safire?" he shouts in from the bedroom.
Charles's favorite place in the apartment is the bed. Mine is the
refrigerator.

"*Safire?*" I shouted back, amazed (a) that Safire was on the
list and I hadn't noticed—William Safire is a big deal—and (b)
that Charles, whose eye runs more to the "Style" section of *The
New York Times,* would have chosen him.

As I loped back into the bedroom, Charles explained, drip-
ping with disdain—how out of it could his boyfriend possibly
be?—"No, not *William* Safire, the columnist. *Sapphire* Sapphire,
the black lesbian."

Oh. Of course.

And let me tell you that if you haven't read *Push,* Sapphire's
novel, and if you can stand very raw, graphic language, it will rip
your heart out. It is a *Huckleberry Finn* for the 1990s inner city.
You will meet a girl named Claireece "Precious" Jones—like no
one you know—and by the end of this short novel, you will
come desperately to care about her.

Anyway, Goddard Riverside is one of several good groups
Charles and I are excited about—Medical Education for South
African Blacks is another great one—not all of them, by any
means, gay.

One that is gay is NLGJA, the National Lesbian and Gay
Journalists Association. After all, what America knows about us,
it knows only two ways: personal contact and the media. In its

earliest days, by going around to editorial boards at the major newspapers and TV networks, face to face, NLGJA woke these folks up. Just as, years earlier, we had had a chance to talk with Mario Cuomo and perhaps shift his perception, so had Roy Aarons, Charlie Kaiser, and a handful of other brave gay and lesbian journalists engaged the opinion leaders of the media.

And it worked.

By September 1993, it was hard to remember that *The New York Times* had first used the word *gay* only seven years earlier. (Prior to that, the policy was that the word could only appear if someone was being directly quoted; the *Times* itself would never use the word.) Now there were 560 gay and lesbian journalists from around the country gathered at New York's Grand Hyatt Hotel at a cocktail reception being *hosted* by *The New York Times* and being welcomed by its publisher, Arthur Ochs Sulzberger, Jr.

Following his remarks, there was a two-hour panel discussion in the ballroom. Bright lights. Video cameras running. And the participants were Judy Woodruff, Robin MacNeil, Dan Rather, and Tom Brokaw. Peter Jennings hadn't been able to come, but ABC News took an ad in the NLGJA journal.

Younger readers may not be able to imagine how extraordinary this seemed to me. But there were these heterosexual media icons talking about our issues and our concerns and our rights as they might have been, though white, at a similar conference held by African-American journalists. And when one of the four drew some audience criticism for what had seemed like a possibly insensitive answer, he said, "Oh, nonsense. My son is gay. I am enormously proud of him and love him very much." Which seemed as good a way as any to make it clear that one might disagree on some of the specifics of how open gay journalists should be in their careers, and so forth, without necessarily being homophobic.

The next morning, I had a chance to "come out," for the first time again, in front of five hundred journalists.

. . .

And then in March 1995, *Out* magazine's cover teased MEET "THE BEST LITTLE BOY"—AUTHOR JOHN REID UNMASKED, along with a couple of photos that made me look adorably neurotic, because the photographer had waited for just the right light. ("Don't you be answering any *fan* mail," Charles warned.)

So I got to come out publicly *again* for the first time.

And then the following month I went up to Harvard Business School at the joint invitation of—get this—the Finance Club and the Gay & Lesbian Students Association (the aforementioned GLSA). Feeling that one's sexual orientation shouldn't be an in-your-face sort of thing, I did twenty minutes on my abortive career as vice president of that once high-flying public company National Student Marketing, comfortable in the knowledge that the questions would be about "that." All the questions were, and once asked, I had a good time telling. "What a good reception," I told one of the gay sponsors afterward. "I'm amazed so many gay HBS-ers would feel comfortable enough to come to a thing like that." (The room was full.) "Most of the audience was straight," he told me.

Governor Clinton had made this topic okay to talk about when he ran for president. And once it was okay, boy did people ever start to talk.

Part of it was just that—giving people the political and cultural cover to sign on. In any movement, to be one of the first takes enormous courage. But then, as you see more and more people you admire signing on, pretty soon you'd feel odd *not* joining them.

This is why I'd gotten so psyched about the Human Rights Campaign's "endorsement project." By the time I heard about it, the late Steve Endean had persuaded literally hundreds of people to sign a simple statement. It was wrong, they felt, to discriminate on the basis of sexual orientation. As of September 1992, the list included *governors* (Republicans Weld of Massachusetts and Carlson of Minnesota among them), *mayors* (Boston, Chicago, Denver, Minneapolis, St. Paul, San Diego, New Orleans, and Spokane, among others), free-floating *political figures* (Jesse Jackson, Eugene McCarthy, Geraldine Ferraro, Paul Tsongas), *religious leaders* (Edmund G. Browning, presiding bishop of the Episcopal Church,* Dr. Paul Sherry, president of the United Church of Christ, Joan Brown Campbell, general secretary of the National Council of Churches of Christ, Alexander Schindler, president of the Union of American Hebrew Congregations, Rabbi Gerald Zelizer, president of the Rabbinical Assembly of America, and eighty-three other bishops, rabbis, and ministers), *entertainers* (Lily Tomlin, Harry Belafonte, Jessye Norman, Richard Gere, Billy Joel), *writers* (Gloria Steinem, Studs Terkel), *civil rights leaders* (Coretta Scott King, Roger Wilkins), *labor leaders* (Douglas Fraser, former president of the United Auto Workers, John Sweeney, president of the Service Employees International Union, Gerald McEntee, president of the American Federation of State, County & Municipal Employees), *psychiatrists* (Judd Marmor, past president of the American Psychiatric Association), *educators* (Keith Geiger, president of the National Education Association, Jonathan Wilson, chairman of the Des Moines Board of Education), *lawyers* (the presidents of the New York, Ohio, and Montana state bar associations, the attorneys general of New York, Illinois, and Minnesota), *models* (Christie Brinkley, Cindy Crawford), *athletes* (Carl Eller, former Minnesota Viking NFL All-Pro, Alan Page, NFL Hall of Fame member). And more.

I sent that list and a personal letter to the CEOs and personnel directors of the country's five hundred largest corpora-

---

* All titles as of 1992. There have doubtless been many changes since.

tions and got only three endorsers. But I also wrote and got Warren Buffett, Paul Newman, Carl Sagan, and Gail Sheehy, among others.

Perhaps the most telling name on our list was "Dear Abby." America was coming around.

(Separately, the following year, there would be a list of 125 university presidents who supported allowing gays and lesbians to serve in the military.)

I think a big poster with all these names should hang on the wall of every congressperson who supports gay rights, be offered to every seventeen-year-old who needs a little help reassuring his parents. *See, Dad? See all the people who support my rights? You admire some of these people, don't you?*

Once Charles and I were a team, just showing up as a couple abetted the ho-hum-ization. When the protocol people at the White House asked us whether we wanted to be announced by the marine guard individually or as a couple—Mr. and Mrs. this, Dr. and Ms. that—we said without a second thought that we were Mr. me and Mr. him. Could this possibly have happened under George Bush? Or under Bob Dole—who is a good man, but who was actually *returning* thousand-dollar contributions from the gay Republicans, so repulsive to some in his "big tent" was the thought of taking their money? (I'm a Democrat, but proud to have helped provide a little of the seed money for Rich Tafel's gay group, the Log Cabin Republicans.)

In some circles it really is becoming ho-hum. (One of my favorite cartoons is of a little kid looking up at his father. "Your mother and I are gay, too," Dad is saying, brusquely. "Now go do your homework.") But of course to many it's *not* ho-hum. At the same time as we were building our broad endorsement list, Dan Quayle—a heartbeat from the presidency—was telling *The New York Times* in no uncertain terms that being gay was a *choice,* that it was the *wrong* choice, and that it was *immoral.* I'd love someone to do a profile of Dan Quayle. Find out from him when he made *his* choice. Was it difficult? What had been the pros and cons as he saw them at the time? Did he have any regrets?

A few people were even picketing gay funerals with signs explaining that God hates fags and that these deaths were well deserved. *Newsweek* reported in mid-1997 that 42 percent of those it surveyed felt the country had gone too far in the effort to secure equal rights for gays and lesbians, while only 23 percent thought too little effort was being made. And homosexuality was so repellent to many on a visceral level—forget the politics—that you had a young man blasting a shotgun hole through the chest of another young man the day after that second young man professed his affection on a daytime talk show. ("Secret Admirers"—next *Jenny*.)

"In a landmark victory for Christian conservatives," reported *The New York Times* on February 12, 1998, "Maine voters have narrowly chosen to make their state the first in the nation to repeal its law protecting homosexuals from discrimination."

Two days later, one Maine homosexual, forty-year-old psychiatrist Charles Mitchell, parked his car in a high school parking lot to go for his usual five-mile jog. His car had a rainbow sticker. The next thing Mitchell remembers is waking up in an emergency room with a fractured skull, a broken cheekbone, and a broken jaw. Falmouth's police chief was quoted saying, "We don't think for one second this was a random attack." Violence against gays increased in Colorado, too, when that state passed *its* antigay referendum.

The conclusion here isn't that most people who voted against us in Maine would condone violence, or even that most Mainers wanted to repeal our civil rights bill. Most Mainers didn't vote. It was largely the deeply motivated Mainers—those passionate to do God's bidding—who roused themselves to go to the polls in this odd February election. It was also those fooled by the religious right into believing we are looking for "special" rights, when in fact that has never been the case. But not condoning violence is not the same as being blameless for it. Those who demonize gays and lesbians, or even just express their distaste, send a message to their kids. In a 1997 study, *The Des Moines Register* found that the average Des Moines high school student hears antigay comments twenty-six times a day— about one every fourteen minutes. The Centers for Disease Control and the Massachusetts Department of Education reported in 1995 that two thirds of gay, lesbian, and bisexual youth had been threatened or injured with a weapon in the previous year. And that gay youngsters were four times as likely as their peers to attempt suicide.

With Maine gone, just ten states included "sexual orientation" in their lists of grounds on which it was illegal to discriminate. In the remaining forty, you could *not* look an employee or a tenant in the eye and fire him or refuse to rent to him "because I don't like Jews" or "because I don't like women" or "because I don't like blacks." That would be illegal. But you *could* look him in the eye and fire or evict him "because I don't like gays."

And, of course, thanks to Senator Nunn and others, the navy, for one, was doing it all the time. (You will recall the case of Timothy McVeigh—not the Oklahoma City bomber but the highly commended seventeen-year naval officer—who was fired because in his private, pseudonymous America Online profile he described himself as gay. To find out who he was so they could fire him—simply for that—the navy not only had to "ask"; it had to strong-arm AOL into violating its privacy covenants.) Which I suppose compels me to tell you about the time I came out to Sam Nunn in the men's room.

Nunn was at a Democratic policy retreat being held at a home that, though totally different in style, would surely rival Vizcaya. (Unbeknownst to many of the eighty or so in attendance, their host was gay.) Nunn, who had already announced his retirement from the Senate, had just given a really sharp defense analysis. You could tell this was a man who had served his country well.

Yet I also knew that he had led the fight against gays in the military, seriously undercutting the efforts of his own party's president; and that he had fired two of his staffers for being gay, one of them a friend of mine.

(It is telling that this gay friend—the father of two and the recipient of both a Purple Heart and a Bronze Star—still says Nunn was "the smartest guy in the Senate," and basically bears no grudge.)

So, always looking for ways to be visible without being confrontational, I found myself at the coffee break in line for the urinal behind Sam Nunn.

"My gosh, Senator," I said. "Why are you retiring? We really need you in the Senate!"

Modest mumble, mumble, handshake, smile.

"There's one issue on which I deeply disagree with you, but otherwise, you're just so dead-on!"

Mumble, mumble, too-smart-to-take-the-bait.

Hmph. Not for nothing did he get this far, I thought, having been unable to pique his curiosity. So I just went for it.

"By any chance do you remember a former staffer named Greg Baldwin?" I asked, genuinely not sure whether he'd remember, or admit to it. (Greg is today partner at Holland & Knight, one of the nation's largest law firms.)

"Of course!" said the senator.

"Well, that's the issue I deeply disagree with you on."

And now it was his turn for the urinal.

No big deal—he wasn't flustered or insulted or defensive. I just figured that even Sam, at his age, if he encounters enough of this, will eventually get a little more used to us, a little less negative. Look at what happened with former Alabama governor George Wallace and the blacks!

· · ·

Returning from that event, I got to ride up from Florida to Washington in a chartered jet with Jack Kemp and Roy Romer. Just the three of us—certainly the most august company, on a concentrated basis, I've ever been in for so long.

Jack Kemp may be wrong in some of his economic views, but he is one great, well-intentioned guy. And Colorado governor Roy Romer would soon become chair of the Democratic party. Listening to them go at it—once the cell phones finally got put away—made one long for the days, if there ever were such days, when politics were civil and congenial. Sure these guys disagreed on a host of things. But they had such *fun* together!

When one of them brought up the name Al Lowenstein— Allard K. Lowenstein—I began to listen even more intently.

Governor Romer had run against Al for the presidency of the National Student Association in 1950. He and Jack began swapping Al stories, of which they had several. Al had been a key liberal voice, a favorite of Eleanor Roosevelt and the Kennedys, William F. Buckley, Jr.'s frequent TV sparring partner (after Al was murdered by a crazed acolyte, Buckley delivered one of the eulogies), and leader of the Dump Johnson movement that helped end the Vietnam War.

Al, father of five, had also been a great friend to any number of young college students and recent graduates, including me. He was a graduate of Horace Mann School, nineteen years ahead of me—we had even had a few of the same teachers—and his uncle had apparently carried on quite a notorious affair with my dad's mother before I was born. He couldn't believe I hadn't known that. (Are you kidding? I didn't even know Mom had a brother.) He had served in Congress only one term, but with the kind of intelligence and energy that made him the Barney Frank of his day.

He is also one of the first people I told I was gay, a subject in which he had great interest on two levels. First was his sense of justice. He had been deeply involved in the civil rights struggle in the South—actively running around places where he could have been shot or bombed or run off the road. He had made numerous trips to South Africa to try to bolster the fragile forces for freedom there. He was involved in Spain. In Czechoslovakia. (You know the Henry Fonda speech in *The Grapes of Wrath*? Wherever there was someone hurting or oppressed, *he'd be there*.) He was a tremendous, passionate, tireless force for human rights. So, naturally, he cared, too, about gay rights, even at this very early stage, just a year or so after the 1969 Stonewall riots.

The second reason he showed a great interest was that he himself felt an attraction to handsome young men.

He was not gay—and certainly not the way I am. You don't become the loving father of five adorable children having a sex drive like mine. But, he would tell me in endless late-night discussions, along with his love of his wife and attraction to women, he had a sort of ancient Greek–style love of maleness.

He never did, or asked to do, anything "improper" with me, and I didn't have the sense he even wanted to. And he wasn't consciously hiding anything from me—*he* initiated these conversations, for the most part. He would construct these long intellectualizations of the type that (on different topics) would leave even William F. Buckley, Jr., sort of wide-eyed, wherein he would explain why he was not gay. It was a different kind of attraction yet a real love that he felt. My own feeling was that he was perhaps kidding himself. But Al was nothing if not a complicated man, and fully entitled, like everyone else, to his complications.

So when the manuscript of *The Best Little Boy in the World* was being readied for press, he was one of the people I showed it to.

I only sent it to a few. In fact, the only other I can remember was Professor George Cabot Lodge at Harvard Business School—

of the "the Lowells talk to the Cabots and the Cabots talk only to God" Cabot Lodges. Professor Lodge was the school's resident Brahmin liberal, assigned to teach courses like "Business Ethics." It was he who introduced us to Garrett Hardin's oh-so-fundamental *The Tragedy of the Commons,* an essay that should be required reading for every citizen in the world, tipped in to every Bible and Koran. And so it was to him I sent a copy of the manuscript in hope of a blurb.

The instant I saw him about it, I felt terrible. Sending it had made this nice straight man feel *so* awkward. It was *so* unLodge-like. He was sympathetic; he was gracious. But it was 1971. Clearly, the place for any such discussion was a therapist's office, in strictest confidence. His name on the back of this book? Heck—I didn't even have the nerve to put *my* name on the book!

Al did not hesitate. In fact, I raised more objections than he did when he offered a blurb. I'm not sure I had even asked him for one! Gosh, could this hurt your chances to get back into Congress? I worried. (They had gerrymandered his district.) Could this lead to rumors that, well . . . *you* know.

Out came the book with his blurb, and only his blurb, on the back cover.

Where do a rare few people get the courage to do what's right no matter how unpopular it may be? To say to the lynch mob—*Stop! You're acting like a lynch mob!* ("Oh, yeah?" responds the crowd. "Let's lynch him, too!")

"Al Lowenstein was a friend of mine!" I interjected excitedly once Romer and Kemp had swapped their stories. I told them about his courage with the book, which led to a nice half hour of impromptu ho-hum-ization.

"So what's the wedding ring?" asked Jack Kemp, former pro-football quarterback (and father of two others). He was genuinely curious.

I chattered on about Charles, made some good-humored

digs at Jack for being a member of a party that deplores our promiscuity yet forbids us to marry . . . we discussed the reasons marriage—the word, not the legal rights that go with it—is a tough marketing challenge . . . I may even have moved Jack a bit when I pointed out that if Charles got sick, I could be barred from visiting him in the ICU for not being a family member . . . and it was a fine little discussion. ("What are you headed to Washington for?" "A board meeting—ZPG." "What's that?" he asked. "Zero Population Growth," I said, surprised someone of his generation hadn't heard of it. "That's the dumbest idea I ever heard of!" He erupted with a laugh. "Look out the window!" But while it's true there's still lots of undeveloped land and forest, we are adding a billion people to the planet every twelve years. It took *ten thousand human generations* to produce the first billion. The toads are dying. We may be getting on Mother Nature's nerves.) We disagreed on a lot of things, but I liked him. I sensed he liked me, too. I know he'll enjoy meeting Charles.

I saw no reason to tell Romer and Kemp the full story of the rings—we were only flying to D.C., not China—but because it involves a genie, I thought it might interest you.

I don't like wearing jewelry, or even a watch, and so hadn't worn a ring since the day the summer of my senior year in college that my high school ring got lost in the surf off Tossa, Spain.

I also have a fear of commitment. "Till death do us part" sounds so awfully . . . final. And I am also more than ordinarily anxious not to promise something unless I can fulfill it. My guilt level over canceling a dinner date—let alone a marriage—is higher than most.

Still, Charles and I had been together for nearly nine months, and as his birthday approached, I thought rings might be a gift he would like. Sometimes this seemed like a very good idea; other times I felt myself growing short of breath. But even when I did think it was a good idea, I wasn't sure precisely how to pull it off mechanically. How do you find out someone's ring size? (And which finger would we wear it on?)

I procrastinated, bought some other, backup presents, decided definitely to go down to Tiffany—but knew I could get 40 percent off if I went through a friend on the board—so I hesitated some more. (Did I really want to bother my friend with this? And isn't it awfully skeevy not to pay full retail for *wedding* rings? Though of course in my mind these were not exactly *wedding* rings—and there *certainly* would be no wedding—they were just a way of saying we were a couple.) And then on the morning of his birthday, having pretty much decided to go for it . . . only now it was too *late* to go for it . . . I got a great idea. I went to a toy store and bought two enormous candy rings. When Charles got ready to open this gift, which I naturally saved for last, I prefaced it by explaining it was just a *symbol* of a gift—he would have to decide whether he wanted the real thing.

He did.

Not that he jumped at the idea. He had a few legitimate doubts of his own. But, yes, we decided to do it. One day soon we'd go down to Tiffany together and pick out rings. Not gold—I don't like gold, and I also didn't want it to look as though I was trying to appear straight. Silver, or platinum. And maybe on the right hand, although we ultimately decided on the left.

With his schedule and mine, and the need to look nice when you go to Tiffany—not having to put on a coat and tie on a summer afternoon is the whole *point* of being a writer—we didn't get around to it immediately. But then one early evening we had to go downtown to a benefit (for a group that puts on talent contests in inner cities, where everyone who comes to try out makes the cut—the purpose isn't finding talent but helping kids develop social skills and self-esteem). So having to don suit and tie anyway, I called Charles and asked if he could leave the office early and meet me at Tiffany.

I got there first, established my ring size, determined the prices—spot platinum at the time was selling for just 5 percent more than spot gold, I knew from CNBC, but Tiffany wanted three times as much for a platinum wedding band as a gold one!—and had pretty much determined the other details, like delivery time, when Charles arrived for his own fitting. A couple of customer onlookers seemed to raise an eyebrow, but the Tiffany rep was totally cool.

The size was easy, but choosing the width, and the price, and we were late—we took her card and said we'd call in our order once we'd decided.

So now we were taking a subway downtown to the benefit (it was rush hour; a cab would never have worked), and now we were walking *very* fast from the subway to the address on the invitation. And now—

"Charles! Wait!"

As if by magic, a genie had appeared in the guise of a guy behind a card table. He was selling silver.

Charles turned without breaking stride, rolled his eyes much as he does when I get stopped, similarly, by the sight of napoleons in a bakery window, and said, "Come on!"

He kept walking, but really: There was a pair of silver rings that looked just like the Tiffany platinum ones, more or less, and when I tried one on—it fit! Which meant it would fit Charles, too, because we had determined he was the same size.

By now Charles had reluctantly doubled back to retrieve me, but I thought it was fate. I bought the rings *without even haggling*—two for ten dollars—and put his on his finger, mine on mine. I thought it was hysterical, not to mention economical. And what great conversation pieces, especially for a guy who makes a living counseling thrift and his boyfriend, who has to put up with it.

I actually thought this might be a good long-term solution. Charles wore the ring but explained that it would be like that awful-tasting thing the dentist puts in your mouth when you get a crown. It's called a "temporary."

In time, Charles got us (wholesale, at least) two platinum bands. Inside each—how do they do this?—is the date we exchanged the rings, August 15, 1995, our respective initials, and what we call each other. ("No," Charles had to explain. "*You* wear the one with my initials. *I* wear the one with your initials.")

Charles said we could keep the silver genie rings as a souvenir. Last I looked, he had them in the cup where we keep the quarters for the laundry.

Did we have a ceremony? people ask. No, we say. We eloped.

"Are you married?" asks my old B–School classmate, whom I've had to call after all these years to solicit a reunion contribution. His son is seventeen; daughter, thirteen—what about me, am I married? "My boyfriend and I have rings," I snap back cheerfully, "but we're not *allowed* to get married." He chuckles and the conversation goes on from there. He sends $2,500.

And then there was that speech to six hundred ninth through twelfth graders and the faculty of Horace Mann School, after which they made me a trustee.

19

"The Crimson *ran a gay guy's thing about*
'today we should all wear Levi's for solidarity.'
Everyone in my final club ran back to change out of jeans."

—gay member of the class of '77

One way of looking at all this "coming out" stuff is . . . *un-comfortably.* After all, most of us grew up knowing homosexuality was simply too shameful to discuss. Murder and mayhem can be regularly televised, but two men or two women holding hands? Decency has its limits.

The better way of looking at it may just be to laugh at God's little joke—wiring 5 or 10 percent of His children differently from the rest. My own feeling is simply to concede what our born-again friends argue: that intimate relations between two people of the same sex are unnatural and perhaps even an abomination before God—*if they're straight.* If they're gay, it's the most natural thing in the world.

The importance of unself-conscious humor in all this cannot be overemphasized. For example:

It is the annual dinner of the Democratic Leadership Council, the group Al From founded and that Clinton had once chaired. The DLC tries to push the Democratic party away from traditional knee-jerk responses and toward progressive policies that will actually work. (Sure, we care about the poor; but the traditional welfare system didn't work. It needed fixing. Sure, we care about jobs and wages at home; but in the long run, free trade *adds* to our prosperity and *increases* our ability to push other countries to improve workplace and environmental standards. Sure, we're grateful to trial lawyers for much of the work they do; but that doesn't mean we should stick with a horribly wasteful, fraud-ridden auto insurance system.) With me are Elizabeth Birch, who left Apple Computer to run the Human Rights Campaign, and Fred Hochberg, who left the business world to advance the cause of gay rights.

Vice President Gore arrives. Like the president, he is a strong supporter of our civil rights.

"Let's go over and say hello," say Fred and Elizabeth in almost the same breath. "He just sat down to eat!" I protest. "Oh, nonsense. No one eats at these dinners." So they get up and I tag along. The vice president rises to greet Elizabeth and gives her a kiss. He shakes Fred's hand.

Fred starts back in mock umbrage. No one else can pull off this kind of thing, but Fred does, beautifully.

"What, Mr. Vice President," he laughs. "Elizabeth gets a kiss and I get just a handshake?"

"Some things take a little more time, Fred," says the vice president, grinning.

A couple of years later Fred was nominated to be the number two guy at the Small Business Administration.

Few have Fred's infectious sense of humor. But Ellen DeGeneres does. Once she broke the ice, it seemed as if virtually every sitcom on TV began having fun with this, too. *It's funny! It's farcical!* And I seriously doubt it's going to turn straight kids gay. I loved *The Honeymooners,* but it never turned me straight.

And still I was having opportunities to come out for the first time. (A well-intentioned 1998 *Miami Herald* headline would announce: BUSINESS WRITER'S HAPPY HE'S FINALLY OUT. *Finally?*)

I introduced Charles into one of my daily Internet columns in 1996. I had been talking about ostrich burgers and I said, parenthetically, that "Charles is in Paris or I'd never get away with this." If people wanted to assume Charles was my chef or something, that was fine, though regular readers would surely know I was not the type to employ a chef. To the few who e-mailed in: "Who's Charles?" I e-mailed back: "My boyfriend."

But the first time I approached the topic head-on was in connection with Ellen's debut. ("Until recently, many people thought being gay was a choice—and a very bad one. Like choosing to be an idiot or choosing to have everyone despise you.") It was a long column that made all the obvious points.

"Enough," the column concluded. "Being gay myself, I can get very boring on this topic—but not Ellen. Apparently, it's a very funny episode. ABC. Tonight. Nine o'clock."

And it *was* enough. I write about money, not sex, for crying out loud, the wild sex scenes in this book notwithstanding. So of the five-hundred-plus Internet columns I've written, only three have been about this topic—the initial *Ellen* column and two follow-ups it occasioned.

But I've sent Charles wandering in and out of a few, just as any columnist might occasionally reference his better half. Why not?

And when my last money book came out, there was "my boyfriend Charles" rolling his eyes on page 159, in the section on buying men's suits for $200 (he has a Prada *backpack* that costs more than I spend in a year on clothes), along with descriptions of gay groups in the section on charitable giving.

Part of the fun with the tour for that book was finding ways to do a little ho-hum-ization. Where once I had dreaded being asked about any of this on the *Tonight* show—to the point I gooked up my hair *twice*—I now found ways to drop it into the conversation myself. I discovered that one of the best ways to convey the spirit of the book—a book about quixotic "money adventures"—was also an easy, nonconfrontational way to slip in my other little point as well.

"You once hired a plane?" the interviewer might prompt me. Or, "Can you give us an example of what you mean by a money adventure?" Whatever the lead-in, I often found myself saying, "My boyfriend and I have a house at Fire Island, and every summer, for years, these *tobacco* planes would fly up and down the beach with their banners—NEWPORT: ALIVE WITH PLEASURE—and it drove me crazy. I mean, there they are saying they don't want to target kids, as if no *kids* would be at the beach in the summer, and for years I kept thinking I just wanted to take a bazooka and shoot them out of the sky. But I knew that wasn't practical, so finally, after four summers of this— which just goes to show you how slow I am—I finally realized, *hey wait a minute! I could hire my own plane!* So I looked in the Yellow Pages and for $200 an hour I hired my plane to follow the Newport plane up and down Long Island. Newport is Lorillard, which is Loews, which is controlled by Larry Tisch, so my plane's banner read"—big hand gesture across the sky, if this was a TV interview—"LARRY TISCH SELLS CANCER STICKS. And they stopped flying. Then the next summer, Parliament, which is made by a different company, had a banner—PARLIAMENT: THE PERFECT RECESS—remember now, they don't want to reach *kids;* this old slogan never had anything to do with *school* recess, right? So I called my guys again and our banner read, PARLIAMENT: THE *PERMANENT* RECESS, and *they* stopped flying. And then the third summer there were no tobacco planes, so on Labor Day I flew a banner that read, THANK YOU FOR NOT SMOKING. And there have been no tobacco planes since."

End of interview. And the thing was, I would just race past that first sentence so that almost everyone would have heard it but then, I hoped, get caught up in the story. And maybe later they'd come back and think, Did he say boyfriend? I think he said Fire Island . . . so, yeah, maybe he did say boyfriend. Oh, well.

Ho-hum.

This was in fact the story I told when Charles and I went up to my twenty-fifth Harvard Business School reunion. I was on a panel called "Public Lives." With me were a classmate from the World Bank, a classmate who had almost become premier of Quebec, and a classmate who had served in Congress. I explained that my own exposure to the political end of things had been pretty much in two areas—tobacco (so I told this story, only starting with the phrase "Charles and I") and auto insurance (so I got to bring them to tears of outrage over the current system and tears of frustration over our inability to fix it). Charles was no secret to anyone—there we were pictured together in the reunion book, just like all the other classmates and theirs spouses—and he was a big hit. All the wives (most of my classmates were guys) wanted his fashion advice; all the husbands were trying to figure out whether they could make a buck launching him in his own line. We had a good time.

None of this is to say "we're there" yet. But going up to Harvard for a reunion reminds me how far we've come. Because condemnation of homosexuality goes back as far at Harvard as anywhere else in America. The Reverend Michael Wigglesworth, author of the Puritan mega-bestseller *Day of Doom,* certainly condemned it. He was Harvard's minister in its earliest years and was once even in the running for its presidency. Yet he lusted after his students. "Lord I am vile," he confided to his diary (portions of it written in code) in 1653.

There was little discussion or understanding of any of this back then, let alone debate over the existence of a gay gene. It was, rather, as Wigglesworth records his doctor's explanation, a condition caused by "a little acrimony" gathering in the mouth, which caused "humours to flow." Marriage, he was advised, "would take away the cause of that distemper." And so Wigglesworth married his cousin Mary "and consummated it . . . by the will of God May 18, 1655." But the news was not good. The very next day he felt "stirrings, and strongly, of my former distemper even after the use of marriage." And this made him "exceeding afraid."

Now here was Harvard—always tuned to the importance of good alumni relations—specifically holding a reception for the gay and lesbian reunion-year HBS alumni.

How times change.

"I thought it was pretty awful being gay at Harvard," says "Bob," one of my college classmates. "After a suicide attempt sophomore year, I was assigned a nationally known Harvard guy as my personal psychiatrist. He wasn't comfortable with the topic or issue or subject or me, so he kind of said, 'So why don't you try this?' and sent me up to group therapy with the Biebers' clinic at the Mass. Mental Health Institute. Aversive shock therapy. They showed us slides. Slides of men gave you a shock; slides of women didn't. Comic in retrospect, but pretty awful at the time."

When I interviewed him for *Harvard Magazine,* the alumni publication, Bob told me he knew of only one person who ever came out of this therapy straight, or at least determined to be straight. (Ironically, others who'd never had any gay experiences—only feelings—met like-minded people at these sessions and "learned the ropes" by being there. So the clinic may actually have helped some people in a completely unintended way.)

Because we were terrified of identifying ourselves, the friends we Harvard undergraduates made were straight. Or we thought they were. Take David Hollander, a few years behind me, who was president of the *Crimson.* At Harvard, he met his current and lifelong boyfriend, Arthur Lubow, who was a couple of years behind *him* and about to become the *Crimson*'s managing editor. Although they were good friends, neither knew the other was gay. They recognized their mutual interest only three years later. David was closeted and abstinent "because I thought my life would be over if I did anything."

During David's stewardship of the *Crimson,* a freshman from Los Angeles named Gene Hightower came to him, saying he had entered Harvard with the express intention of starting a gay student group. He asked David whether he could get a notice in the *Crimson.* "I said I could get him a front-page notice, so I dummied it, and it didn't run. And then again the next night. And finally I realized that Pat, our Roman Catholic typesetter, was just throwing it out and leaving a little extra white space." So David went to him and said, "Pat, I know you may not like this, but it is *going* to run in the *Crimson* tomorrow." So it did—the first such notice ever. But David himself didn't uncork his sexuality until the second year of Harvard Law School, even though he had realized as a teenager, way back in Tell City, Indiana, that he was gay. "I had seen *Advise and Consent* and thought that's what happened to people—you ended up killing yourself. Being gay was just not an option for me." And Harvard at the time did nothing to change his mind.

(David went on to edit *New Times* magazine, to manage a successful entertainment-law practice, and to chair GMHC, the nation's largest AIDS services organization. He and Arthur, who writes for *The New Yorker* and elsewhere, have a town house in Manhattan, a country home, and the world's most enthusiastic golden retriever. Gene Hightower, for his part, alive and well in San Francisco, did manage to help start Harvard's first undergraduate gay organization, but recalls how difficult it was. "We had to get ten signatories to qualify," he says, "but it was very hard finding ten students to do this. They were terrified." Once the ten had in fact been found, one of the deans,

Archie Epps, was good enough to go before the board that char-
ters student groups and vouch for the fact that the requirement
had been met—he had verified the list—and asked the board
just to take his word for it rather than publicly identify the signatories. They said okay. But it was a struggle. Harvard's president at the time, Nathan Pusey, threatened to shut down the
group if it tried to incorporate, Hightower recalls; and the Cambridge post office more than once just discarded outgoing mail-
ings rather than deliver them.)

It seemed from the interviews I did for my story that *most*
gay Harvard undergraduates were, until recently, like "Bob" and
David and me. We simply repressed it or faked it or lived in terror until sometime after graduation.

"I knew I was gay but had no experiences at all at Harvard,"
recalls a hugely best-selling author a few years my senior. "I had
major crushes on some guys, but never let anyone know." Nor
did he realize at the time that at least one of the guys in his stair-
well, whom he would later meet, was gay, too. Yes, he says,
"there were some obvious theatrical gays. But they were stereo-
typical. There was no real discrimination against them. They sat
together and were the fags." (*Gay* is a word he heard just once
in college.) Unlike me, he wasn't homophobic. "I wasn't attracted to them because they were too nelly and flamboyant.
But I wasn't threatened by them, either. They were as nice as
they could be to everyone."

He dated a little at Harvard but didn't have sex with a
woman until he was twenty-five. "She seduced me. She took
my glasses off and put them in her underpants and said, 'If you
want them, get them.' " He has worn contacts ever since, he
says.

That he doesn't feel comfortable being identified by name
speaks volumes. He's independently wealthy by now, after all,
much celebrated, and acknowledges that everyone who knows
him knows—and that everyone who doesn't know him, if they

think about it, would at least suspect (handsome, never married, etc.). But, he says, there is a deep-seated shame, inculcated over a lifetime, that these relatively accepting, liberated last few years simply can't remove. You will not find him attending gay political meetings or marching in Gay Pride parades.

So, yes, we have a way to go. But not every old alum is as reticent as that hugely best-selling author.

Todd Jennings, Harvard class of 1971, amicably divorced father of three, *is* marching—behind the Harvard banner in New York's 1996 Gay Pride parade. Out from the St. Regis and into the street come a gentleman from the class of '52 and his wife. They haven't any idea what the parade is about—they're just leaving their hotel. They spot the Harvard banner and go right over to Todd.

"'Fifty-two," says Frank, the alumnus, extending his hand. "What is this?"

"The Pride march," Todd explains.

Well, Frank and his wife are as proud as anyone, and they begin marching too. "What are these other contingents?" he asks after several blocks.

"It's the *Gay* Pride march," Todd explains.

Whoosh—they're gone.

As an undergraduate, and later at Harvard Business School, Todd was active in the Owl Club. Not long ago, he went back for the Owl's hundredth anniversary. "I had been a board member, too, so I knew most of the hundred forty people who attended the dinner, and I had decided I wouldn't make an issue about my sexuality there." But two drinks into the eleven-hour evening, someone from the class of '67 said, in reference to something else, that he never imagined the Owl would have a gay member. "One of my classmates spoke up before I could. '*Todd* is gay,' he said. 'And not just that, he's an activist. And we all think that's great.' The other guy got embarrassed and moved off to the other end of the room for a while, although we started talking again later. Much of the rest of the night I spent talking about the Employment Non-Discrimination Act, the Defense of Marriage Act, and lots of gay issues. My primary memory of the evening was the near-total support and unaltered camaraderie I got from nearly everyone. One guy gave me a big kiss good-bye around two in the morning—friendships run deeper than homophobia for most people."

And now for the impossible question: If Harvard had been an open, supportive place when Todd was an undergraduate, as it more or less is today, and the country had been gay-friendly— would he have gotten married? Had kids? Been happier now or less happy?

"Your impossible question is one I've pondered a lot recently," says Jennings. "My first thought is that I had such a wonderful childhood that I've always wanted to have children myself to share those memories with—and I'm very glad that I do. Maybe, in your hypothesized world, I would have decided that godchildren and nieces and nephews could have filled that need. I hope I would not have married a woman, at least not as a closeted gay man."

When he entered Harvard, Todd didn't know he was gay. "But that may be because everyone said nirvana would come when I got to sleep with a woman," he says. "Deep down, I think I knew. I guess the answer is this: In the Harvard world you hypothesize, I would not have married a woman, but I would have had kids, and I'd have been happier not working in a homophobic environment and not having the years of worry about cheating on my wife."

Harvard Magazine, circulation 220,000, had asked me to write about all this. When I finally handed the piece in, a year late, they gave it fourteen full pages and put the first paragraph, in huge type, on the cover.

The reaction was mixed.

Samuel T. Rhodes, MBA '57, was "appalled, shocked, disgusted and saddened."

A member of the class of '52, who went on to get his Harvard Law degree in 1957, likened *Harvard* to *Hustler*—he too was "sickened"—and asked to be removed from the mailing list.

"Alumni parading their homosexuality," wrote Carl Stiefel, who had been at the Divinity School in 1937–38, "is a monstrous evil in view of the anatomical structure of male-female, clearly intended by nature and Nature's God to be heterosexual."

"Utterly disgusting" and "nauseating," wrote an architect who lives not far from me in South Florida and who got his master's degree in 1940.

Edward Sergant, class of '34, wrote a poem about a fictional gay Harvard tutor. It concluded:

[O]ne day he found to his great dismay
That he had AIDS as a result of his sin.
So one day he went out in one of his moods
With the devil in hand when no one was out,
He took out a gun
And blew his brains out!

("I never realized they hated you so much," President Clinton told a group of gay rights advocates at one point in the gays-in-the-military debacle.)

One of the strikingly hopeful things about the negative letters is that they came mostly from senior citizens.

By contrast, the debating topic at my old high school the month the *Harvard* article appeared was "Should Homosexuals Be Allowed to Adopt?" After the pros and cons were ably presented, reported the *Horace Mann Record,* a majority of the student audience sided with the pro-adoption position. Could teens be smarter about some things than venerable Harvard alumni?

A reader from Dallas, with a 1963 law school degree, wrote that he had "read the article one more time and have one more time found it disgusting. Please cancel my subscription." So disgusting he read it *twice*?

The last negative letter of note came from Dr. Charles Socarides. Socarides is father of the (now quite small) homosexuality-can-and-should-be-cured school of psychiatry—and also father of *Richard* Socarides, his only son, White House liaison to the gay community. It's hard to say which Socarides is more chagrined by the other.

Noted Socarides Senior:

> It is a matter of professional responsibility and public health to respond to Andrew Tobias's article. Mr. Tobias, emboldened by the huge success of the gay propaganda machine, has dared to come out of the closet (and bring others with him) and by his act has attempted to reduce the burden of what Joseph Conrad once termed "the cross one has to bear" since his early childhood, and beautifully described in his book *The Best Little Boy in the World*.
>
> This is understandable. And as a psychoanalytic clinician to whom homosexuals come to resolve the intrapsychic conflicts which are causative of this disorder, one can only be empathic and compassionate. What is completely misleading, however, if not outrageous, is the false assertion that homosexuality is simply an alternative lifestyle, not only to be tolerated, but cultivated as well as embraced by all—homosexuals, their parents, the Harvard community, and the public at large.
>
> Even more serious, however, Mr. Tobias, in his lengthy essay, is claiming a freedom to alter the basic design of life itself and thus to promote the most radical of all social move-

ments. Beneath his confessional lies the statement that all forms of sexual relations are equal and indistinguishable. But this freedom, I submit, is not ours to fulfill. It is a freedom that goes too far, because it undoes us all. It is a freedom that seeks to overturn not only the history of the human race, but to subvert its future as well—a freedom that dares to re-form the most basic institution of society, the nuclear family, an institution that is written in our natures, and evolved over eons.

Needless to say, I do not seek to turn straight people gay (can that be much easier than turning gay people straight?), subvert the future, or re-form the nuclear family. I myself emerged from a *wonderful* nuclear family.

Over lunch in the White House mess one day, gay son Richard Socarides was discomfited as usual when talk turned to his dad. He loves him. But he notes that his own former ten-year gay relationship compares favorably with the tenure of any of his father's four marriages.

The positive letters came from readers old *and* young. One was from a recent Harvard Law School graduate who wrote about her brother.

> My brother graduated Phi Beta Kappa with a double major in biology and chemistry from the University of Pennsylvania. He went on to graduate from the Baylor College of Medicine in the top of his class. Due to an unfortunate decision made while he was still in denial about being gay, he went to medical school on an Air Force scholarship. So, after finishing his residency in psychiatry, he spent four years not asking and not telling in the military. He was promoted to Major and received a medal of distinction. (He never bothered to pick up the medal. One of his colleagues from the Air Force presented it to my parents at his memorial service.) Less than a

year after being honorably discharged, during what should have been the happiest point in his life up to then, he drove his car to the Golden Gate Bridge on a Monday morning and jumped. June 9, 1997. I think he did it because he was gay and he couldn't deal with it. As hard as he tried to accept it in himself, he just couldn't. . . .

One wonders how much of the depression and suicide come from being gay and how much from the stigma heterosexuals *place* on being gay. My own guess is that it's almost entirely the latter.

I must tell you that for the most part, my friends and I—having come to accept ourselves—have happy, productive lives.

20

It is August 1997. My fax machine begins to whir. Out crawls *New York* magazine's cover story, TROPHY BOYS, illustrated with a shirtless guy taking sun. "They adorn the pools and the private lives of A-list gay men, parlaying muscle tone and conversation into Rolexes and Range Rovers and (even) real estate."

Well, hasn't *New York* gone beefcake, I thought as I settled in to read what turned out to be a long article playing off the murder of Gianni Versace.

And from the first sentence I realized why a friend was faxing it to me.

"It was a balmy Fourth of July," began the article, "and at the Fire Island Pines beach house of a prominent gay writer"—hah! me!—"the annual Independence Day bash was in full swing."

Were they going to tell the story of the lobsters in the hot tub with the pitchforks?

"The guest list included the A-Gays—the aristocracy of gay society [oh, please]: entertainment mogul David Geffen and super-agent Sandy Gallin, Congressman Barney Frank chatting with Clinton apparatchik Bob Hattoy"—now, *that* was odd, I thought. Barney has never been to one of the lobster parties. Like most politicians, he has to march in Independence Day parades back in his district. That's a pretty big "fact" to get wrong in the first paragraph of a cover story, I thought. It's not as though the paragraph listed fifty so-called gay aristocrats; it named five, at least one of whom had definitely not been there.

("Your writer," Barney would later write the editor, "appears to have confused a party on Fire Island with either a parade in Natick, Massachusetts, or the parade sponsored by the Cape Verdean Veterans Association in New Bedford.")

"Troughs of lobsters and corn had been carted in by caterers in crisp white aprons." You mean my pal George Wurfelman from The Fish Store? And the two high school girls he brings to help out? They're clean, certainly, but I never thought of them as caterers in crisp white aprons.

"Up on the sun deck, men in polo shirts and Bermuda shorts discussed no-load mutual funds and Janet Reno and their golf swings." And their *golf swings*? I don't *think* so. Bruce Stanwich was the only gay golfer I had ever known, and he, poor guy, had died years earlier. "But if you'd looked poolside, you'd have seen a dozen smooth young Adonises in slivers of bathing suits, lazily batting a giant beach ball across a volleyball net." Well, not exactly. If you had come a few hours earlier, you might have seen us playing water volleyball—the foreign-currency trader who stops the whole game every time it's his turn to serve as he slides under the surface and emerges to get the hair out of his eyes . . . "the tree," a Dartmouth grad who speaks fluent Russian and does high-level database programming for a small consulting firm . . . "the duke"—who is many wonderful things but by no stretch an Adonis. But you certainly would not have seen any of this by the time the party started, inasmuch as the party starts at six. By then the volleyball net is long gone, the sun is at an angle not conducive to lazy pool lolling, and those previously sliver-clad are now fully dressed, plastic cupful of beer-from-the-keg in hand.

And that was just the first paragraph.*

I wouldn't have much cared except that the story went on to give a really tacky impression of this slice of gay life overall.

"The boldfaced respectability upstairs contrasted notably with the anonymous gym rats frolicking below. . . . There was no denying the tinge of commercial enterprise in the air. The laughter of the boys, if you got close enough, had the forced cheer of actors playing to the cameras on the set of a music video. . . . If the deck below wasn't really a stage, the action taking place on it was nevertheless something of an audition. For these men, the Establishment types on the deck represented opportunity—a chance to pump their careers or, at the very least, their bank accounts."

A less sensational article might have begun with a quote from the 1953 Marilyn Monroe classic *How to Marry a Millionaire.* And the point, explicit from a different lead and editorial framing, might have been: "It's the oldest story in the world— and not just the straight world." Attractive young people *are* often sought out by wealthy or powerful older people, and vice versa. (Stop the presses!) But anonymous gym rats in the pool trying to boost their bank accounts? Nah.

For me, Fire Island is largely about sitting on the deck playing Scrabble, listening to the eternal washing of the waves.

My favorite music.

So here's my point: Forget about all these suicides and all the self-loathing. There are lots of reasons to be unhappy or self-

---

* "I must confess I have been a guest at the 'prominent gay writer's' home," Barney's letter continued, "[and] that I have even been present at the location when volleyball games were going on. But on those occasions I was a participant rather than a spectator from above, and candor compels me further to acknowledge that the bathing suit I wear on this and other occasions is composed of considerably more material than a 'sliver.' "

loathing, but being gay or lesbian is not, per se, one of them. Your gay son or daughter can grow up to have a happy, wonderful, constructive life and make you proud. To tell him or her otherwise, directly or indirectly, is to be the *cause* of unhappiness and self-loathing. It's not your "fault" your child is gay. (Nor is it his.) But it may be partly your fault your child is unhappy about it, or about himself.

On November 8, 1997, three months after the TROPHY BOYS story appeared, Charles and I got to attend a Human Rights Campaign dinner honoring Ellen DeGeneres. It was black-tie, 1,500 people, and featured as its keynote speaker the president of the United States. C-SPAN covered it live. It was the first time in American history any president had ever publicly addressed a gay and lesbian group. Slowly and deliberately he laid out our case:

> For more than two centuries now, our country has had to meet challenge after challenge after challenge. We have had to continue to lift ourselves beyond what we thought America meant. Our ideals were never meant to be frozen in stone or time. Keep in mind, when we started out with Thomas Jefferson's credo that all of us are created equal by God, what that really meant in civic political terms was that you had to be white, you had to be male, and that wasn't enough—you had to own property. Which would have left my crowd out when I was a boy.
>
> Over time, we have had to redefine the words that we started with, not because there was anything wrong with them . . . but because we were limited in our imaginations about how we could live and what we were capable of and how we should live. Indeed, the story of how we kept going higher and higher and higher to new and higher defini-

tions—and more meaningful definitions—of equality and dignity and freedom is in its essence the fundamental story of our country.

Fifty years ago, President Truman stood at a new frontier in our defining struggle on civil rights. Slavery had ended a long time before, but segregation remained. Harry Truman stood before the Lincoln Memorial and said, "It is more important today than ever to ensure that all Americans enjoy the rights [of freedom and equality]. When I say all Americans, I mean all Americans."

Well, my friends, all Americans still means all Americans. We all know that it is an ideal and not perfectly real now. We all know that some of the old kinds of discrimination we have sought to rid ourselves of by law and purge our spirits of still exist in America today. We all know that there is continuing discrimination against gays and lesbians. But we also know that if we're ever going to build one America, then *all* Americans—including you and those whom you represent—have got to be a part of it. To be sure, no president can grant rights. Our ideals and our history hold that they are inalienable, embedded in our Constitution, amplified over time by our courts and legislature. I cannot grant them—but I am bound by my oath of office and the burden of history to reaffirm them.

All America loses if we let prejudice and discrimination stifle the hopes or deny the potential of a single American. All America loses when any person is denied or forced out of a job because of sexual orientation. Being gay, the last time I thought about it, seemed to have nothing to do with the ability to read a balance book, fix a broken bone, or change a spark plug.*

---

* Applause interrupted much of the speech, but I sensed particularly large lesbian reaction to the line about the spark plug.

For generations, the American Dream has represented a fundamental compact among our people. If you take responsibility and work hard, you have the right to achieve a better life for yourself and a better future for your family. Equal opportunity for all, special privileges for none—a faith shared by Americans regardless of political views. We believe—or we all say we believe—that all citizens should have the chance to rise as far as their God-given talents will take them. What counts is energy and honesty and talent. No arbitrary distinctions should bar the way.

So when we deny opportunity because of ancestry or religion, race or gender, disability or sexual orientation, we break the compact. It is wrong. And it should be illegal. Once again I call upon Congress to honor our most cherished principles and make the Employment Non-Discrimination Act the law of the land.

I'd like to say just one more word. There are some people who aren't in this room tonight who aren't comfortable yet with you and won't be comfortable with me for being here.

On issue after issue involving gays and lesbians, survey after survey shows that the most important determinant of people's attitudes is whether they are aware—whether they knowingly have had a family or a friendship or a work relation with a gay person.

Now, I hope that we will embrace good people who are trying to overcome their fears. After all, all of us can look back in history and see what the right thing to do was. It is quite another thing to look ahead and light the way. Most people are preoccupied with the burdens of daily living. Most of us, as we grow older, become—whether we like it or not—somewhat more limited in our imaginations. So I think one of the greatest things we have to do still is just to increase the ability of Americans who do not yet know that gays and lesbians are their fellow Americans in every sense of the word to feel that way. I think it's very important.

When I say, "I believe all Americans means all Americans," I see the faces of the friends of thirty-five years. When I say, "all Americans means all Americans," I see the faces of the people who stood up when I asked the people who are part of our administration to stand tonight. When I say, "all Americans means all Americans," I see kind, unbelievably generous, giving people back in my home state who helped my family and my friends when they were in need. It is a different story when you know what you are seeing.

So I say to you tonight, should we change the law? You bet. Should we keep fighting discrimination? Absolutely. Is this Hate Crimes Conference [we are about to have] important? It is terribly important. But we have to broaden the imagination of America. We are redefining, in practical terms, the immutable ideals that have guided us from the beginning. Again I say, we have to make sure that for every single person in our country, all Americans means all Americans.

After experiencing the horrors of the Civil War and witnessing the transformation of the previous century, Walt Whitman said that our greatest strength was that we are an embracing nation. In his words, a "Union, holding all, fusing, absorbing, tolerating all." Let us move forward in the spirit of that one America. Let us realize that this is a *good* obligation that has been imposed upon our generation, and a grand opportunity once again to lift America to a higher level of unity, once again to redefine and to strengthen and to ensure one America for a new century and a new generation of our precious children.

Thank you and God bless you.

The full speech ran twenty-five minutes, interrupted by constant applause and even a well-intentioned heckler. (*"People with AIDS are dying!"* he shouted. "People with AIDS *are* dying," the president responded. "But since I've become president, we're spending ten times as much per fatality on people with AIDS as on people with breast cancer or prostate cancer. And the drugs are being approved more quickly. And a lot of people are living normal lives. We just have to keep working on it.")

For a gay man or lesbian my age, it's hard to read that speech without getting choked up. If only it could be read at least once in every eighth or ninth grader's history class.

With an eye toward those history classes, a young gay director named Jeff Dupre created a documentary called *Out of the Past.* It begins with the aforementioned Reverend Michael Wigglesworth in 1653 and traces gay and lesbian history in America up through the present—all in an hour, and with a contemporary story woven through it. The contemporary story is of a young woman named Kelli Peterson, who at the age of seventeen in 1995 started a small gay and lesbian club at her Salt Lake City high school. Two of my favorite clips in the documentary are from Bryant Gumbel and, separately, Tom Brokaw, reporting on what became a national story. You may remember it. "The city school board has voted to ban all—all—nonacademic clubs," Gumbel explained, wide-eyed, "rather than allow one—one—for gay and lesbian students." Deadpanned Brokaw: "Included in the ban will be the chess club, the ski club, and the Bible club. One student called the decision of the school board 'stupid.' "

And so it came to pass that the students—the *straight* students—boycotted East High in protest, and eventually the courts found in Kelli's favor.

You must see this documentary.* And if it strikes you as it

---

* If you missed it on PBS, send $25 to GLSEN (the Gay, Lesbian, and Straight Education Network), 121 West 27th Street #804, New York, NY 10001.

has me, you must try to get someone at your old high school to show it.

For helping to raise a portion of the money for *Out of the Past,* Jeff made me "executive producer." That was the sum total of my creative input—zero—and yet it entitled Charles and me to fly out to the Sundance Film Festival. *Out of the Past* was one of hundreds of documentaries submitted to Sundance and one of the sixteen selected to be shown.

Our quick trip got off to a rocky start as the best little boy in the world, a genius at saving money, showed up at Newark Airport with his $238 round-trip tickets—for a flight that left from Kennedy. That little mistake (which TBLBITW seems to make regularly once every twenty years) cost me $1,616, and as you can tell, I'm *still* agonizing over it. The screening that night, January 17, 1998, was fine, but it was basically ninety-five creative geniuses, many of them sallow from years in the editing room, in a depressing little hole of a theater. Had we really gotten up at four-thirty and come all the way out to Utah for *this?* But the screening at noon back in Salt Lake City the next day erased all doubts. It was in a packed 450-seat theater only three blocks from Kelli's high school.

The audience *cheered.* When Kelli and her girlfriend were asked to stand, they cheered again.

And they, not the elders of the Mormon church (fine people, but *old*), are the future.

Out of the Past won Sundance's Audience Award for Best Documentary.

And now GLSEN's eighty chapters will attempt to get it shown in tens of thousands of high school classrooms over the years to come. It will be a tough sell in many schools, but having the imprimatur of PBS and Sundance should help. Attaching a copy of President Clinton's November 8, 1997, speech couldn't hurt, either.

. . .

As you know, I am happiest with my knees up in the fourth row. But for this Salt Lake screening we decided to sit way in the back, in the last row, to be able, in effect, to watch the audience watch the film.

When it was over, Jeff Dupre (who had apprenticed with Ken Burns, which is why the style of *Out of the Past* may remind you of PBS's *The Civil War* or *The West*) rose at the front of the theater to take questions. Many were less questions than comments. One woman stood to say she had been suspended from her teaching position for using the word *homosexual*. Crying, she thanked Jeff for making this film. "Thank *you*," said Jeff, unsure of what to say. Another person asked whether the So-and-So listed among the major donors to the film was actually the same So-and-So who was the nationally known Republican whose views we all knew were so reprehensible. Jeff was even less sure how to answer *that*, so I found myself rising from the back of the theater—to Jeff's relief—and explaining that yes, this was the same guy he was thinking of but that, in the first place, he was a very *good* guy—some Republicans *are* very good guys—and one I had known for twenty-five years. We make a mistake, I suggested, if we feel automatically superior to those who, on some issues, disagree with us. We should be very grateful to this guy, I said, for his money and for having the courage to be publicly identified with the film. (That said, I don't want to make a whole big deal out of this for him. If you're really curious, just get the film and watch the credits.)

I would go further and suggest that far from not dismissing Republicans or conservatives (no small handful of whom are gay), we should not demonize even the "religious right," except perhaps for a few of its most cynically malicious leaders.

But how *do* you deal with people who have it on the highest authority—God's—that our "lifestyle" is simply unacceptable?

21

"I have caused great calamities.
I have depopulated provinces and kingdoms.
But I did it for the love of Christ and his Holy Mother."

—Queen Isabella of Spain

All this stuff about turning the other cheek and "blessed are the meek"—could Jesus actually have meant to say we should massacre each other in his name? Taunt the meek kid in the class (guess which one *he* is) and beat him up?

Here's a fun question to ask your more religious friends. It was asked in a Broadway play called *Twilight of the Golds:*

If you or your wife were just *one day pregnant* with a child you somehow knew carried the gay gene, would you have an abortion? Or would you carry the fetus to term and then despise it the rest of its life?

Any good Christian will tell you it's the sin, not the sinner, he despises. (And there may not literally be a gay gene, though clearly *something* not of my doing got my hungry yearnings reversed.) But that doesn't solve the conundrum. It merely rephrases it: Okay, so you wouldn't despise the child. But would you hope he never experienced intimacy? Hope he would trick a woman into marrying him and live a life of deceit and shame?

It's too easy, it seems to me, to say you'd do none of the

above—you'd hope for a miraculous conversion. Conversions just don't seem to work.

"I was gay from as far back as I can remember," Mitchell Adams told his church congregation a few years ago. "My way of coping was to attempt to manage a great deception; to pretend that I was just like everyone else; to act like I was having a good time, when I was in fact very uncomfortable; to fake enthusiasm, when in fact there was great fear. I was in pain and I was confused."

At Harvard, which Mitchell attended first as an undergraduate, then for his MBA, it got worse. He began a course of psychotherapy, once a week with a psychiatrist, once a week in group, without interruption for seven years. *Seven hundred sessions* all told, give or take. "The single objective of all this therapy was to change my sexual orientation. To make me straight." He even tried electric shock to discourage the wrong kind of fantasies. (If all this sounds amazing, remember that even today there are people who believe he just didn't try hard enough.)

"The stresses at work on me were very, very powerful. These are the forces which have driven some people to despair, depression, alcoholism, to suicide. Some are never relieved of this pain. But by the grace of God I was," says Adams. Gradually, he came to accept himself, then to tell others and—to his great relief—to find that they accepted him, too.

In 1970, a year after graduating from B-School, he roomed with his friend Bill Weld, though he didn't discuss his sexual orientation while they were roommates. Over time, he says, "it just became obvious, by osmosis," not least because Mitchell's partner of the last seventeen years, Kevin Smith, was until recently chief of staff for the former Massachusetts governor. (Adams serves as the Massachusetts commissioner of revenue.)

Adams and Smith live in Dedham. Kevin's mother lives with them. His father lived with them also until he died. Mitchell is the godfather of three. "Our house," he told the congregation at St. Paul's, "is full of kids, infants, and golden retrievers."

Michael Wigglesworth would have been appalled—but that was 1653. "One of the greatest life mysteries for me," Adams says, "is, Why me? Why am I so fortunate when so many others are so much less fortunate than I? There isn't anything I want out of life that I haven't gotten already, except to become myself a better person, a more Christian person."

Would it have been better to abort Mitchell Adams? Condemn him to a life alone? Why do some people feel so threatened by a family like the one Adams and Smith have formed? With which Christian would Jesus have been more comfortable—Queen Isabella or Massachusetts commissioner of revenue Mitchell Adams?

Though I'm not religious, I do have my heroes. Martin Luther King, Jr., is one. Jesus Christ is an even bigger one, though I don't believe he walked on water.* From what I've read, I just know he would have favored honesty and love over deception, loneliness, and misery.

I understand that the reason he himself did not marry and was surrounded by all-male disciples was that he was divine, preoccupied with matters that transcended mortal flesh. I can buy that, although it's not so hard for me to imagine that one of the things that may have set him apart and driven him into the wilderness was the same thing that led many another talented youngster to retreat into a world of his own.

Clearly—and meaning no disrespect—Jesus, this product of a doting mother and a distant father, was the best little boy in *the history of* the world. Even those who don't believe he was the son of God are the better off for his teachings, I among them.

---

* Or that God parted the Red Sea for Moses.

So isn't there some sort of face-saving compromise here? One that would allow even the most devoutly religious Christians and Jews (and others) to be true to their faith but also allow gay people to live happy, loving, honest lives?

I say again: Why can't we just all agree that intimate relations between two people of the same sex *are* unnatural—even an abomination before God—*if they're straight*—while if they're among God's gay children, it's the most natural thing in the world.

It's that simple, really.

I've had two prime chances to try my pitch. Once was to a Mormon financial writer and his wife, whom I actually flew out to Utah to visit. He may have assumed I was coming to discuss penny stocks, but after getting the tour of his home and the rundown on his latest ventures, I told him I had come because of the things he'd been writing in his newsletter about gays and lesbians. (His is a far-ranging financial newsletter.) He and his wife couldn't have been more friendly. They readily admitted that they had never actually talked with an openly gay man before, in all their sixty-odd years. They seemed interested in what I had to say. They argued that I should find conversion through Christ; I explained that it just didn't work that way. He revealed that he had gone through a period of addiction to prostitutes— I must say I was surprised to hear this—and that when he confessed this to the elders of the church, expecting to be expelled for his adultery, they counseled him to *get a grip* through Christ, which he did. The Lord showed him the way, and he has been faithful ever since. I was happy for him, but tried to point out that overcoming the impulse to cheat on your wife was at least one order of magnitude less impressive than ridding oneself of lust altogether, let alone somehow switching it from lust for women to lust for men (or, in my case, vice versa).

Why not just let straight people be straight, gay people be

gay, and judge people by the quality of their civic contribution rather than by their sexual orientation?

I felt all but sure I had made my case until the next issue of the newsletter arrived. In it, he described my visit (he called me Joe) and reassured his readers that while he felt sorry for me, he could never condone such a terrible sin. And the S&P 500 looked as if it might soon be breaking out to the upside.

I did much better with a hugely successful mutual-fund manager who had several years earlier elected Jesus Christ chairman of his board. He and his wife are nice, nice people, and he promised he would do what he could to moderate some of the more hateful rhetoric of several of the people whose photos he had up on his wall (Oliver North, Ralph Reed—that crowd).

It is important for every homosexual to know his Bible.

"Jesus preached and talked against a whole gamut of sins," former president Jimmy Carter, a good born-again Christian, told the *San Francisco Chronicle* on January 10, 1997. "He never mentioned homosexuality at all."

So where do all the far-righteous Christians get their scriptural ammunition?

The most damning biblical passage I know of is in Leviticus, which basically says that men who lie down with men will be put to death. (Women appear to be exempt.) But the very same Scripture goes on to say that adulterers and adulteresses "shall also surely be put to death." People who touch the skin of a pig—which is to say any American who ever played football—and people who wear clothes made from two different fabrics—which is to say cotton/Dacron sweat socks—are also in hot water with the Lord.* Shave your beard? Same deal.

---

* Charles tells me that at work they refer to wool-linen blends as the "abomination fabric."

I don't mean to trivialize Scripture, but this is what it says. So if it clearly does not apply, a few thousand years later, to sweat socks or the NFL or men who shave, maybe there's a more modern way to look at the men-lying-with-men part of it, too. Remember: When the Old Testament was written, the Jews were struggling for survival and procreation. Infant mortality was terribly high; life expectancy, low. Having seen world population swell from 2.5 billion when I was born to 6 billion today, I hardly think this remains an issue. And pork won't kill you, either.

Christians will tell you that the New Covenant specifically lifted those proscriptions. But as a lawyer named John Tally asked in the *San Francisco Examiner* a couple of years ago, what of the New Testament notion that anyone who remarries after divorce commits adultery (Mark 10:11)? When did the Reverend Jerry Falwell ever condemn Ronald and Nancy Reagan for this great sin? What of the New Testament regulation that women should remain silent, not teach, and have no authority over men (1 Timothy 2:11)? And doesn't "slaves, obey thy masters" (Colossians 3:22)—"with fear and trembling," no less (Ephesians 6:5)—pretty well convey divine blessing on the institution of slavery? There is no corresponding exhortation I know of in either the Old or the New Testament to "masters, free thy slaves."

Shouldn't the Bible be interpreted based on its underlying lessons of love and kindness and honesty rather than millennia-old specifics?

Ask your religious friends, as John Tally suggested: "When Deuteronomy [23:21] prescribes death for nonvirgin brides shortly before it claims no homosexual shall be a son of Israel, do you agree with both those moral laws?"

Though Jesus never mentioned us in his teachings, could he really have wanted his followers to treat gays and lesbians with anything other than love and respect? Would he have condemned an employer for offering medical care to the ailing same-sex partners of its employees? Can even the most minimally thoughtful fundamentalist really imagine that Jesus would have called on his followers to boycott Disney, as some Southern Baptists did, for extending this helping hand to the sick?

Not the Jesus I've long admired.

The problem, of course, is that many fundamentalists are *not* thoughtful. They just follow the leader. It is their leaders, some of them cynically using us to increase the financial returns of their direct-mail appeals, who should be stoned in the public square, because they know better.

22

So what, finally, is the homosexual lifestyle?

If it were strictly a matter of economics, it would be socially desirable if more men and women were gay. A single gay man earning $35,000 a year pays more in income taxes than a family of four with the same income (they have three additional exemptions) yet gets only about one fourth as much garbage hauled away, takes up only one fourth as many seats on the taxpayer-subsidized subway, and pays to educate that family's children but, typically, none of his own.

If he has adopted children, he serves the social interest a different way. Kids in orphanages and institutions cost society a lot to care for, and few get the degree of love and nurturing they would in a real home. I happen to agree that a traditional mom-pop-and-a-collie home is ideal—it worked for me—but the ideal is frequently not attainable. Who is to say that the millions of children growing up fatherless are better off than they would be with *two* fathers? Or that the millions who shuttle back and forth between a divorced mom and dad are better off than they would be in a home with two loving parents of the same sex?

Each case is different. Not all gays and lesbians would make suitable adoptive parents. But that's true of heterosexuals as well.

Of course, whatever economic advantages there are to being gay are really just the advantages of being childless. But childless heterosexuals can't be fired from their jobs or denied a marriage license simply for being childless, so there is less reason to write about the economic advantages of that condition.

Yes, in the current era, the gay male is likely to impose higher medical costs on society because of AIDS. But in the first place, one likes to think that in the thousands of years to come—as in the thousands of years past—the few awful decades of this plague will be regarded as a onetime "extraordinary item," as the corporate accountants would say, rather than a routine operating expense.

The economic flip side of AIDS, in any event, is that lesbians—about the least likely group on the planet to contract it—should be exalted. And that those gay men who do contract AIDS, while they impose a medical cost on society, relieve society of elder-care costs. They pay in to Social Security but then, quite often, don't live to collect it.

Obviously, human rights should not be determined economically. But it's worth noting that on balance, gays and lesbians shoulder at least their fair share of the defense budget, the education bill, and all the rest.

You could argue that, well, no, we don't, because by and large, we don't pay the cost of raising the next generation. But the solution I'd suggest is not to stigmatize the childless (or, as it has worked out in practice, only the gay childless) but to allow gays to marry and adopt.

These days, some openly gay and lesbian couples are going a step further. Through a variety of arrangements that should make family law a challenging field, they are having children of their own.

Two gay lawyers I know have a daughter with two lesbian lawyers *they* know. She's eight now, raised primarily by the moms. Can having four loving parents be all that bad? Among them, they have seventy-six years of education and a combined disposable income greater than Kentucky's. No guarantee of happiness, of course, but perhaps a leg up.

Another couple I know, Joey and Laurent, have two daughters. In their case . . . well, let me back up, because it's a nice story. I met Joe Cherner in 1981, shortly before he graduated from Columbia Business School and went to work for Kidder Peabody trading treasury securities. By 1988 he would be named Kidder's "Man of the Year"—he made them a *lot* of money—and by 1990 he would take a year off from his senior vice presidency to battle the tobacco companies. That year has now stretched to eight. *Joe Cherner became the tobacco industry's worst nightmare.* He succeeded almost single-handedly in having all tobacco advertising removed from New York City buses and subways, having the Marlboro Man removed from Shea Stadium, having cigarette vending machines banned from New York, having New York's restaurants go smoke-free—and much more. Those VIRGINIA SLIME and COME TO CANCER COUNTRY posters you may have seen atop New York City taxicabs? Joe's.

So one day in the summer of 1984, while still very much in the trenches at Kidder Peabody, he was flying back from Paris with his boss and had somehow been assigned to a seat in the smoking section. This would not do. Yet there were no empty seats. Well, one thing led to another and a terrific young Air France flight attendant managed to work it out. Joe, who is fluent in French, spent much of the flight conversing with that flight attendant.

When they landed at Kennedy, Joe asked his boss if it would be all right to give the flight attendant a lift into the city. Joe and Laurent have been together, through thick and thin, from that day on. Their daughters, courtesy of a surrogate mom who lives three thousand miles away but with whom they remain friendly, are beautiful, happy, computer literate, and trilingual.* There is no live-in help; Joey and Laurent are very much hands-on parents. Two doting grandmothers assist from time to time when they pass through New York, and there's the baby-sitter. Joey says he doesn't know whose sperm produced which child—they combined teams in a turkey baster and let the best swimmer win. In any event, the girls, now seven and five, are doing beautifully.

Charles and I have thought about doing something like this, or adopting. He'd make a great dad. Our kids would grow up with *rules*. I'm not sure I'd make such a good dad. I don't know where I'd find the time. And I'd be terrified of having a child I didn't . . . well, like. (I know: You *always* love them when they're yours.) If we could arrange to skip the first three years, I'd be a lot more interested.

I did once get as far as a sperm bank.

It was before I knew Charles. A woman I knew and loved, who was more keen on children than on husbands, asked me if I wouldn't mind supplying some DNA and perhaps some orthodontia and tuition as needed. She'd do most of the hard stuff. I thought this was probably a swell idea; in any event, going to the bank was just the first step, not an irrevocable decision.

And so it was that I found myself in the middle of the day going up to an office in the Empire State Building to . . . well, you know. I've always actually quite enjoyed you-knowing ever since, as related in the last book, I accidentally learned how to do it sophomore year in college.

---

* Joey and Laurent speak English and French interchangeably; the baby-sitter speaks only Spanish. And not wanting their daughters to grow up watching TV, the dads decided to do without it. From birth, the only TV the girls saw were Disney tapes—in Spanish. They have about a hundred of them. For a while, Joey says, the girls didn't realize that the TV could speak anything *but* Spanish.

But doing it on command? In a faux-leather chair under fluorescent light?

"You might want a couple of these," said the young para-banker as he handed me copies of *Playboy* along with my plastic cup and cubicle key.

Then, remembering I had told him I was gay—"Low sperm count?" . . . "No, gay" is my vague recollection of how the conversation went—he laughed a little self-consciously as I arched my eyebrow and took just the cup and the key.

Now, they probably don't care a hoot how long it takes you as long as you finish by closing time and they get their $400 plus semiannual maintenance fees. It's not as if there was a line of people waiting for my cramped, windowless, music-less, fluorescent-lit cubicle. Still, I felt the pressure to perform—and that wasn't helping. I could hear people walking past from time to time, a couple of feet away on the other side of the door, the quiet sounds of the office—the phone, the copier, the door chime.

It was not erotic.

The cubicle was not quite spacious enough to lie full out on the floor. (And wasn't that a charming prospect, anyway? Who knows the last time it had been cleaned?) So it was the faux-leather club chair or nothing.

But that didn't work. No, success was finally achieved lying on my back, knees bent so I'd fit, light switched off, concentrating on one of those early fantasies sure to enliven even the dreariest party—and trying to be completely silent, lest a passerby hear my foot shoot out against the cheap hollow door—*thwhack*—and know I was abusing myself. Which, though it was precisely what I was supposed to be doing, seemed illicit and dirty all the same. (I was supposed to be a *straight* guy doing it.)

No shower? I thought as I collected myself and my essential milliliters. *Not even a sink in this awful cubicle?*

I handed in my cup and key and was later told, by phone, that I had done a good job.

For reasons involving the X chromosomes rather than the Y, our equation did not ultimately compute. But especially now that I'm at no risk of actually being responsible for the child, I can tell you that she or he would have been one cute, smart kid. Maybe even musical. (The André Previn gene clearly skipped *me,* but could have resurfaced in vitro.) Straight? Gay? I'd have mildly preferred straight, just as I'd have mildly preferred a boy. But either would have been fine. Anything but Republican.

Okay, Republican is fine, too. Obviously. But so is gay. I've already explained why the religious objections seem bogus to me and why, economically, gay is good—what other issues are there?

Procreation

Many people—well, Jack Kemp, for one—think concerns about overpopulation are silly. Malthus redux. And they may be right. You can make a pretty persuasive case on both sides. But compare the alternatives:

If it proves a false alarm, where's the harm? Too *few* people? If *under*population ever emerged as a threat, we could resolve it in virtually a single night of global merrymaking. (I exaggerate, but you get the point.)

But what if the concerns prove valid? What if overpopulation cuts into our species's quality of life—perhaps even throws out of kilter the billion-years-in-the-making delicate ecological balance that has so nicely sustained human life? What would be the solution then? A single night of world slaughter? How would you ever get the population back down from 10 billion fifty years from now to, say, today's 6 billion or 1948's 2.5 billion?

Not to be concerned with population is to take a huge,

species-threatening, and *unnecessary* gamble. It would be beyond awful ever to get to the point in the world where we actually felt involuntary population limitations, of the type imposed in China, were the lesser of two evils. It's precisely to avoid this, among other things, that support for population education and efforts to curb unwanted pregnancies are, in my view, important.*

The notion that "homosexuality threatens the human race" is just preposterous. If anything, those who would like more than two kids should be delighted that some of us have none.

Recruitment

"Homosexuals can't reproduce so they *have* to recruit." This is equally preposterous. Who recruited *me*? Surely not that fellow at the Museum of Natural History who, when I was sixteen, as recounted in the last book, touched me *down there* and offered me a blow job. Who recruited Mitch Adams, who spent seven hundred hours in therapy trying not to be gay? Quite the contrary: If one's sexual orientation were based on recruitment (as if you were deciding between the army and the navy), then surely we would all be straight. What kid grows up not knowing that in straight sex lies happiness?

Could the idea really be that most men secretly are not turned on to women's breasts after all? That what most men really desperately want—but, unlike me, have been too disciplined to succumb to—is to wrestle around with *other* guys?

I feel certain that an awful lot of adolescent boys really *are* heterosexual, really *will* want to have sex with girls no matter how many gay sitcom subplots they see, no matter how many of their high school teachers are gay.

If morality and fidelity and family are important to a healthy society—and they are—then the best way to encourage them

---

* If you have access to the Internet, see www.zpg.org for more on this, or to join.

among gays and lesbians is to encourage, rather than prohibit, marriage (and adoption).

It is completely inappropriate to offer a sixteen-year-old a blow job—whether you're a lonely guy in a museum or a female hooker ("Hey, sweet thing"). But it is not a life-changing, let alone a sexual-orientation-changing, event. In my own case, not knowing exactly what a blow job was, it simply drove me deeper into my terror. (When I finally did find out, I couldn't believe it—why would anyone want to do *that*? In this reaction, I readily admit to being within a minority of a minority. To each his own.)

Child Molestation

This is a terrible thing. The gay men and lesbians who molest children should be condemned. But it's worth noting that most child molesters—even the men who rape little boys, to say nothing of those who rape little girls—are *straight*.

If I had a child, I wouldn't object to her being taught by a heterosexual. But like any good parent, I'd keep my eyes open.

The Military

The Israelis have allowed gays in their military for decades and yet are considered to have one of the world's best armies. Conservative Barry Goldwater said it best in June 1993: "You don't have to be straight to fight and die for your country. You just need to shoot straight."

Promiscuity

Listen: Men are pigs. (I actually own a letter from Albert Einstein to a female colleague who was devastated by her husband's infidelities. What should she do, Herr Professor? And, paraphrasing loosely, that's what he says: It's unfortunate, but men are pigs. If in most respects he's a good husband, you may just have to live with it.) So the first dynamic here is that where no female is involved—women are not pigs—it may be in the nature of things for there to be more promiscuity. Beyond that, of course, neither party has to worry about pregnancy. (AIDS, though it has surely had a mitigating effect, is a Johnny-come-lately to the gay culture.) And beyond *that,* society has long told gay men they are engaging in illicit behavior and has held out no role models for, or social approbation of, committed gay relationships. So, heck—if you're gonna be illicit, you may as well enjoy it. Add to that the fact that sex can become addictive, and the lack of shared children to be concerned with . . . and you have a prescription for promiscuity.

Nor is promiscuity the end of the world, even the moral world. There is the health issue—the promiscuous must practice safe sex—but surely syphilis was an issue in Don Juan's day, and yet somehow we do not equate Don Juan with the devil (the devil-may-care, perhaps, but not the devil).

Promiscuity is not a "gay" thing. If sex before marriage is a problem, or multiple sex partners before marriage is a problem, it is surely a problem irrespective of sexual orientation.

My own experience has been one of "serial monogamy," with very occasional lapses. Assuming that Dr. Socarides, the self-avowed protector of the human species, has been monogamous in each of his four marriages and each of the additional nonmarital relationships he has had, his record on promiscuity may be about the same as mine.

The problems with promiscuity are threefold. First: health. Second: infidelity—but only when you're in a relationship (you're not cheating on anyone when you're single). Third: what might be called the desensitizing effect. If a person does somehow manage to remain chaste until he or she meets that perfect person, sex becomes associated only with that person and takes on an almost sacred meaning. (Not for nothing was virginity such a big deal.) Once sex becomes no more dramatic than scratching an itch in a dark room, it's harder—not impossible, I should think, but harder—to form a really strong, mutually supportive relationship. And while that may not be much of a concern to a gym-buffed guy in his twenties or thirties, for the *latter* half of a full, happy life—the second forty or fifty years—it's the relationship, not the sex, that most matters.

That said, it seems to me that where cheating and dishonesty are not involved, and where people play safe, this is no one's business but their own. There is no single route to personal happiness—and no automatic higher moral ground for those who remain in miserable relationships rather than divorce and remarry.

Love

Now, *there's* a tricky subject. It sort of just grabs you and . . . good luck! I certainly don't consider myself wise about this. And logic—my strong suit—may be just the wrong tool for trying to understand it. What's logical about love? I do think that among gays more than straights there may be the phenomenon of the lover and the lovee; this notion that one party is more smitten than the other. At its extreme, it's Sal Mineo worshiping James Dean (you haven't seen *Rebel Without a Cause?*). But you have that in straight relationships, too. All I can tell you is that we gay people are just as sappy and romantic, and can be just as fiercely loyal and deeply committed, as our straight brothers and sisters. Love is love.

Gay Marriage

My first thought, when I heard someone propose it, was: *Are you nuts?* Have you no marketing savvy *at all?* Language and imagery are so important—why not just call it something else? Then you can get all the equal rights and protections with just 10 percent of the fight.

But there are problems with this, including the problem that tens of thousands, if not millions, of local laws and private contracts use the term *marriage*. So unless you're going to amend thousands or millions of laws and contracts, it doesn't work that well to find another word. And what would that word be? We're getting *committed*? Sounds like the loony bin. We've become partners? Sounds like a law firm.

Andrew Sullivan argues all this far better than I could.

Frankly, marriage makes me nervous. Would Charles and I have to negotiate a prenup? I can just see *that*. I don't want to be together because I am legally bound to be but because I *want* to be.

Still, why are some straight people so threatened by this concept? Why would those who deplore promiscuity not want to extend to gays and lesbians the very institution that does more to discourage promiscuity than any other?

"What we are dealing with here is the defining civil rights issue of this decade," Representative Ed Fallon told his colleagues on the floor of the Iowa House of Representatives in February 1996. Iowa was debating a "defense of marriage" act much like the one Congress passed (and the president reluctantly signed into law) later that year.* "There isn't a limited amount of love in Iowa," Fallon, a heterosexual, argued. "It isn't a nonrenewable resource. If Amy and Barbara or Mike and Steve love each other, it doesn't mean that John and Mary can't. To suggest that homosexual couples in any way, shape, or form threaten to undermine the stability of heterosexual unions is patently absurd."

---

* The Republicans had timed DOMA as a wedge issue for the 1996 election. Either the president would veto it, threatening his reelection, or sign it, hurting his support among gays and lesbians. Presumably, he felt it would be ruled unconstitutional and was not worth risking reelection over.

. . .

"What does it mean when someone tells me they don't condone my lifestyle?" Colonel Margarethe Cammermeyer has
asked. "Does it mean they don't approve of my having a job and
paying taxes? Does it mean they don't approve of my going to
church? Does it mean they don't approve of my having four
sons of whom I am very proud? Or does it really mean that, assuming I am not celibate, they do not approve of what I may or
may not do in my own bedroom?"

Finally, a few lifestyle topics separate from the moral debate but
perhaps worth a word or two:

The Gym

It may be a sexual obsession, but it's a heck of a lot healthier
than The Bar or The Baths that it's partly replaced. My own
routine for the last twenty-five years has involved the floor and
a towel. Step one: Lay towel on floor. Step two: Do a couple
million scrunches (which would be sit-ups except you only
come up a quarter of the way). Step three: Do twenty or thirty
or forty push-ups (but good ones). Elapsed time: five minutes.
Annual membership dues: zero. Travel time and likelihood of
catching the flu in the steam room or from leaving the gym with
wet hair: also zero. This is very efficient and works fine. For the
aerobic exercise needed to round out the regimen, one can buy
a StairMaster, but if one lives in anything but a ranch house, one
can use actual *stairs.* I don't do this yet because I am terribly lazy,
but whenever I check into a hotel I fully intend to spend twenty
minutes walking up and down the back stairs.

This simple regimen, combined with a sensible diet, guar-
antees you a good body. The purpose of the *gym,* needless to say,
is simply to show it off. Well, and to socialize. And to acquire the
inspiration to do all this boring stuff in the first place. If Charles
ever leaves me, I think my first step would be to join a gym.

The Jinx

Speaking of which, let's be frank. There is always the possibility Charles *will* leave me, or that prenup negotiations would erupt into civil war. I raise this issue to try to foil the jinx—namely, the tendency of people and things to self-destruct after being written about. No sooner do Rod Jackson and Bob Paris publish a book about their relationship than—oops, they split up. No sooner does famed investor Victor Neiderhoffer publish *The Education of a Speculator* than his $135 million hedge fund gets entirely wiped out. I don't want to jinx Charles's and my partnership with this book, so I hereby acknowledge the problem, hoping that will keep it at bay. (I am also wearing a garlic clove and typing this paragraph with my fingers crossed, which is easier than it sounds when one types, as I do, with just two fingers.)

Cuddling

For those younger readers hoping to form lasting relationships, I have just two thoughts, one huge, one tiny. The huge thought, obviously not original with me or needing much elaboration, is: Work at it. If one is entirely self-centered and uncompromising, one is headed for trouble when one is no longer twenty-six. But take heart: I am *almost* entirely self-centered (and Charles is not exactly Mother Teresa), yet we have done pretty well. The tiny thought is that it's actually okay if you're someone who doesn't like to cuddle all night. Yes, you will have to find someone who feels the same way, *but you needn't feel guilty about this,* as I did for about a decade. My liberation on this score came one day in a doctor's waiting room, reading a newspaper that carried Dear Abby. And there, as if she were writing to *me,* was an answer to someone (Sleepless in Seattle?) who felt awful that he didn't like holding his girlfriend all night as she wanted him to, and what should he do about it? Dear Abby replied that he shouldn't do *anything* about it—that some study she cited showed that 37 percent of all human beings don't like to touch once they actually roll over and go to sleep. A minority, I recognized, but such a large one as virtually to defy marginalization. Well, I saw that statistic and realized there would be hope for me after all. My God—37 percent is almost a majority!

The End of History

Not that it's likely to happen anytime soon—or happen entirely *any*time—but what if we actually succeeded? What if almost everyone came to accept gay people just so long as, like straight people, they didn't impose their desires on the unwilling (or underage)? Oppression, evil though it is, does nonetheless confer upon the oppressed a sense of purpose, a sense of community, and a sense of righteousness. The struggle gives life *meaning*. Without it, other challenges will surface to inspire our best instincts—this is no argument for continued oppression. But let's face it: The experience of growing up a secret agent, special, enrolled in a secret society—and the experience of overcoming all that terror and confusion—is, for many of us, at the core of our identity and our community.

The Pill

In the last book I asked whether, if there were some miraculous pill that could switch one's sexual orientation, I would take it—and the answer was no. That would make me an entirely different person and would be, thus, like killing myself. Twenty-five years later I feel exactly the same way. A pill to make me a little taller or younger I would take. A pill to grow more hair on my head or brain cells *in* my head—especially read-faster cells or remember-more cells—I would take. A pill that would let me wake fresh and clear after just six hours instead of eight I would kill for. But a pill to make me straight? No thanks.

23

Charles and I turned ninety. I don't look fifty! He doesn't look forty! I know this shouldn't matter to us! It does!

Knowing Charles, it was not a surprise to me that there would be a surprise party. By the time it rolled around, I even knew the time and the place—Saturday night at the Sony store.

But what a party! I had rehearsed my line: "Surprised? Surprised is not the word!!!" Yet no such legal niceties were needed, as my jaw dropped lower and lower. (Again, the three chins.) There was Matt from *San Francisco*! There were Sal and Larry and Bryan from *Miami*! There was my old soccer coach from Horace Mann! There was Tom Moore from L.A.! (There was my cousin-in-law having a heart attack in the back, and Charles's brother's boyfriend, Dr. Matt Caleb, saving his life.) There were Peter and Ann up from Washington! There were, I calculated, about 180 people for what wound up being a 120-minute party, giving me approximately forty seconds with each. People had given up their weekends in the country or flown across the country and I got to spend forty seconds with them.

If only it could have been a three-day convention instead of a late-evening surprise party.

This being the Sony store, there were TVs playing everywhere, each with one of my favorite movies.

There was food.

There was a cloud bank of silver balloons.

There was a jazz band Charles had discovered playing in Central Park.

"Have you seen the invitation?" someone asked me in the middle of all the excitement—and in a way that suggested there was something remarkable about it. "No!" (That's right! There must have been an invitation.)

She handed me an envelope, and by the time I had gotten the card just halfway out, I was convulsed. SUPRISE, it read in huge block letters.

One of the small benefits of being the world's slowest reader—I still basically read with my lips—is that I am one of the world's most natural proofreaders. Apparently, this thing had passed Charles's approval, several of his siblings, and the printer without anyone noticing that—SUPRISE!—it was misspelled.

So for Charles's fortieth a couple of months later, we printed up virtually identical invitations, only with the word SURRPRISE!

In my mind, they were one big party separated by a ten-week intermission. Sony was perfect for me, because I love gadgets. We held Charles's at a flower store . . . we went into Central Park and engaged the same terrific jazz band. It was all very symmetrical.

His cake for me had been this extraordinary replica of a bookshelf with my books. The one his siblings and I got for him came from the same oven, but with a representation of one of his dresses that had been in *Vogue*.*

---

* Gone was the Erotic Baker; now we were dealing with the Expensive Baker.

I did indulge my weakness for buying in bulk. In case anyone was hungry, we had one of those six-foot hero sandwiches (with a sign over it: CHARLES IS OUR HERO). In case anyone was dirty, we had 120 "soaps-on-a-rope" with Charles, age fourteen or so, pictured on the front. All the guests now have them hanging from their shower heads at home. In case anyone needed to write a note, we had 120 pens with Charles's initials—click them and they played "Happy Birthday"—and 120 five-hundred-sheet memo cubes. These had a color photo of Charles in front of the Eiffel Tower on two sides (I took the photo!), a little poem on the third side ("At one he bawled, at two he crawled, at three he scrawled—the rest is FASHION HISTORY"), and a list of "Charleses in Charge" on the fourth side (Charles the Great, Charles de Gaulle, Charles Revson, Charles Nolan). In case anyone wanted to look really, really stupid, we had 120 propeller beanies with pins that read: LOOK WHO's 40!

We were ninety. Kind of fun.

Sandwiched between our two birthday parties were the 1997 Felipa Awards, an annual presentation by IGLHRC (rhymes with "gigglejerk"), the group I had gone over to Russia with. Felipa de Souza lived in the town of Salvador, Brazil, during the Inquisition. In 1592, she was run out of town for being, in the words of emcee Kate Clinton, a "mmm-mmm." (There was no word for lesbian back then.) When she left, quite a few of the wives in town sorely missed her—Kate's drift seemed to be that Felipa was not the only mmm-mmm in Salvador at the time.

The event was being held in New York, and I had been assigned the task of introducing two of the year's three nominees. (For the third, a magnificently eloquent woman from Namibia, we had had the privilege of providing housing.) One, a young man from Albania, had actually managed to get the Albanian parliament to decriminalize homosexuality. Yes, he lost his job and basically had to flee the country as a result, but even so, he had had the courage to do this. (He worked as a waiter in one of the elite dining halls for the lawmakers. They knew and liked him—and it's hard to hate someone you know and like. He persuaded a few of them that gays should not be imprisoned merely for being themselves.) The other, a Turkish woman named Demet Demir, had been born a man. She was at least six feet tall, in a tight-fitting red gown. And she made me nervous.

I don't think I had ever before met or talked to a transsexual. So for me this was not unlike a straight person talking with a gay person for the first time. She just seemed so . . . different. And the notion of—well, for one thing, don't you have to have things *cut off*? I didn't ask! Don't tell!

In other words, in my gut if not my head, I was probably as uncomfortable with this person, or nearly so, as would be your average conservative from Kansas. Not least because the profession listed in her bio was "sex worker." (This, someone clued me in, meant prostitute.)

So TBLBITW, who'd tried very hard to be just like all the other guys, and who had a little difficulty (even though he knew he shouldn't) even with the profession *hairdresser,* was now at the lectern introducing to the assembled a transsexual prostitute.

And my point is this: Even in Turkish, through a translator, this woman, Demet Demir, projected more nobility and courage than all the Turkish police who had ever beaten or imprisoned her, who had ever murdered half her transsexual coworkers. They are prostitutes, Demet explained, because in Turkey this is the only "job" open to transsexuals. And then they are arrested and beaten and sometimes killed for it.

Is it odd to be transsexual? Surely. Is it odd to be an elephant man or to be born like the Daniel Day-Lewis character in *My Left Foot*? Absolutely. But when we open our ears and our minds to these stories, our instinctive discomfort is often replaced with empathy. In my case, with Demet, discomfort was displaced by admiration.

. . .

Time doesn't heal *everything*. It certainly doesn't bring people back to life. The AIDS crisis is not remotely over. But a lot of my friends who were going to die have died, and a lot of others—thanks to protease inhibitors and expected future advances that many in the gay community have helped finance—seem to be doing amazingly well. One of my Valmare housemates has been HIV-positive for fifteen years, yet his viral load is now undetectable. After having retired to enjoy what little was left of his life, he's *un*retiring.

It seems a long, long time since the AIDS Project Los Angeles benefit that, above the big-name performers on stage, featured a constant, silent roll call of names projected onto a screen in the rafters. One after another. Three seconds per name. With no explanation, except that it quickly became clear that these were the names of people audience members had lost. Bruce Weintraub . . . Joe Peckerman . . . Greg Bauer . . . Rick Froeschl . . . Jack Fitzsimmons . . . Paul Jabara . . . Tom Johnston . . . Tom Fortuin . . . Gary Kalkin . . . Perry Ellis . . . Rock Hudson . . . Jerry Pfeiffer . . . Roger LeClaire . . . Ron Lohse . . . Tom Lowe . . . Garry Hammond . . . Luis San Jurjo . . . Freddy Souza . . . Jimmy Kirkwood . . . Michael Bennett . . . Michael Richardson . . . Jason Richardson . . . Jeff Arnson . . . David Peterson . . . David Oliver . . . Doug Reynolds . . . Doug Watt . . . Greg Roehrs . . . Peter Scott . . . Lee Wright . . . Kip Trafton . . . Clarke Taylor . . . John Cacciatore . . . Mark Cordray . . . Mark Diamond . . . John Curry . . . Josh Lukens . . . Bill Miller . . . Deyen Popovic . . . Paul Popham . . . Chris Hill . . . Richie Hill . . . Ira Barmak. . . .

I was mesmerized by this list. And when Scot's name flashed on the screen, time seemed to stop. And . . . well . . . it *did* stop. Scot's name just stayed up there on the screen. And stayed. And stayed. For two or three *minutes*. The entertainment continued onstage; but for those of us who had noticed, it was like something out of *The Twilight Zone*. I flashed back to meeting Scot and to pignapping him . . . to the weekend I'd been stuck in town working but flew out to the beach and surprised him . . . to the scene of this poor, sweet kid with a tube down his throat and his little hands strapped down to keep him from ripping it out, attached to the respirator, not wanting to leave . . . and *still* his name was up there.

It was only a glitch in the computer program—the same thing happened the two other times these thousand-plus names cycled around. But wouldn't Scot have been embarrassed—and yet amused, and perhaps even a little triumphant?

In the fall of 1997, the president nominated James Hormel—heir to the Spam fortune—to be United States ambassador to the Godforsaken Principalité of Luxembourg. Jim is one of San Francisco's best-known philanthropists, on the board of both the symphony and the chamber of commerce. Gentle, thoughtful, modest. But faced with the prospect of *a gay man* representing our nation in Luxembourg—whose strategic and economic importance it is hard to underemphasize—the forces of righteousness sprang into action. For one thing, they discovered that Jim had underwritten the gay and lesbian center of the San Francisco Public Library . . . and that *in* that center were all manner of ghastly books, ranging from *Hard to Imagine: Gay Male Eroticism in Photography and Film from Their Beginnings to Stonewall* (Thomas Waugh; 1996) to *Good Vibrations: The Complete Guide to Vibrators* (Joani Blank; 1982).

Hormel supporters note that these same books are in the Library of Congress—as is *Susie Sexpert's Lesbian Sex World*. They wonder whether the conservative congressmen who voted to approve the appropriation for the Library of Congress are also unfit to serve.

Granted, it's not quite the same thing. Neither the congressmen nor Jim selected the specific books; but a bookplate with Jim's name does appear in each of the books in San Francisco because of his financial support. And unlike the conservative congressmen, he might actually feel it's okay to allow free expression of this type. *What might this do to our relations with Luxembourg?*

At this writing, his nomination has been floundering endlessly.

And let's take one more minute on this, shall we? San Francisco and Manhattan have long been the two gayest, most lesbian places on earth. More than enough time for our moral decay to have destroyed neighborhoods, blighted economies, and sent tourists fleeing. And yet—what's that?—San Francisco and Manhattan would actually appear to be among the world's most successful communities, economically and culturally and in their worldwide allure. It's Oklahoma and Arkansas, the home states of the senators leading the opposition, that have not yet attained world-class status.

Around the same time Jim was nominated, I went out to address a group of four hundred mostly gay and lesbian Minneapolis business executives. Their periodic meetings rotate among the big companies headquartered there. This one was hosted by General Mills. I was introduced by its chairman, Steve Sanger—which left me with very mixed feelings. On the one hand, I was appalled to realize that I was five years *older* than the chairman of General Mills. On the other hand, I thought it was terrific he'd take the time to support his gay and lesbian employees. Like more and more events, this one was attended by respected, contributing gay men and lesbians—one of them the gay president of a General Mills division—who could show their faces happily, knowing that as far as their company's chairman was concerned, and as far as their nation's president was concerned, and as far as a growing majority of Americans was concerned, all Americans really *does* mean all Americans.

. . .

Braver souls will shout angrily about all the things that haven't been done—and they will be right to do it. Why *can't* Charles and I have the same rights as any other couple? Why *is* it legal in so many parts of this country to deny a job or a house to someone just because he's gay or she's lesbian? Why *do* gays risk derision or assault in many parts of the country just for walking down the street holding hands?

But there's room also for those of us less brave (and maybe just older) to recognize the progress we *have* made and say thank you.

Proposed Epilogue

We told them. And told them and told them. Gradually, all but a hard-core few came around. Society began treating gay men and lesbians with respect. That placed a burden on gay men to act more responsibly themselves. Some of them did; some of them didn't. Just like straight men.

Along the way, our friends stopped dying. One of them had been living with AIDS for *thirty-seven years* and had just won the seniors-division tennis tournament at the 2018 Gay Games. Charles and I cheered him on from the stands.*

Most important, over enormous opposition from the trial bar, California became the last state in the union finally to adopt Michigan-style no-fault auto insurance. After forty-five years of

---

* The biggest roar of applause at the Games' closing ceremony rose for Jesse Helms. Not because he had now taken the late Strom Thurmond's place as the oldest man in the Senate but because, George Wallace–like, he had seen the light. "Ah still buhleeve it's an abomi-nashun before God for people o' the same sex to lie down with one another," he said, paus-ing for effect, "if theyuh hetro-sexchul. But God made gays and lesbians, too. Some damn fahn ones. So ah say to y'all this beautiful eve-nun: God bless America."

seeing injured Michiganders far better compensated, and at significantly lower cost, the voters of California finally decided to give it a try.

I was seventy, but to some youngsters my tales of auto insurance reform became all the more sexy.

This made Charles very cross.

Cut out this page—or just send a note with the same information.

The Human Rights Campaign
1101 14th St., N.W., Suite 200
Washington, D.C. 20005

[ ] I want to join HRC. Enclosed is my $20 membership contribution. (Because HRC lobbies, this is not tax-deductible.)

Name: _____

Street: _____

City and State: _____ Zip: _____

www.hrc.org

"Teaching Respect for All."
The Gay, Lesbian, and Straight Education Network
121 West 27th Street #804
New York, NY 10001

[ ] Please send me OUT OF THE PAST, winner of the Audience Award for Best Documentary at the 1998 Sundance Film Festival. I have enclosed a check for $25 made out to GLSEN.

Name: _____

Street: _____

City and State: _____ Zip: _____

www.glsen.org

PFLAG
Parents, Families and Friends of Lesbians and Gays
1101 14th St., N.W., Suite 1030
Washington, D.C. 20005

[ ] Sign me up! Enclosed are my $30 annual dues.

Name: _____

Street: _____

City and State: _____ Zip: _____

www.pflag.org

About the Author

ANDREW TOBIAS was born in New York and graduated from Harvard, where he ran the student business organization, and Harvard Business School. His books, magazine articles, and software have been concerned mostly with financial topics. He lives in Miami, New York, and cyberspace—atobias@aol.com.

ABOUT THE TYPE

This book was set in *Bembo,* a typeface based on an old-style Roman face that was used for Cardinal Bembo's tract *De Aetna* in 1495. Bembo was cut by Francisco Griffo in the early sixteenth century. The Lanston Monotype Machine Company of Philadelphia brought the well-proportioned letter forms of Bembo to the United States in the 1930s.